BUILDING ENHANCED
# HTML HELP
WITH **DHTML & CSS**

ISBN 0-13-017929-9

90000

9 780130 179296

# Hewlett-Packard® Professional Books

**OPERATING SYSTEMS**

| | |
|---|---|
| Fernandez | Configuring CDE: The Common Desktop Environment |
| Lund | Integrating UNIX® and PC Network Operating Systems |
| Madell | Disk and File Management Tasks on HP-UX |
| Poniatowski | HP-UX 11.x System Administration Handbook and Toolkit |
| Poniatowski | HP-UX 11.x System Administration "How To" Book, Second Edition |
| Poniatowski | HP-UX System Administration Handbook and Toolkit |
| Poniatowski | Learning the HP-UX Operating System |
| Poniatowski | UNIX® User's Handbook |
| Rehman | HP Certified, HP-UX System Administration |
| Sauers, Weygant | HP-UX Tuning and Performance |
| Stone, Symons | UNIX® Fault Management |
| Weygant | Clusters for High Availability: A Primer of HP-UX Solutions |

**ONLINE/INTERNET**

| | |
|---|---|
| Amor | The E-business (R)evolution |
| Greenberg, Lakeland | A Methodology for Developing and Deploying Internet and Intranet Solutions |
| Greenberg, Lakeland | Building Professional Web Sites with the Right Tools |
| Ketkar | Working with Netscape Server on HP-UX |
| Klein | Building Enhanced HTML Help with DHTML and CSS |

**NETWORKING/COMMUNICATIONS**

| | |
|---|---|
| Blommers | OpenView Network Node Manager: Designing and Implementing an Enterprise Solution |
| Blommers | Practical Planning for Network Growth |
| Lee | The ISDN Consultant |
| Lucke | Designing and Implementing Computer Workgroups |

**ENTERPRISE**

| | |
|---|---|
| Blommers | Architecting Enterprise Solutions with UNIX® Networking |
| Cook | Building Enterprise Information Architectures |
| Pipkin | Halting the Hacker: A Practical Guide to Computer Security |
| Pipkin | Information Security: Protecting the Global Enterprise |
| Sperley | Enterprise Data Warehouse, Volume 1: Planning, Building, and Implementation |
| Thornburgh | Fibre Channel for Mass Storage |
| Thornburgh, Schoenborn | Storage Area Networks: Designing and Implementing a Mass Storage System |

**PROGRAMMING**

| | |
|---|---|
| Blinn | Portable Shell Programming |
| Caruso | Power Programming in HP OpenView |
| Chaudri, Loomis | Object Databases in Practice |
| Chew | The Java™/C++ Cross-Reference Handbook |
| Grady | Practical Software Metrics for Project Management and Process Improvement |
| Grady | Successful Software Process Improvement |
| Lewis | The Art & Science of Smalltalk |
| Lichtenbelt, Crane, Naqvi | Introduction to Volume Rendering |
| Mellquist | SNMP++ |
| Mikkelsen, Pherigo | Practical Software Configuration Management |
| Norton, DiPasquale | Thread Time: The Multithreaded Programming Guide |
| Wadleigh, Crawford | Software Optimization for High Performance Computing |

**IMAGE PROCESSING**

| | |
|---|---|
| Crane | A Simplified Approach to Image Processing |
| Day | The Color Scanning Handbook |
| Gann | Desktop Scanners: Image Quality |

**OTHER TITLES OF INTEREST**

| | |
|---|---|
| Kane | PA-RISC 2.0 Architecture |
| Markstein | IA-64 and Elementary Functions |

BUILDING ENHANCED
# HTML HELP
WITH **DHTML & CSS**

## *Jeannine M. E. Klein*

Hewlett-Packard Company

www.hp.com/go/retailbooks

Prentice Hall PTR
Upper Saddle River, New Jersey 07458
www.phptr.com

**Library of Congress Cataloging-in-Publication Data**

Klein, Jeannine M. E.
    Building enhanced HTML help with DHTML and CSS / by Jeannine M.E. Klein.
        p. cm
    Includes index.
    ISBN 0-13-017929-9
    1. HTML (Document markup language) 2. DHTML (Document markup language) 3.
Computer graphics. I. Title.

    QA76.76H94 K48 2000
    005.7'2--dc21

                                                00-058444


Editorial/production supervision: *Laura E. Burgess*
Acquisitions editor: *Jill Pisoni*
Marketing manager: *Julie Tiso*
Manufacturing manager: *Maura Goldstaub*
Editorial assistant: *Justin Somma*
Cover design director: *Jerry Votta*
Cover designer: *Nina Scuderi*

Manager, Hewlett-Packard Retail Book Publishing: *Patricia Pekary*
Editor, Hewlett-Packard Professional Books: *Susan Wright*

Published by Prentice Hall PTR
Prentice-Hall, Inc.
Upper Saddle River, New Jersey 07458

Prentice Hall books are widely used by corporations and government agencies for training, marketing, and resale.

The publisher offers discounts on this book when ordered in bulk quantities. For more information, contact Corporate Sales Department, Phone: 800-382-3419; FAX: 201-236-7141; E-mail: corpsales@prenhall.com Or write: Prentice Hall PTR, Corporate Sales Dept., One Lake Street, Upper Saddle River, NJ 07458.

Microsoft Developer's Network, Front Page 2000, Home products, HTML Help Workshop, HTML Help Image Editor, Internet Explorer, Notepad, Office, Visual Interdev, Web Embedding Fonts Tool, Windows 98, Windows 95, Windows 2000, Windows NT, Wingdings, ActiveX, and JScript are either trademarks or registered trademarks of the Microsoft Corporation in the United States and/or other countries. SoftQuad HoTMetaL Pro is a registered trademark of SoftQuad. Dreamweaver, Flash, and Shockwave are either trademarks or registered trademarks of Macromedia, Inc. Paint Shop Pro is a trademark of JASC, Inc. GIF Animator, SmartSaver Pro, and PhotoImpact are trademarks of Ulead, Inc. GIF is a service mark of CompuServe Incorporated. ForeHelp and ForeHTML Pro are either trademarks or registered trademarks of ForeFront, Inc. HomeSite is a trademark of Allaire Corporation. Coffee Cup is a trademark of CoffeeCup Software, Inc. JavaScript is a trademark of Sun Microsystems, Inc. Netscape Navigator is a trademark of Netscape Communications Corp. HP, OpenView, and ManageX are trademarks of Hewlett-Packard Company. Adobe Acrobat, PageMaker, and FrameMaker are trademarks or registered trademarks of Adobe Systems Incorporated. AltaVista is a registered trademark of AltaVista Company. WexTech and Doc-to-Help are trademarks of WexTech Systems, Inc. Blue Sky, RoboHelp, and WinHelp are trademarks or service marks of Blue Sky Software Corporation. Macintosh is a service mark of Apple Computer, Inc. Yahoo is a trademark of Yahoo!, Inc. UNIX is a registered trademark licensed through X/Open Company, Ltd. All other products and company names mentioned herein are the trademarks or registered trademarks of their respective owners.

Printed in the United States of America
10  9  8  7  6  5  4  3  2  1

ISBN 0-13-017929-9

Prentice-Hall International (UK) Limited, *London*
Prentice-Hall of Australia Pty. Limited, *Sydney*
Prentice-Hall Canada Inc., *Toronto*
Prentice-Hall Hispanoamericana, S.A., *Mexico*
Prentice-Hall of India Private Limited, *New Delhi*
Prentice-Hall of Japan, Inc., *Tokyo*
Pearson Education Asia Pte. Ltd.
Editora Prentice-Hall do Brasil, Ltda., *Rio de Janeiro*

# Dedication

This book is dedicated to my boss, Doug McBride, whose committment, passion, and vision have guided the ManageX team through the past years, and whose support and belief in my abilities allowed me to achieve two life goals: moving to California and writing a "real" book. Thanks, Doug.

Special thanks also to my manager, Laurence Sweeney, whose unwavering support and common sense made it all a lot easier.

Thanks to all members of the ManageX team for patience and forbearance in listening to endless discussions of "The Book," but especially to Doug Albright, Matt Deter, Sunil Joseph, Larissa Miller, Keith Rogers, and Steve Wolfe, who worked through specific scripting, installation, and style sheet issues with me.

Thanks to the Learning Products and Information Engineers at Hewlett-Packard, particularly Linda Schoenhoff, Greg Larsen, and Judie Lew, who shared their problems and discoveries, adding insights into the process.

Continued thanks to Bob Patten and Linda Driskill, my mentors in graduate school. Never doubt your influence extends far beyond the hedges.

And, as always, the most heartfelt thanks of all to my daughter April, whose love makes life brighter.

# Table of Contents

# 2 So How Does It Work? Process & Product Overview

## 3   Bringing It Together: HTML Topics & Templates

# 4 Doing It In Style: CSS [Cascading Style Sheets]

# 5 Making Waves: DHTML (Dynamic HTML)

# 7  Navigating the Waters: Table of Contents

# 8  Out of Many, One:  Merging Modular Files

# 9  Accelerating Links:  Cross-Referencing Options

# 10 Making It Happen: Distribution & Installation

# It's Not Just Help, It's HTML Help

*"Users don't use help."*

*"People don't want to read long documents online."*

How often have you heard these statements? It often seems that the two abiding truths in the world of the Help author are "no one reads manuals" and "no one uses help." For the online content provider, one of the central truisms seems to be "no one wants to read on a computer."

But who is this mythical "no one"? Does such a person really exist? The evidence suggests otherwise.

On the one hand, a significant proportion of the World Wide Web explosion centers on the search for content, for information, even for complete documents and electronic books. One extremely popular author's online release of his latest mystery caused a virtual traffic jam online; medical sites are bombarded by requests for downloads of complex medical texts; ebook initiatives are springing up everywhere; and the most popular online bookstores have added electronic delivery options.

At the same time, online Help is growing in unprecedented ways. User assistance is being added to everything from stock portfolios to online museums, whether distributed over the Web or on CDs. Certainly "someone" is reading online and using the new generations of Help.

And the most exciting possibilities of all arise from the merger of the two worlds, combining the best of HTML with the best of online Help—quite possibly, in a new format from Microsoft® that is called *compiled HTML Help* (figure 1.1).

HTML Help goes miles beyond the boring yellow pages with tiny type that have become the de facto Windows help standard. The "HTML" components possess the capability to be both dynamic and interactive, presenting a style as strong as the content. Web technologies enhance the system with cascading style sheets (CSS) for control over layout, and with dynamic HTML (DHTML) that allows the author to customize content and design presentations that literally move the information to meet the user's needs. These enhancements are not merely aesthetic tricks, but

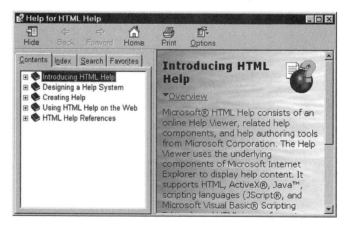

*Figure 1.1 The compiled HTML Help window. HTML Help's tripane window (top button bar, left navigation pane, and right topic pane) lets users keep navigational facilities onscreen at all times, providing a better sense of how the current topic fits into the overall picture.*

legitimate tools that allow the writer to appeal to the needs of all types of learners and all sorts of situations. These needs are also addressed by the strong architectural and navigational components that the "Help" part of the equation brings to the table. Drawing on the Windows help tradition, HTML Help supplies built-in tools for creating indexes, full-text search (FTS), and tables of contents that are synchronized to the user's current page.

As its name implies, HTML Help is designed for online Help in the Web era. It is the new standard in Microsoft Windows 98® and 2000® and is ever more commonly used in applications that run on these platforms, including Microsoft® Office. While the Office systems are easily identifiable as HTML Help, many other HTML Help systems are less easy to spot. Most of the Microsoft Home products push the HTML Help envelope in their format and approaches. But more surprising (and more difficult to see) are the third-party tutorials and online books being published with HTML Help. An amazing wealth of content-rich, visually complex works are now being published from the HTML Help platform, including encylopedias and works of literature—and the online fanatic's guide to at least one wildly popular television show!

And the best part of the HTML Help revolution is that it's not difficult to join in. While the full world of HTML, Help, CSS, and DHTML is stunningly wide, you need not master it all to create rich, useful, and attractive HTML Help systems. In this book, you can learn everything you need to get started and successfully produce your own HTML Help system enhanced with Web technologies. After that, the only limit is your own imagination.

# Basic ideas & their corollaries

The basic idea underlying this book is that HTML Help can and should be an enhanced format for online user assistance and information publishing, taking advantage of the best of both HTML *and* online Help.

HTML Help merges the world of the Web and the world of online user assistance (commonly known as "Help" or "what you get when you press F1"). Online help has a long history of developing useful content (whether or not "anyone" reads it). On the other hand, the enormous growth of the Web in recent years suggests that users prefer and are more comfortable with the Web model of information gathering than with the traditional Help models. HTML Help offers the best of both worlds.

One of the easiest paths to that "best of both worlds" scenarios is through compiled HTML Help, which is the method discussed in this book. In general, *HTML Help* can mean any system that uses standard HTML pages to create an online help system; in practice, HTML Help most often refers to Microsoft's version of compiled HTML Help, while other systems are referred to as *HTML-based Help*. HTML-based Help systems have the advantage of running on any computer with any Web browser; however, generic HTML-based Help does not offer any easy way to create a table of contents, indexing, or search facilities. In addition, the user must have as many .htm files as there are pages in the Help system. (Some third-party systems supply the navigational components, but the multiple file restriction remains.) Also, Help systems designed to run "in any browser" must deal with an incredible number of variations in the ways that different browsers implement Web technologies such as HTML, DHTML, and CSS. In practice, these variations force authors to create "browser-sniffing" scripts, multiple implementations for multiple platforms, or design only for the lowest common denominator, doing away with tables and frames (not to mention DHTML and CSS).

Microsoft's system, referred to as *compiled HTML Help*, requires users to have Internet Explorer® 3.01 or above on their systems, although they need not use it as their default Web browser. The Internet Explorer installation (a standard component on Windows 98 or 2000 machines) allows HTML Help to provide built-in contents, index, and searching facilities. It also lets you use most of the special capabilities available to HTML, CSS, and DHTML. Since HTML Help uses the Internet Explorer engine, it avoids the difficulties of testing and coding for various browsers. Finally, the compiled version allows you to distribute only a single file (.chm) for your help system.

## The corollaries

One of the strongest lessons learned from the popularity of the World Wide Web is that *style aids substance,* that the two are inseparable partners. HTML Help used for user assistance or online publishing must have content; but there is no reason why it should not also have style and sizzle.

Writers can use HTML Help's access to Web-publishing features such as cascading style sheets and dynamic HTML to quickly and efficiently add both style and substance, customizing the content and presentation to the user's needs. And the Web-based approach of HTML Help opens the field to people who are not dedicated tech writers and Help authors. As "everyone" becomes familiar with basic HTML, HTML Help will open a new world of online publishing to anyone with basic HTML knowledge.

## A note on terminology

The full Microsoft system can be referred to either as *compiled* or *compressed* HTML Help. The most common term to date is *compiled* HTML Help. However, these systems are *not* compiled in the strictest sense (the final file doesn't run on its own but requires the Internet Explorer engine), but they are *compressed* (compare the total size of all the included files to the total size of the final .chm file). Microsoft documents are beginning to refer to these systems as "compressed HTML Help," but most of the Microsoft Web site and most technical writer conversations use "compiled HTML Help." The term used in this book is "compiled HTML Help."

# The enhanced proposition

The information in this book is based on knowledge that I have gained in two years of creating real-world HTML Help systems for the Hewlett-Packard™ Company. The first of these systems shipped in 1998, when HTML Help was definitely bleeding-edge technology. Many of the lessons I learned with that first system are presented as examples in Chapter 2, "So How Does It Work," in the hopes that they will keep you from "bleeding" quite as much as you first enter the wonderful world of HTML Help.

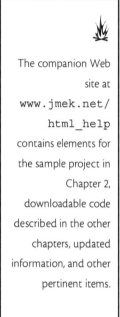

The companion Web site at www.jmek.net/ html_help contains elements for the sample project in Chapter 2, downloadable code described in the other chapters, updated information, and other pertinent items.

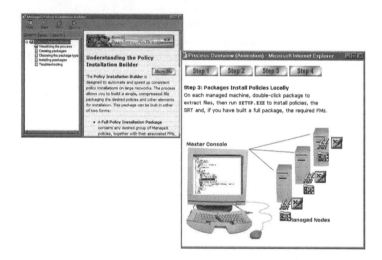

*Figure 1.2 Adding functionality and sizzle. One of the enhancements to the ManageX™ help system is a DHTML-based* Show Me *that provides an animated explanation of processes. In the example above, when the user selects the appropriate button for steps 1 through 4 of the process, the explanatory text changes and the directories (folders), policies (pads), and agents (running men) move between the Master Console to the Managed Nodes.*

Since its first release in 1998, my original HTML Help system has been repeatedly enhanced as it lived through a variety of upgrades, spin-offs, repurposings, and external adoptions (figure 1.2); the lessons learned from these changes provide the real-world testing backing up the theories and techniques described throughout this book. Over time, the systems have been well received by customers, developers, and other writers. Perhaps the greatest tribute is the number of fellow Hewlett-Packard writers around the world who have not only adopted my basic system, but have consistently made it their own with adjustments and enhancements as new technologies become available and as new minds envision new approaches. I believe that the ability to consistently "grow" an HTML Help system is one of the truest benefits of this technology.

# A complete process

The presentation of HTML Help in this book suggests a complete process for creating enhanced HTML Help—a process based on real-world experience as well as theoretical exploration and experimentation. The underlying concept is that you can most efficiently create HTML Help as an iterative process whereby you begin with an overview of your project, then craft each element as the necessary materials and information become available. In other words, create content when information is available; design graphics when stylistic parameters are determined; and craft scripts and style sheets as needs become obvious. The key is to create each element in a reusable and revisable form so that it is always "good enough," but is also always getting better. This approach lets you make the best use of your time by working in a serial fashion on the multiple "threads" involved in HTML Help—an approach not unlike the "componentization" currently advocated and practiced by many software development teams.

# Basic HTML Help+DHTML+CSS = Enhanced HTML Help

The multiple threads of HTML Help allow you to combine basic Help system functionality with Web capabilities to create enhanced HTML Help systems. HTML Help brings with it the rich heritage of Windown help, with navigational and other features not easily available in HTML. Specifically, the Windows help heritage gives HTML Help advantages over standard HTML that include:

- built-in expanding and contracting, hierarchical table of contents, with the ability to merge contents from multiple projects;

- automatic index creation based on keywords in individual files or defined in the HTML Help project;

- ability to create shortcuts that open other Microsoft Windows programs (or even specific locations within other programs);

- automatic full-text search without an additional search engine or any coding;

- ability to ship and run an entire system from a single file;

- in short, access to most Windows help capabilities.

From the other side, HTML brings the exciting new world of Web technologies, such as dynamic HTML and cascading style sheets. Specifically, HTML and other Web technologies add the following advantages to the equation:

- dynamic content that can modify itself based on user response;

- Web graphic standards that support rich design with small file sizes;

- dynamic graphics that can change over time or in response to user interaction;

- in short, access to most Web-based capabilities.

Finally, in addition to the Windows help and HTML capabilities, HTML Help brings its own rich set of functionality, including the following:

- Single tripane window simultaneously displays content and navigation.

- Synchronized table of contents allows users to visualize their location within the system's hypertextual structure.

- Boolean (AND, OR, NOT) capabilities are available in the full-text search pane (figure 1.3).

All combined, the equation adds up to rich online assistance or ebook publishing—that is, an enhanced HTML Help system.

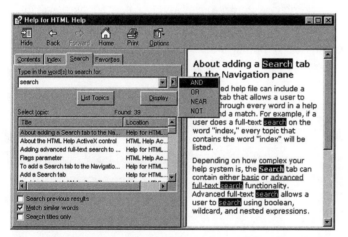

**Figure 1.3 HTML Help's FTS.** *HTML Help provides built-in full-text search (FTS) facilities, including advanced capabilities such as Boolean search terms* (and, or, not, near) *and searching within previous results.*

All work in this book can be done within the HTML Help Workshop (freely downloadable at `msdn.microsoft.com/library/tools/htmlhelp/`) or in Windows Notepad. No other tools are needed.

# Who should read this book

This book is designed for anyone who wants to package a collection of information in a single-file format that incorporates the attributes of HTML, including the sophisticated design and interactivity of cascading style sheets and dynamic HTML, plus convenient navigational facilities. Although the primary audience consists of Help authors and documentation specialists interested in moving to HTML Help, the book should also prove useful to others who want to publish writing in a highly functional, self-contained package that takes advantage of the explosion of technologies and access available on the World Wide Web.

Overall, no previous knowledge is assumed beyond a general familiarity with using Windows Help systems and the World Wide Web. Novices to Web and Help authoring should be able to learn the essentials required to build enhanced HTML Help; at the same time, experienced Help and Web authors should find enough new material to challenge them to enhance their existing systems.

On the one hand, this book does not attempt to provide a complete course in every aspect of HTML Help, DHTML, and CSS; however, it does provide all the information necessary to build a more-than-adequate—in fact, an *enhanced*—HTML Help system. Hefty chapters on HTML, DHTML, and CSS each provide a bit of background and an overview of what is possible with the technology; detailed descriptions of the tags, attributes, and other bits of coding employed by each technology; and pre-canned code bits pertinent to HTML Help systems.

On the other hand, this book *is* designed to provide a substantially complete guide to HTML Help—the framework that brings all the other aspects together. Individual chapters cover specific aspects of HTML Help, including the project file, the table of contents, navigational facilities (indexing, search, etc.), merged projects, and final distribution to your audience.

This book takes a "purist" approach to building HTML Help, avoiding dependence on third-party tools. Although individual chapters discuss (and occasionally recommend) specific tools for building HTML Help, HTML files, cascading style sheets, and dynamic HTML, the approaches explained in this book do not use any specific tools beyond Windows Notepad and Microsoft's HTML Help Workshop (free and downloadable from the Microsoft Web site). The idea is that you will get "under the hood" and understand what you are doing, rather than relying on knowledge that a third party built into their tool. You may want to use one of the many available tools, but a knowledge of HTML Help itself will allow you to better work around the "bugs" and limitations of the tools and to take advantage of new capabilities before the tools can incorporate them.

# What you can learn from this book

This book should provide everything you need to know to efficiently create an attractive *and* useful compiled project in Microsoft's HTML Help—whether that project be for online user assistance or for a self-contained ebook. You can learn how to create the necessary HTML code, cascading style sheets, and dynamic HTML scripts, in addition to how to manipulate the HTML Help Workshop to add navigational functions (table of contents, index, full-text search) and compile the completed project.

New users can learn:

- the structure and elements of compiled HTML Help systems

- functionality, tricks, and tips for using the HTML Help Workshop

- inner workings of the HTML Help table of navigation pane (table of contents, index, and full-text search)

- standard HTML markup and structure necessary to create HTML Help content, together with templates for creating HTML pages and information about two dozen standard HTML tags

- essential elements of cascading style sheets, including 50 frequently used properties for paragraph, font, list, and heading elements

- basic dynamic HTML coding in JavaScript™, with pre-canned code for pop-ups and other common items

More advanced users can discover:

- Microsoft's sitemap format used for HTML Help tables of contents and indexes

- window definitions, their meanings, parameters, and available values

- how to open HTML Help code and "tweak" elements not accessible via the HTML Help Workshop

- known bugs in the HTML Help system, together with "under-the-hood" tips and tricks for working around the bugs

- 50 CSS properties, together with the "gotchas" for the HTML Help implementation

- detailed information about the values and pitfalls of merged modular systems, together with step-by-step instructions for creating these systems

# Limitations

This book is not meant as a standalone work on HTML, DHTML, or CSS for general use on the World Wide Web. Its applications are focused on uses within HTML Help.

Within the Help authoring universe, this book focuses on compiled HTML Help as implemented on Microsoft Windows platforms (95, 98, NT, 2000, and forward). Although much of the information on HTML Help (and all of the information on the HTML, CSS, and DHTML) applies to other products written in HTML, this book does not provide any specific information on HTML-based (uncompiled) Help, JavaHelp, or other variations of online user assistance systems; nor does it address questions pertinent to help on operating systems other than Windows.

Finally, this book is meant for authors, not program developers, and so does not delve into the mysteries of of the HTML Help API that developers use to connect an application to an HTML Help file. For developer information, I strongly recommend the Microsoft™ Developer Network (MSDN™), available online at msdn.microsoft.com, with more extended content available by subscription from Microsoft.

# Chapter overviews

This book begins with an overview of the HTML Help concept and a complete walk-through of a sample project. Then the next three chapters—on HTML, CSS, and DHTML—explain the three core Web technologies used in HTML Help. Learning these technologies and applying them to your projects gets you set up for rapid content and product development. These chapters are presented from the simplest technology (HTML) to the most complex (DHTML), but you should find yourself using them in an iterative fashion as you create templates for your HTML Help topics, enhance them with CSS and DHTML, then return to the basic HTML pages to add more information and to the CSS and DHTML to add new formats supporting the new content. Each chapter closes with a section explaining the ways in which HTML Help specifically works with and clashes against the technology—along with workarounds, where available. The final section of five chapters focuses on HTML Help-specific elements built within the HTML Help Workshop itself—the project file, the table of contents, navigational elements (such as indexes, full-text search, and related topics), and merging modular files—before describing the steps necessary to distribute the final product. More specific chapter descriptions follow.

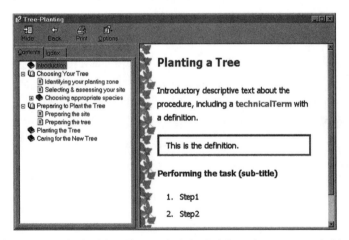

*Figure 1.4. Learning by doing. Chapter 2 includes the information necessary to build a sample HTML Help project using HTML, CSS, and DHTML, plus the merge facilities.*

**Chapter 1, "It's Not Just Help, It's HTML Help"** is the chapter you're reading now. It provides general background describing what HTML Help is, how it can be enhanced with other technologies, and an overview of the remaining chapters.

**Chapter 2, "So How Does It Work?"** supplies a hands-on **"Process & Product Overview."** Based on a belief in learning by doing, this chapter presents a walk-through of all the procedures required to create an HTML Help project. The chapter works through every step of the process, from assessing your audience and choosing your tools; through building the style sheets, dynamic HTML, HTML topics, table of contents, and index; and closes with a description of the procedures required to compile the project and prepare it for merging with other projects. Along the way, this chapter includes a case study of an HTML Help system that Hewlett-Packard shipped with a Windows NT application. In addition, the chapter walks you through the steps required to create the sample HTML Help system on a gardening topic (figure 1.4). Sample files required for the project are posted on the book's companion web site, www.jmek.net/html_help.

**Chapter 3, "Bringing It Together: HTML Templates & Topics,"** provides both the starting and ending points for the builder of HTML Help systems. It *starts* out the system by helping you identify and design the templates which will define the overall structure of your topic pages before you enhance them with CSS and DHTML. It *ends* the system building by teaching the HTML that structures the information content as you write each topic page. But this is a cyclical process as new content suggests alterations to the template, which in turn provides new possibilities for the content and its presentation. This chapter evaluates some of the most popular tools for creating HTML, including third-party software as well as the HTML Help Workshop's facilities. The chapter then describes the basic concepts of writing HTML (even in a plain text editor) and discusses the syntax for two dozen tags commonly used in HTML Help. It also offers cut-and-paste code "recipes" for standard online Help formats.

**Chapter 4, "Doing It In Styles: CSS; Cascading Style Sheets,"** explores the wonders of adding formatting to Web pages with the same sophistication that style sheets offer in word processing and desktop publishing programs. Cascading style sheets define the look of your HTML Help system's look and feel quickly and efficiently, allowing changes to a single style sheet to automatically flow throughout hundreds of HTML pages. This chapter not only describes the basic concepts underlying CSS, it also presents relevant syntax, values, and examples for some 50 CSS properties.

**Chapter 5, "Making Waves: DHTML (Dynamic HTML),"** uses JavaScript to add dyamics to the style and structure of your HTML topic pages. This chapter explains what DHTML is and what it does, together with its advantages over other interactive technologies. It walks you through Microsoft Internet Explorer's DOM (Document Object Model), discussing the objects, properties, values, methods, parameters, and events most commonly used in HTML Help, along with "recipes" ready to cut and paste into your own HTML Help system.

**Chapter 6, "Creating Magic: The HTML Help Project File"** introduces the project file, the primary container for information about and pointers to all elements of the HTML Help project. This chapter explains how to create a project file (in the HTML Help Workshop or a text editor), integrating the various topic files with the table of contents, index, and search features before compiling the project. Special attention is given to window types, Workshop definitions specifying the size, placement, and other attributes of the primary and secondary HTML Help windows.

**Chapter 7, "Navigating the Waters: Table of Contents"** delves into the table of contents, one of the primary navigational elements in HTML Help systems. The expanding table of contents is an integral part of the standard HTML Help window, remaining synchronized and available whenever the system is open. This presents a distinct advantage over earlier online Help implementations, where the contents disappeared and reappeared in a never-ending dance with the topic pages. HTML Help's contents also allows presentation of links from other files in a merged modular system.

**Chapter 8, "Out of Many, One: Merging Modular Files"** describes the concepts and procedures required to merge multiple HTML Help files into one apparently seamless system. These systems support the creation of "plug-in" modules that can be sold or downloaded separately, but still appear as part of the main HTML Help in the table of contents, index, and search facilites. They are also useful in updating content on the fly and in managing extremely large systems.

**Chapter 9, "Accelerating Links: Cross-Referencing Options"** presents navigational options beyond the table of contents. This chapter explains how to create an index, full-text search, and other methods for cross-referencing information in your HTML Help system that are not available with the standard links of basic Web site technology.

**Chapter 10, "Making It Happen: Distribution & Installation"** details the steps required to let users access completed HTML Help systems. This chapter describes the vagaries of HTML Help installation on various Windows releases, including Windows 2000. It also lets you look "under the hood" at some of the libraries, executables, and ActiveX® controls that enable HTML Help on the end user's system.

# 2

# So How Does It Work?
## Process & Product Overview

Creating HTML Help combines Web technologies (HTML, CSS, DHTML) with technical writing skills (audience analysis, information acquisition, organization, writing, grammar), and graphic design talents (layout, conceptualization, color management). Making the pieces fit can feel like putting together a particularly rough-edged jigsaw puzzle! Windows help procedures seem flat and lifeless compared to the power of HTML; color schemes that work beautifully in print dither into mush on Web browsers. You switch from application to application, using different tools for writing, HTML editing, graphic design, interactive scripting....

So how can you get a handle on it all? One of the best ways is by walking through the process yourself. This chapter presents a high-level view of an entire HTML Help project, from start to finish. The opening design sections describe the types of choices you must make before beginning your project, while subsequent divisions detail the steps required to create an HTML Help system.

At each step of the walkthrough, you will find both case study information gleaned from the first HTML Help project I ever created and the actual

If you don't want to key in the tree planting project elements, you can download them at the companion Web site:
`www.jmek.net/ html_help.`

steps you'll need to take to create a sample project that guides a home gardener through the process of planting a tree, from the conceptual task of choosing an appropriate species to step-by-step directions on planting the particular specimen. While the topics of the tree-planting project are accurate, they are not extensive. (For example, the choice of species is limited to two!) The focus is on creating HTML Help rather than on actually planting a tree.

The case study describes the help for ManageX, a Windows NT-based system administration application from Hewlett-Packard's OpenView software division. Developed at a time when very few non-Microsoft applications had been released with HTML Help systems, this foray into the new technology presented both challenges and opportunities. The challenges stemmed from the need for a rapid transition to the new system and from the trials of working with a "bleeding edge" development tool (Microsoft's HTML Help Workshop), including some of its quirkier features (notably, merged Help files). The opportunities brought in the wonderful (and bleeding edge) technologies of the World Wide Web, including dynamic HTML(DHTML) and cascading style sheets (CSS). Both the challenges and the opportunities should be familiar to anyone who has worked with HTML Help. Usability studies conducted on the Hewlett-Packard product show that our audiences felt the challenges were met successfully. Following this chapter's walkthrough should help you meet the challenges as well.

NOTE: In order to follow along with the procedures in this chapter, you must have Microsoft's HTML Help Workshop installed on your system. The Workshop is available as a free download at `http://msdn.microsoft.com/library/tools/htmlhelp/`. You may also need an HTML editor; in a pinch, you can write and edit HTML pages in the Windows Notepad or any other editor that produces plain text. Do not use a full-fledged word processor unless you know how to make it save your documents in a plain text format with an `.htm` extension.

# What the process looks like

One of the confusing aspects of the HTML Help process is the multitude of different parts, each using its own file type. Basically, the process involves the following steps:

## 1. Planning system design:

Plan the overall Help system, addressing both traditional online help decisions (audience analysis, high-level organization, navigation model) and HTML-specific questions (compiled or uncompiled projects, style sheet design, interactive elements). This is a good time to set up your directory structure.

## 2. Crafting reusable elements & content:

Use an HTML editor or Notepad to write individual topic files (*.htm). Identify and create required reusable elements including graphics, style sheets, and DHTML snippets. Combine these elements into HTML files that can be used as templates.

## 3. Creating & testing the HTML Help project:

Use the HTML Help Workshop or a third-party product to define the HTML Help project (*.hhp), combining the individual topic files, specifying project parameters, and building the navigation system (table of contents, *.hhc, and index, *.hhk). Finally, compile the project into the distributable file (*.chm), and troubleshoot the results.

## 4. Merging modular projects [optional]:

If you will combine several help projects into a single master project (for example, if your documented application has components that are only available in certain packages), create a master project file (*.hhp) that specifies the constituent .chm files as "Merged Files" in the .hhp and with "INCLUDE" statements in the .hhc.

# Notes on file types & extensions

As the previous list shows, HTML Help involves many different file types, each with its own extension and special requirements. The following list and table (table 2.1) summarize the different file types, their extensions (and the extension of the Windows help counterparts), their uses, and their requirements.

.Hhp, .hhc, and .hhk files are plain text files. You can create them in the HTML Help Workshop, a third-party editor or, if you're brave, in Notepad.

- Reusable elements can include cascading style sheet files (.css) to specify formatting; boilerplate text (in .txt files for unformatted language or in .htm files for formatted text); dynamic HTMLcode snippets (in standard .txt format for cut-and-paste or in separate JScript .js files). These can be combined into *.htm files that function as templates.

- Individual topics are contained in standard HTML files (.htm).

- The project file (.hhp) specifies such things as window definitions, compiler options, included files, and the default page for the help file.

- The contents file (.hhc) creates the expanding table of contents. It lists each displayed contents entry with its associated HTML file and icon. The file is similar to an unordered list <UL> in HTML.

- The index file (.hhk) defines the index. It lists each displayed index entry with its associated HTML title and HTML file. It, too, is similar to an undented list <UL> in HTML.

- The distributable help file then consists of a single file with the .chm extension. (One exception: If you're creating a modular system, you will have multiple .chm files to distribute, one for each module.) You create this file using the HTML Help Compiler (in the Workshop) to combine the .htm, .hhp, .hhc, and .hhk files.

TABLE 2.1 FILE TYPES & EXTENSIONS FOR **HTML** HELP COMPONENTS

| EXTENSION (.HLP COUNTERPART) | FILE TYPE | CREATED IN | PURPOSE & USE |
|---|---|---|---|
| .chm (.hlp) | compiled help file | HTML Help Workshop | contains all elements of the Help system (text, graphics, styles, scripts, contents, index, search) in a single compressed file distributed to the end user |
| .css | cascading style sheet | HTML editor, specialized CSS tool, or text editor (Notepad) | contains format definitions (font, size, color, etc.). The .css extension identifies an external file that HTML files link to. |
| .hhc (.cnt) | help contents file | HTML Help Workshop or text editor (Notepad) | contains table of contents for the project; in modular projects, may contain references to external .hhc files |
| .hhk | help index file | HTML Help Workshop or text editor (Notepad) | contains a specific list of indexed terms and associated topics. Does *not* include either Alinks or Klinks, though Klinks may be merged into the index during compilation. |
| .hhp (.hjp) | help project file | HTML Help Workshop or text editor (Notepad) | contains information about the project, including window definitions, included files, compiler & compatibility options, default page |
| .htm, .html (.rtf) | Web page | HTML or text editor, or Workshop | contains actual text and graphics of the project's Help topic pages |
| .js | JavaScript or JScript | scripting tool or text editor (Notepad) | scripts for dynamic presentations or interactivity The .js extension identifies an external file that HTML files link to. |

# Planning the system design

Before diving into the project, plan as much as possible. Planning is an essential part of any documentation project, but it's even more important when working with a new format that brings new expectations and new possibilities. HTML Help brings into play traditional online Help decisions (based on audience and needs analysis as well as choice of tools, organization, navigation, and presentation models) as well as the newer demands of a Web-savvy audience for style and interactivity.

In most software development projects, the Help developer has some "dead time" at the beginning of the cycle when the programmers are wrestling with the backend code. Planning before the development code is ready can save enormous amounts of time during the inevitable "crunch" at the end of the production cycle. Pre-designing individual elements (such as outlines, graphics, and scripts) for the ManageX help system allowed me to take advantage of HTML Help's opportunities without destroying the final production schedule. Our sample tree-planting project doesn't have the same schedule constraints, but planning will still help to insure a useful and well-designed help system.

## Traditional online help decisions

### Audience/needs analysis

As much as possible, interview actual users of your product (or similar products) to determine their needs, desires, and expectations. If you can't talk to users directly, gather data from your company's technical support group (or usability lab, if you have one). Connecting with this team can provide valuable insight into what users are actually saying about the product. And don't let your information sources just feed back "received wisdom." Prod users and support groups for ideas about what they might like if they could wish for the moon; show them new ideas and see what they say. You may be surprised. Remember: in the early days of the Web, black type on a gray background was on the outer limits of "cool."

When starting the new ManageX HTML Help system, I looked back at the old system and the responses it had received. I was fortunate to have access to user comments. ManageX has a very active technical support and consulting community which frequently passes user comments back to the development team.

What the tech support professionals had to say convinced me that you can never assume you know what users want. ManageX users are network engineers, IT professionals who often come from a UNIX background that deals with "man pages" of white text on a black background, accessible only if you already know how to spell the proper command. I expected their navigational and aesthetic requirements to be limited, with more focus on code and commands. But once these users moved to an NT environment, they wanted full navigation capabilities (contents, index, full-text search) plus pictures, pictures, and more pictures (figure 2.1)!

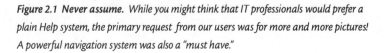

*Figure 2.1* **Never assume.** *While you might think that IT professionals would prefer a plain Help system, the primary request from our users was for more and more pictures! A powerful navigation system was also a "must have."*

Within my development team, the mandate was to be on the "cutting edge" of Windows-based technologies. Because of this, management supported the move to a new system (even if it did require installation of Internet Explorer; see *Compiled or not?* later in this chapter), and the developers were willing to learn new ways to hook help into the application. The developers and managers had also been bitten by the Web bug and agreed with users that graphic appeal and easy navigation are essential, not optional, requirements.

These comments helped guide me toward the compiled form of HTML Help, which automatically provides full-text search and makes it easy to add contents and indexing. In addition, I designed a simple but attractive banner graphic combining logo elements with a "signpost" identifying the component of the application covered by the topic. The users responded enthusiastically to these and other easy-to-implement enhancements such as colored headline text and a lightly textured background (contrary to most usability recommendations). Usability tests conducted on the released product included many positive comments about the "snazzy" help!

For our sample tree-planting project, talk to friends and neighbors, particularly ones who may have been landscaping recently. Among my sources, the requests included:

- **Simple terminology.** When botanical terms are necessary, definitions for the layperson should be immediately available. The tree-planting project can meet this need by using a simple dynamic HTML script to show and hide definitions with a click of the mouse.

- **Simple, attractive design**. Gardeners are interested in aesthetics (or why would they plant trees and flowers?). So the project uses a cascading style sheet to create a simple design that pleases the eye without distracting from the pictures required by the desire for....

- **Pictures to identify specific trees.** This one is fun and (if you have good clip art or a digital camera) easy to implement. We'll also add small map graphics showing appropriate planting areas for each tree.

- **Quick access.** If someone suggests a Santa Cruz redwood, users want a picture and planting requirements *right now.* HTML Help's full-text search capability, indexing, and "favorites" tab will meet these requirements.

## Organization: reference vs. task

Most online help use one of two organizations: a command-reference orientation that follows the menu structure of the application or a task orientation that walks users sequentially through the steps required to perform tasks. Neither one is necessarily better; the choice depends on a combination of user analysis, application design, and the other available materials.

In the case of the ManageX system, the technical focus of our users combined with the task-based printed manuals allowed me to use a command-reference orientation for the online help. In addition, the organization of the application itself pointed in this direction. ManageX works as a "snap-in" to the Microsoft Management Console, but ManageX itself is composed of several "extension snap-ins." A user may add or remove extensions at will; in addition, different versions of ManageX may include different sets of extensions. For these reasons, it made sense to organize the help system around the individual extensions. In addition, I made the help system modular. The help system for each extension is composed of a single .chm that merges into the master help file. Thanks to the ability to merge help files at run time, I can keep up with the different versions of ManageX by adding and removing individual .chm files from the list of installed files.

From a user's point of view, this modular, reference-based system presents only those items that are available in the currently installed product. From the developers' point of view, they could "easily" add context-sensitivity at the extension level. (Unfortunately, this "ease" proved elusive and was one of the main places we noticed the "bleeding" edge of the HTML Help API.)

The tree-planting project involves both a task orientation (to walk users through the steps involved in choosing a tree and then in planting it) and a reference orientation (for the "encyclopedia" of specific trees). We can plan to expand our project (and future sales) by setting up for run-time merging of separately purchased reference modules for specific geographical areas. (Don't forget that the company's sales and marketing departments are an important secondary audience!)

## Navigation model

Once you decide on the basic organization, consider how users will navigate through it. Compiled HTML Help's tripane format uses the left pane for navigation tools (figure 2.2).

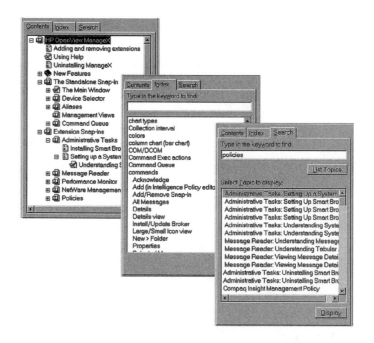

*Figure 2.2 Basic HTML Help Navigation Pane. Compiled HTML Help uses a "tripane" format with the left pane devoted to navigation tabs. The three standard tabs are the* Contents, Index, *and* Search *tabs. A Favorites tab is also available for storing users' most frequently referenced pages.*

The **Contents** tab provides an expanding/collapsing table of contents that "auto-syncs" to the user's current location in the Help system. The Help author specifies the hierarchy, the page titles, destination for the links, and identifying icons.

The **Index** tab provides access to author-defined keywords. The Help author can code the keywords into the individual HTML files or create a separate index (`*.hhk`) file created within the HTML Help workshop. The keywords need not actually appear in the Help file, making this navigation aid useful for providing synonyms (e.g., creating new topics, adding new topics, drafting new topics, etc.)

The **Search** pane provides automatic full-text search capabilities. When the user types a word and clicks List Topics, HTML Help searches through all words in the Help project. The Help author does not have to specify any keywords, but the word that the user types in must actually appear in the text of the Help topic.

The **Favorites** tab (not pictured) allows users to save their most frequently used topics in an easily accessed location. (The ManageX system was created under HTML Help 1.1; Favorites were not available until version 1.2, so it does not appear in the sample pictures taken from this project.)

All of these navigation aids are part of the HTML Help setup. You may want to include additional cues for users. For example, since the ManageX program was made up of multiple modules, I wanted a quick way to notify users of their current location. HTML Help's "Auto-sync" in the table of contents provides users one clue, but I decided to also use graphic "headers" that varied according to the extension. Because they depended only on high-level groupings, these headers were one of the elements I could design before the product was ready for more detailed documentation. The sample tree-planting project could also use zone maps for additional cues.

## Tools

The HTML Help Workshop is a free download. Beginning with version 1.3, the download is at `msdn.microsoft.com/library/tools/htmlhelp/`.

While analyzing audience and application needs, don't forget to consider your needs as well; specifically, what tools will you use? At a minimum, decide whether to use Microsoft's HTML Help Workshop directly or to access it through one of the available third-party tools. Also choose an HTML editor and, possibly, specialized tools for creating CSS style sheets and interactive DHTML elements.

Microsoft's HTML Help Workshop may prove to be the best choice for creating your HTML Help projects. This new technology is moving so quickly that the third-party tools have difficulty keeping up with the newest features. On the other hand, the third-party tools may provide "add-ons" that make it easier to keep up with the technology. So it's usually best to try the demos and see for yourself. Three leading products are:

- ForeHelp™ from ForeFront℠, `www.ff.com`
- Doc-to-Help™ from Wextech™, `www.wextech.com`
- RoboHelp™ from eHelp™ (formerly Blue Sky℠), `www.blue-sky.com`

As Blue Sky, eHelp's zealous marketing department won RoboHelp a large market share based on corporate purchases. However, ForeHelp carries the votes of many actual users based on both product functionality and service after the sale. (At the leading Help author conferences in 1999, ForeHelp won Author's Choice from the WinWriters Conference as well as Best Overall Windows help Authoring Tool and Best HTML Help Output from Help University). In addition, Doc-to-Help has long been the favorite for authors who single-source online and printed content.

For the ManageX HTML Help project, I decided to work directly in the HTML Help Workshop. When writing Windows help, I used third-party tools and never got "under the hood" to deal directly with the Help compiler. As a result, I never felt I understood the product as thoroughly as I would like. At this point, I want to really understand the technologies; so when I ultimately settled on HTML Help, I decided to put the project together and compile it directly in Microsoft's HTML Help Workshop. I deliberately did not use any third-party help authoring tools; in fact, I often find myself editing the project files with Notepad. This is not to denigrate third-party tools, but sometimes you can learn more working in a hands-on mode.

As for the HTML pages themselves, the goal is to find an editor that writes clean code and moves quickly and transparently from raw code editing to a more polished graphical user interface (GUI). Ideally, it should also have sophisticated tools for creating more complex elements. It is important that the editor not require the distribution of special additions (such as the Microsoft Front Page® extensions), inhibit you from moving among tools, or add extraneous and/or proprietary code that might conflict with HTML standards (or the HTML Help Workshop requirements). For example, a common problem involves the superfluous use of <DIV> tags. Some HTML editors separate HTML pages into "divisions" using <DIV> tags before applying other tags, even when there is absolutely no need to add the <DIV> tags. Since <DIV> has other, special uses in HTML, this just adds clutter and the potential for misinterpreted HTML code. Once you've located an editor that writes clean code, look for one that also supports "assets" or "libraries"for reusable text, graphic, or code elements for drag-and-drop insertion and enhanced productivity. Other things to look for are internal tools for creating image maps, cascading style sheets, and dynamic HTML, as well as site management tools that make sense to you.

My personal favorite for working with HTML is HoTMetaL Pro® from SoftQuad® (www.softquad.com), which writes beautifully clean code and provides asset and site management, image map tools, a CSS editor, and a great links checker. For dynamic HTML, I use Dreamweaver™ from Macromedia™ (www.macromedia.com), which includes a number of extremely useful "pre-canned" DHTML effects. In particular, the timeline feature (which lets you show, hide, and move elements at predefined time intervals to create a low-overhead online "movie") is worth the cost of the program. Dreamweaver has good site and asset management tools, but its basic code is somewhat cluttered.

*HTML editor*

Many HTML editors are available, so choose your favorite. You may still find yourself using Notepad for quick edits. Instructions in this book require only Microsoft's HTML Help Workshop and a basic text or HTML editor.

# HTML aspects

## Compiled or not?

At the current time, the main decision point in adopting compiled HTML Help will be users' reactions to the requirement of Microsoft Internet Explorer (IE). Without IE, you can only use the uncompiled version of HTML Help, which requires an entire "web" of HTML files and lacks features such as full text search and associative links. Compiled HTML Help provides built-in contents, index, and searching facilities (although these facilities have their own "bugs"). It also supports most of the special capabilities available to HTML, such as cascading style sheets and dynamic HTML. Since HTML Help uses the Internet Explorer engine, it does away with the difficulties of testing and coding for various browsers. Finally, compiled HTML Help allows you to distribute Help in a single file (.chm).

However, compiled HTML Help works only if the user has IE 3.02 or higher installed. When Windows 2000 becomes the dominant Windows platform, this will no longer be an issue (since IE 5 is built into the system). Under current versions of Windows 9x or NT, full HTML Help functionality requires IE 4.0 or higher. To provide this functionality without requiring users to upgrade to IE 4.0, Microsoft's MSDN Web site (http://msdn. microsoft.com /library/tools/htmlhelp/wkshp/download.htm) provides a freely distributable file (hhupd.exe) that updates the user's system without installing the full Internet Explorer 4.0 componentry. You can include this file as part of your application's installation, providing virtually transparent installation. This is another place where it pays to plan ahead, letting your installation engineer know requirements in advance.

The sample tree-planting project's requirements for full-text search and a favorites tab dictates using compiled HTML Help as well. (Adding full-text search to an uncompiled HTML Help project requires adding a third-party search engine, which is beyond the scope of this book.)

# Graphical look and feel [CSS]

Cascading style sheets—like styles in Microsoft Word®, Adobe™ PageMaker® or FrameMaker®—define the visual appearance of the page. Style sheets can determine such things as fonts, point sizes, colors, background graphics, and bullet styles. Specific style "classes" can specify consistent formatting for code examples or important notes. Most of this planning and design work can be done at the outset of the project, before the application is completely ready for documentation.

One of the first decisions is the type of cascading style sheet to use:

- inline style sheets, located on each page, directly within the code, near the element they describe;

- embedded style sheets, located on at the beginning of each page;

- linked style sheets, located in an external file (.css), but referenced at the beginning of each individual HTML page.

The reusability and centralization of linked style sheets enhances productivity. All the HTML Help files in a project can link to one or two style sheets stored in separate text files. Then, if the requirements used in the early planning and design change and you need to modify the basic project font from Verdana to Arial Narrow, changing a few lines in the style sheets will flow the new design to literally hundreds of HTML pages.

For the ManageX project, I chose a background graphic that mimics lined pads, providing a familiar environment. In addition, using lined paper rather than "bond paper" look provides a more casual feel I also experimented with different colors of lined paper, hoping to provide an affordance or subtle visual clue signaling the type of information: conceptual topics had a pale gray background, while procedural topics had pale yellow. While the overall look tested well for usability (the pattern is subtle enough to add interest without making the text difficult to read), the difference between colors proved too subtle. Learning from this experience, the tree-planting project uses a single background—white with a leafy border. This sample project also adopts the linked style sheet model.

## Action & interactivity [DHTML]

Dynamic HTML takes Web pages another step, adding easy interactivity. Dynamic HTML combines CSS with scripting (usually JavaScript or JScript) to layer information, change colors, display movement, and otherwise provide interactivity and movement. For example, one of the simplest (but most useful) tricks is a few lines of code to show or hide extra information whenever the user clicks on a graphic or piece of text. The sample tree-planting project uses such a "show/hide" script to provide the immediate definitions that users requested. (We could use HTML Help's built-in pop-up facility, but it is limited to plain text and an unreliably colored background.)

Like the cascading style sheets, DHTML comes in various types, including embedded scripts defined in each HTML page's header and linked script files. Again, the embedded approach provides the most rapid development path. When I first began designing the ManageX project, I created reusable snippets of code and stored them in a simple text file, cutting and pasting the code into HTML pages as needed. Even with the external .js files, you may want to keep a text file of the code for calling the script (since the actual call must be made within the individual HTML file at the text location). You may also want to investigate Dreamweaver and other HTML editors that provide pre-canned scripts and special storage approaches.

For the tree-planting project we'll use a single script that displays and hides botanical definitions when the user's mouse pauses over the scripted section of text. (We could also use the HTML Help Workshop's pop-up functionality, but then you're limited to text only. The JScript allows the use of pictures as well.)

## Directory structure

HTML Help has some specific preferences on directory structure. In particular, it prefers that the project and output files (`*.hhp`, `*.hhc`, `*.hhk`, and `*.chm`) be on a directory level *above* the project's component parts. For this reason, I recommend the following directory structure.

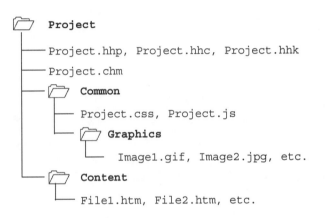

```
📂 Project
├── Project.hhp, Project.hhc, Project.hhk
├── Project.chm
├── 📂 Common
│   ├── Project.css, Project.js
│   └── 📂 Graphics
│       └── Image1.gif, Image2.jpg, etc.
└── 📂 Content
    └── File1.htm, File2.htm, etc.
```

---

### Tree Project 1: Set up the directory structure

On your hard drive, create a directory named `Tree`, with subdirectories named `Common` and `Content`. The `Common` directory should have its own subdirectory, named `Graphics`.

---

# Crafting reusable elements & templates

Once the planning is done, begin to create the HTML Help system's reusable elements—even if the application is not yet ready for documentation. You may be able to begin writing some topics and use these to identify the necessary reusable components. Then you can begin creating style sheets, DHTML, and graphics, even before the application is far enough along to be fully documented. Although it may seem odd to start working on stylistic elements before writing the text itself, this "plan ahead" approach and the use of templates can prove invaluable both in terms of speed and user satisfaction.

Templates, in the sense used here, are sample HTML files that combine the reusable elements (graphics, CSS, DHTML) with boilerplate text for common tasks. Rapid development can occur once the templates are complete and the application is ready for documentation: Simply open the appropriate template, save it under another name, and make edits as necessary to reflect the individual application concepts and procedures.

The question of speed always arises at deadline time. Experience leads most technical writers to expect a very small window between the moment when the developers stop changing the application and the day when the documentation is due. (In fact, I have even had the distinctly uncomfortable experience of having a documentation deadline fall *prior to* code freeze.) Designing the resuable elements and assembling them into templates in advance allows time to focus on the writing during the inevitable end-of-cycle "crunch."

In addition, the extra time put into designing the "style" elements pays off with users. While it's essential that the content be solid, the style first catches the eye. Style should not take precedence over substance, but why not have both?

# Create the reusable elements [graphics, CSS, and DHTML]

The audience analysis and other planning steps should provide a good list of elements that will be required by the HTML Help system. In the ManageX project, I knew I needed graphics for the headers to identify each ManageX module as well as designs for the background; a cascading style sheet that would cover common elements for concepts and procedures; and DHTML snippets for expanding lists and show/hide definitions.

For the sample tree-planting project, the previous audience analysis and planning sections provide the following list of reusable elements that can be created before writing the topic:

- **Graphics:** a pale green textured background and a "zone map" identifying planting areas for each tree

- **CSS:** a simple but attractive design to appeal to the aesthetics of gardeners

- **DHTML:** a show/hide snippet for definitions of botanical terms

## The graphics

A course in creating graphics for the Web is beyond the scope of this book. However, you should at least keep these two points in mind:

- **File format:** HTML Help requires Web-style graphics. In general, the file format should be .jpg (best for images with continuous tones, such as gradient fills photographic styles) or .gif (best for images with sharp differentiation between color areas, such as small icons or items with text that needs to be readable).

- **Color palette:** Anything that will be displayed in a Web browser window (including HTML Help) should be confined to the 216 colors of the browser-safe palette.

For the ManageX project, the graphics included small headers for each project module; icons denoting cautions and hints; and two background papers. This book's companion Web site allows you to download the required graphics for the sample project, including

- the page background (`green.jpg`)

- pictures of different trees (`tree1.jpg`, `tree2.jpg`, etc.)

- zone maps (`zone1.gif`, `zone2.gif`, etc.)

## The style sheets (CSS)

The style sheets for the ManageX project were created in the HoTMetaL style sheet editor and refined in Notepad (don't forget that style sheets are just plain text files). These style sheets defined the general elements expected in the project (BODY, P, FONT, HTML, H1, H2, and TABLE with its associated headers, data, and rows; ordered and unordered lists), specifying for each the font family, font size, line spacing, and color.

### ManageX CSS [excerpt 1]

```
BODY    { font-style: normal; font-weight: normal;
          font-size: 9pt; line-height: 150%; font-
          family: "Verdana"; color: black;
          background: transparent
          url(..\GRAPHICS\paper.JPG); }
P       {font-size: 9pt; line-height: 150%; font-
          family: "Verdana";}
FONT    {font-size: 9pt; line-height: 150%; font-
          family: "Verdana";}
HTML    { font-family: "Verdana"; }
H1      { font-weight: bold; font-size: 12pt; line-
          height: 140%; font-family: "Verdana";
          color: #CC0000;}
H2      { font-style: normal; font-weight: bold;
          font-size: 10pt; margin-top: 10pt; font-
          family:"Verdana"; color: black; }
```

```
TABLE    {font-size: 9pt; line-height: 50%; font-
         family: "Verdana"; }

TH       {font-size: 9pt; line-height: 150%; font-
         family: "Verdana"; }

TD       {font-size: 9pt; line-height: 150%; font-
         family: "Verdana" }

TR       {font-size: 9pt; line-height: 150%; font-
         family: "Verdana"; }
```

In Excerpt 1, notice that this style sheet specifies the font ("Verdana") in every case. Under the style sheet's rules of inheritance, specifying the font for the BODY or HTML should carry through to the other element's font; however, experience showed that such meager specification produces erratic results, especially in tables. It's easiest to simply specify the font for every element in the style sheet—and it's *still* shorter than specifying the font for every occurrence of every element in every file!

For more details on CSS, see Chapter 4, "Doing It In Style: CSS (Cascading Style Sheets)."

## ManageX CSS [excerpt 2]

```
OL       {font-size: 9pt; line-height: 150%; font-
         family: "Verdana";}

UL       {font-size: 9pt; line-height: 150%; margin-
         top: 0pt; font-family: "Verdana"; list-
         style-type: square;}

LI       {font-style: normal; font-weight: normal;
         font-size: 9pt; line-height: 150%; margin-
         top: 6pt; font-family: "Verdana"; color:
         black;}

.INFO    {font-size: 9pt; line-height: 150%; font-
         family: "Verdana"; border-style: ridge;
         border-color: #CCECFE; padding-left: 16px;
         padding-top: 6px; padding-bottom: 6px;
         padding-right: 2 px;}
```

Excerpt 2 presents the portion of the ManageX style sheet defining bulleted and unbulleted lists. Style sheets provide a great deal of control over list items, specifying the bullet type, margins, etc. Note that you can specify items such as line spacing (line-height) in absolute terms (for example, points) or in relative terms (here, a percentage of the font size). The 150% gives more "air" to the look (standard line spacing is approximately 120% of the font size).

In addition, the special class for INFO paragraphs specifies a colored border and extra padding (space between text and border), providing a consistent way to highlight important information. Once this class is defined, prefacing any paragraph in the HTML files with <P CLASS="INFO"> automatically adds a ridged blue border and extra space around it.

In figure 2.3, the bordered paragraph prefaced with "Note" uses the code shown in the adjacent text box. Note the efficiency of using a class tag

```
<P CLASS="INFO">
<IMG
SRC="Info.gif"
WIDTH="16"
HEIGHT="16"
ALIGN="BOTTOM">
<B><FONT
COLOR="#006699">
NOTE:</FONT></B>
<BR>Paragraph
text</P>
```

```
<UL>
<LI><B>Item 1,</B>
description1;
</LI>

<LI><B>Item 2,
</B>
description2;
</LI>
```

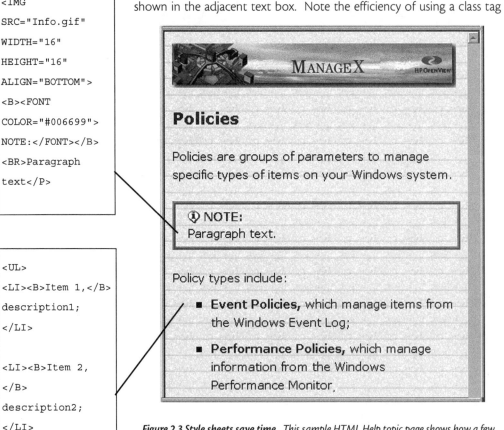

**Figure 2.3 Style sheets save time.** *This sample HTML Help topic page shows how a few lines of CSS code can save time and avoid repetitive coding in the topics. Callouts show HTML coding used to create the topic elements.*

`<P CLASS="INFO">` in the HTML page. Without the CSS, each "Note" would require the following additional lines of code:

```
.INFO { font-size: 9pt; line-height: 150%; font-
        family: "Verdana"; border-style: ridge;
        border-color: #00699; padding-left: 16px;
        padding-top: 6px; padding-bottom: 6px;
        padding-right: 2 px}
```

### Tree-planting style sheet

The style sheet for the sample project borrows from the ManageX style sheet, but is adjusted to suit the previous audience analysis. For example, the ManageX style sheet uses colors and graphics determined by the company—the signature red of the product (ManageX) and the signature blue of the corporation (Hewlett-Packard). The tree-planting project reflects the look of the garden with green and brown colors as well as leaf and tree graphics. Also, we'll suit the hobbyist audience with a larger, more casual font to enhance readability and approachability. Finally, we'll adapt the INFO class as a DEF class to display easily identifiable pop-up definitions.

## Tree Project 2: Create the style sheet

Create the tree-planting style sheet by typing the text below into a Notepad file named `tree.css` or downloading it from the companion Web site: `www.jmek.net/html_help`. Be sure to store the file in the `Tree\Common` directory.

```
BODY   { font-style: normal; font-weight: normal;
        font-size: 11pt; line-height: 160%; font-
        family: Tahoma, Arial;  color: black;
        background-image:
        url(..\GRAPHICS\LeafBkgrd.gif);background-
        color: white; margin-left: 40px;}
P      { font-style: normal; font-weight: normal;
        font-size: 11pt; line-height: 160%; font-
        family: Tahoma, Arial; color: black; }
```

The style sheet continues on the next page.

```
HTML     { font-style: normal; font-weight: normal;
           font-size: 11pt; line-height: 160%; font-
           family: Tahoma, Arial;  color: black; }
LI       { font-style: normal; font-weight: normal;
           font-size: 11pt; line-height: 160%; font-
           family: Tahoma, Arial; color: black; }
H1       { font-weight: bold; font-size: 15pt; line-
           height: 200%; font-family: Tahoma, Arial;
           color: green;}
H2       {font-weight: bold; font-size: 11pt; margin-
           top: 10pt; font-family: Tahoma, Arial; color:
           black; }
OL       {font-size: 11pt; line-height: 150%; font-
           family: Tahoma, Arial;}
UL       {font-size: 11pt; line-height: 150%; margin-
           top: 0pt; font-family: Tahoma, Arial; list-
           style-image: url(TreeBullet.gif); }
LI       {font-weight: normal; font-size: 11pt; line-
           height: 150%; margin-top: 6pt; font-family:
           Tahoma, Arial; color: black }
.DEF     {font-size: 11pt; line-height: 150%; font-
           family: Tahoma, Arial; border-style: inset;
           border-color: rgb(51,204,153);  padding-left:
           16px; padding-top: 6px; padding-bottom: 6px;
           padding-right: 2 px }
.DEFTERM   {font-weight: bold; color:
           rgb(51,204,153);}
```

## The dynamic HTML (DHTML)

The ManageX project used snippets of DHTML to create collapsing lists and other bits of interactivity. One of the most useful of these tricks involves a few lines of code that show or hide extra information whenever the user clicks on a graphic or piece of text. This simple trick requires no external or embedded styles, just some code in the text to control display of the hidden text. The tree-planting project incorporates this code to create pop-up definitions and/or pictures when the user's mouse moves over specialized terms.

```
Previous text:  Whatever lines of text might
         precede the coded section.
<SPAN ONMOUSEOVER="IDx.style.display=''"
         ONMOUSEOUT="IDx.style.display='none'">
         <SPAN CLASS="DEFterm"> clickableTest </
         SPAN> </SPAN>
         with a definition. </P>
<P CLASS="DEF" ID="IDx" STYLE="display:none"> This
         is the definition. </P><P CLASS="DEF"
         ID="IDx" STYLE="display:none"> popupText </P>
Following text: Whatever lines of text might
         follow the coded section.
```

The code sample shows a reusable snippet that displays the `popupText` whenever the user's mouse passes over the `clickableText`. When the user's mouse moves past the `clickableText`, the `popupText` disappears.

Certain elements need to be customized for each use of this DHTML:

- `IDx` is the placeholder for the identification code given each instance of show/hide text, with *x* reminding us that each identifier must be unique within a given HTML file. If a single file contains multiple terms requiring pop-up definitions, each term and its definition must be given a unique ID (at a minimum, ID1, ID2, etc.).

- `clickableText` is the placeholder for the trigger point, the text that triggers the display or hiding of the extra information.

- The `previous text` and `following text` paragraphs show how the coded text fits within the larger HTML file.

For the tree-planting project, store these lines in a simple text file or as part of a template. Then cut, paste, and modify whenever needed (you could even add a picture to aid with the definition, if desired). For example, to

This onMouseover snippet is one of the easiest ways to write show/hide code. More elegant approaches using scripts and an external .js file are explored in Chapter 5, "Making Waves: DHTML (Dynamic HTML)."

Making the placeholder text a single word (`IDx`, `clickableText`) makes it easy to select with a double-click when it's time to customize the code.

create a definition of *deciduous,* use the following customization of the code:

```
You may choose a tree that is
<SPAN
  ONMOUSEOVER="ID1.style.display=''"
  ONMOUSEOUT="ID1.style.display='none'">
<SPAN STYLE="DEFterm">deciduous</SPAN>
</SPAN>
or one that is
<SPAN
  ONMOUSEOVER="ID2.style.display=''"
  ONMOUSEOUT="ID2.style.display='none'">
<SPAN STYLE="DEFterm">evergreen</SPAN></SPAN>
<P CLASS="DEF" ID="ID1" STYLE="display:none">
        Losing its leaves in winter. </P>
<P CLASS="DEF" ID="ID2" STYLE="display:none">
        Retaining most of its leaves all year. </P>
```

# Assemble the templates

For the ManageX project, I began by creating templates for the three general purposes: overviews of each extension (figure 2.4), explanations of concepts, and directions for carrying out procedures. As the project continued, patterns of application behavior emerged, allowing the creation of additional templates for common procedures and tasks.

For rapid, efficienct project development, templates should include:

- **HTML page title:** The title appears in your Help system's title bar and as the default identifier elsewhere in the project. Adding

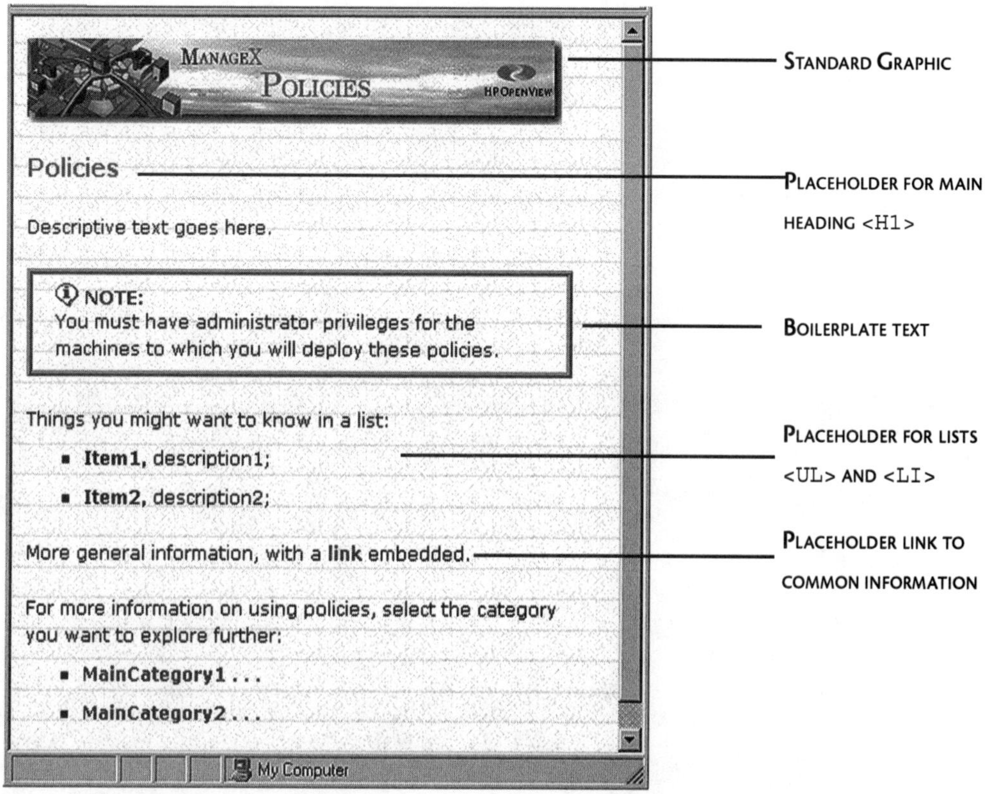

STANDARD GRAPHIC

PLACEHOLDER FOR MAIN HEADING <H1>

BOILERPLATE TEXT

PLACEHOLDER FOR LISTS <UL> AND <LI>

PLACEHOLDER LINK TO COMMON INFORMATION

*Figure 2.4  Template elements. This topic page was designed as a template for overview pages within the ManageX project. It provides for a general description, a frequently used warning, and two types of lists. The bottom list uses DHTML to allow each Main Category to expand and display its subcategories.*

`<TITLE>My Application Help </TITLE>` within the `<HEAD>` tags insures that you'll never have a blank title. It also provides a consistent search term when you want to create a more meaningful title.

- **CSS and JS links:** External stylesheet `(*.css)` and script `(*.js)` files provide the most efficient way to make global format changes or add new bits of DHTML.

- **Standard graphics:** For example, you may want a page header. Where appropriate, also include icons for tips and cautions, etc.

- **Layout placeholders:** Easily identifiable text to hold the space for standard layouts elements, including such things as level 1 headers, descriptive paragraphs, and lists of procedural steps.

- **Boilerplate text:** A timesaver for commonly repeated warnings or procedures. Since online Help is nonlinear, information must be repeated in multiple locations. Sometimes you'll want a link to another file, but short or important information should be repeated with boilerplate text.

---

## Tree Project 3: Create the template (optional)

The tree-planting project uses a single basic template. If you plan to write the topic files `(*.htm)` yourself, create this template by typing the text below into a Notepad file named `Template.htm` within the `Tree\Content` directory. You can also download the template from the Web site: `www.jmek.net/html_help`.

You can skip this step entirely if you plan to use the prewritten topic files from the Web site.

The following HTML lines create `ProcedureTemplate.htm`:

---

```
<HTML>
<HEAD>
<TITLE>Tree-Planting Help</TITLE>
<LINK REL="STYLESHEET"
      HREF="..\Common\tree.css">
<! - - The following lines are for projects with
      external script files.
<SCRIPT LANGUAGE="javascript"
      SRC="..\Common\tree.js">
</SCRIPT>
- -!>
</HEAD>
<BODY>
<H1>Procedure Title</H1>
<P>Introductory descriptive text about the
      procedure, including a
<SPAN ONMOUSEOVER="ID1.style.display=''"
      ONMOUSEOUT="ID1.style.display='none'">
      <SPAN CLASS="DEFterm"> technicalTerm
      </SPAN>
      </SPAN> with a definition. </P>
<P CLASS="DEF" ID="ID1" STYLE="display:none"> This
      is the definition. </P>
<H2>Performing the task (sub-title)</H2>
<OL>
<LI>Step1</LI>
<LI>Step2</LI>
<LI>Step3</LI>
<LI>Step4</LI>
</OL>
</BODY>
</HTML>
```

The template provides for an external JavaScript file, which is not used in the chapter's sample project files. These files use only a single bit of JavaScript, which is included in topic files as needed.

This code produces the HTML template shown in figure 2.5.

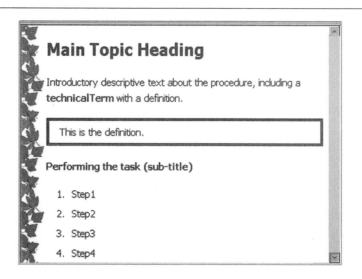

*Figure 2.5 The reults. The HTML in step 3 creates this procedural template page.*

## Write the individual pages

Once the templates are complete, you're ready to begin documenting the application as soon as it's available! For each page, open the template, save it under a more descriptive name, and edit away.

### Tree Project 4: Create the topic files

For the tree-planting project, you won't need to create the topic and graphic files; just download the following from the book's companion Web site. Store topic (`*.htm`) files in the `Tree\Content` directory. Graphic files (`*.jpg,*.gif`) go in `Tree\Common\Graphics`.

| | |
|---|---|
| `Main.htm` | `LeafBkgrd.gif` |
| `Choose.htm` | `Ch_Site.htm` |
| `Ch_Zones.htm` | `ZoneMap.gif` |
| `Ch_Species.htm` | `SantaCruz.htm` |
| `SantaCruz.jpg` | `Oak.htm` |
| `Oak.jpg` | `Prepare.htm` |
| `Prep_Site.htm` | `Prep_Tree.htm` |
| `Plant.htm` | `Planting.gif` |
| `Care.htm` | |

# Creating the HTML Help project

The HTML Help project file specifies and manages the parameters and files of your help system. It brings the required elements (topics, graphics, style sheets, script files, contents, indexing) together with the project parameters (window definitions, compilation parameters, etc.), ultimately compiling all the pieces into a single distributable HTML Help file (*.chm).

While the project file can be created directly in Notepad or another text editor, Microsoft's HTML Help Workshop (and third-party HTML Help editors) provides a graphical interface and helps insure that the project file's structure and syntax are correct. Later chapters will describe times and places when you should edit the project file directly; for this overview, we'll use the HTML Help Workshop.

You can download ready-made project files from the companion Web site, but you'll learn more by following through the rest of this chapter and creating your own.

## Project definition

### Create the project & add its topic files

Creating the new project is as simple as selecting FILE>NEW from the HTML Help Workshop's menus and then following the NEW PROJECT Wizard. The HTML Help Workshop automatically creates a file with the bare minimum required settings, including the file list, default topic and compiled filenames, language and compatibility settings, and compile settings.

Be sure to immediately add as many topic files to the project as possible. The HTML Help Workshop makes it difficult to specify project parameters until you define the set of working files.

## Tree Project 5: Create & populate the project file

1.  In the Workshop, go to the File menu and select New. When asked to Specify what to create, choose Project and click OK.

2.  In the New Project wizard, select Next to bypass the first page (asking if you want to convert Windows help project).

3.  On the Wizard's New Project – Destination screen, use the Browse button to locate the top level Tree directory you created earlier for this sample project. Once within the directory, type Tree as the project file name. Click Open to verify the selections, then click Next to continue.

4.  On the Wizard's New Project – Existing Files screen, select only the HTML files (*.htm) option so that you can quickly add the downloaded topic and graphic files. Click Next to continue.

5.  On the Wizard's New Project – HTML Files screen, click Add and then use the standard file Open box to navigate to the Tree\Content subdirectory. First select the main.htm file and click Open. (The first file selected is both added to the project and set as the project's default topic.)

6.  Back on the Wizard's screen, New Project – HTML Files you'll see Content\Main.htm has been added to the list. Click Add again and use ctrl-click and shift-click to select the rest of the topic files. (You could also add the graphic and style sheet files now, but we'll do that outside the Wizard.) Click Next to continue.

7.  Click Finish to have the Wizard create the basic project file (*.hhp) and display the result as shown on the next page.

    If you opened tree.hhp in Notepad, it would look exactly like the left pane of the Workshop shown here, with the

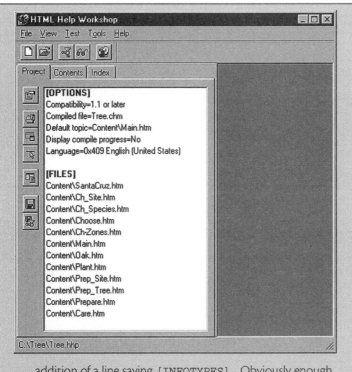

addition of a line saying [INFOTYPES]. Obviously enough, the [FILES] section reflects your choices in the New Project Wizard. In the [OPTIONS] section, the compiled file name is the one specified on the first page of the New Project Wizard, while the default topic is the first .htm file chosen in the Wizard. The other options are the Workshop defaults (more later).

8. In theory, the HTML Help compiler automatically adds all files referenced in your topics. In practice, this seldom happens, so it is necessary to manually add graphic, style sheet, and script files.

To add the graphic files to the project, click the ADD/ REMOVE TOPIC FILES button (second from the top on the left side). In the resulting dialog, click ADD and navigate to the Tree\Common\Graphics folder. Force the Workshop to display the graphics files, by typing *.* in the FILE NAME text

> box and pressing ENTER. Select all the graphics files and
> click OPEN to add them to the project. Repeat this
> procedure to add `Tree\Common\Tree.css` to your
> project. Click **OK** to return to the main part of the
> Workshop.
>
> 9.    From the FILE menu, choose SAVE ALL FILES.

## Specify parameters

The HTML Help's New Project Wizard defines the following default parameters:

- **Compatibility=1.1 or later:** This setting allows your HTML Help system to be backwardly compatible. (Version 1.0 was available for only a short time and did not offer all the functionality of 1.1 and later versions.)

- **Compiled file:** Specified by you from within the Wizard

- **Default topic:** The first topic (.htm) file selected in the Wizard's NEW FILES page.

- **Display compile progress=No:** Setting this parameter to "Yes" causes the compiler to display the file currently being compiled in the right window of the HTML Help Workshop. This option can be useful for troubleshooting a compiled project.

- **Language=0x409 English (United States):** By default, this is the language set as your machine's default locale (in the Regional Settings of the Windows Control Panel). Be aware that language settings other than English may experience difficulties in using the full-text search capability.

For the sample tree-planting project, we'll accept the default options and add two more:

- **Title:** Determines what displays in the title bar at the top of the compiled HTML Help project.

- **Compile full-text search information:** Allows the user to search for any word that appears anywhere in the text of the topics.

## Tree Project 6: Specify additional project options

1. In the left window of the HTML Help Workshop, double-click [OPTIONS].

2. On the GENERAL tab of the OPTIONS dialog, type *Tree-Planting* in the text box labeled TITLE.

3. Click the COMPILER tab. Select the COMPILE FULL-TEXT SEARCH INFORMATION option.

4. From the FILE menu, choose SAVE ALL FILES.

Now we'll go on to the slightly more complicated option of defining the default window.

## Window definition: size & styles

Window types are one of the tricky parts of the HTML Help Workshop. Although the New Project Wizard does not specify a default window type, erratic behavior is common in projects without one. In addition, HTML Help seems happiest if the default window type is named "main," especially in merged projects. You can modify this window in the WINDOW TYPES dialog.

## Tree Project 7: Define the default window

1. In the HTML Help Workshop, click the ADD/MODIFY WINDOWS DEFINITIONS button (third from the top on the left)

2. In the ADD A NEW WINDOW TYPE dialog, type **Main** for the window type name.

3. On the GENERAL tab of the WINDOWS TYPES dialog, type **Tree-Planting** as the TITLE BAR TEXT.

4. Click the NAVIGATION PANE tab. If you've been experimenting and have created any other types, make sure that the WINDOW TYPE text box shows **Main.**

   - Set the NAVIGATION PANE WIDTH to 200.

   - Select the AUTO SYNC option to make sure that the topic in the navigation (left) pane of your HTML Help system always places the highlight on the topic pertaining to the currently open MAIN window.

   - Choose **Contents** as the DEFAULT TAB.

5. Click the POSITION tab and make sure that **Main** is the currently selected WINDOW TYPE. Then click the AUTOSIZER button. Drag the model AUTOSIZER window to the upper right corner of your screen, then resize the window to a comfortable size. This sets the size and location in which your HTML Help system opens by default. Click **OK** and you'll see your choices reflected in the WINDOW SIZE AND POSITION fields (I recommend a width of about 550 and a height of about 400).

6. Back in the POSITION tab, select SAVE USER DEFINED WINDOW POSITION AFTER FIRST USE to allow your users the courtesy of sizing and positioning the window to their liking. Click **OK** to save all choices.

7. From the FILE menu, choose SAVE ALL FILES.

# Building the navigation system

## Contents

HTML Help's Table of Contents feature is right on the *bleeding* edge. Things change without warning and you're often not sure what you did to fix it! In version 1.0 of the HTML Help compiler, for example, books often lost their settings and became pages, while the indent level changed apparently at random. Most of this seemed fixed in 1.1, but such behavior is still reported occasionally. At least three bugs persist through version 1.3.

- Adding a contents entry using the list of **HTML FILES** in the **ADD PATH OR URL** dialog is apt to add the wrong file. In figure 1.6, taken from the ManageX system, the HTML title ("Configuring Console Policies") is

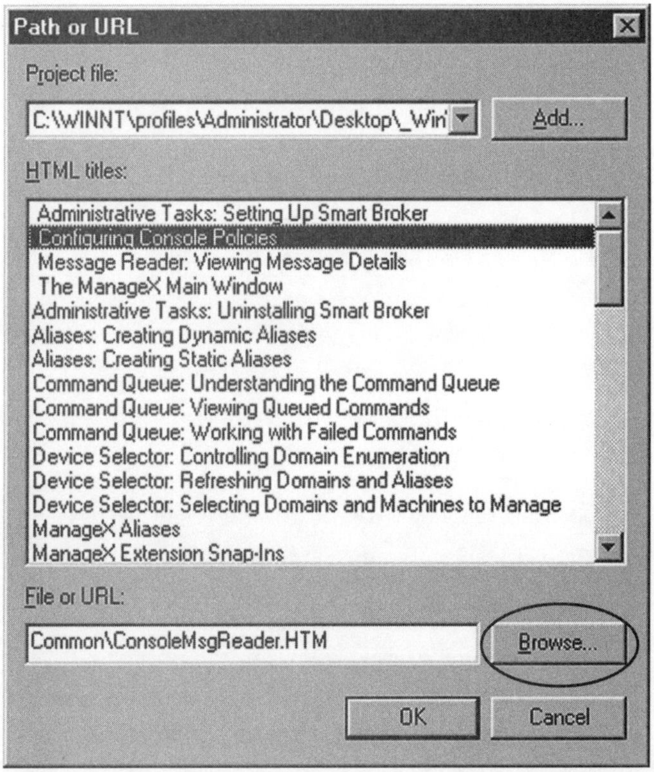

*Figure 1.6 Bug alert. The* Add Path or URL *dialog loses the synchronization between* HTML titles *and* File or URL paths. *Choose the correct file by using the* Browse *button.*

the title of a file named CP-configuring.htm. The filename shown as the **File or URL** (Common\ConsoleMsgReader.HTM) actually refers to the third item in the HTML files list ("Message Reader: Viewing Message Details"). The workaround? Use the BROWSE button to access a standard Windows browse dialog where you can choose your topics by their filename.

- There's also a video refresh bug: If your table of contents grows longer than the window can show, the display does not refresh when you close the TABLE OF CONTENTS ENTRY tab after adding a new entry. You must force a refresh by going to one of the other tabs and back again.

- It takes two tries to assign a non-standard icon to a contents entry. If you add an entry (book or page) on the GENERAL tab and go directly to the ADVANCED tab, the IMAGE NUMBER spin control will not work. You must click **OK** to exit the dialog, then select the new entry in the contents list and click on the EDIT icon (the pencil). Now when you go to the ADVANCED tab, you will be able to change the icon image.

---

## Tree Project 8: Create the table of contents

1. To create a new, blank contents file, select the CONTENTS tab of the HTML Help Workshop. When a dialog labeled TABLE OF CONTENTS NOT SPECIFIED appears, choose CREATE A NEW CONTENTS FILE and click **OK.** In the SAVE AS dialog that appears, navigate to the TREE directory and type **Tree** as the FILE NAME, then click SAVE.

2. To tie the contents to your default window, click the CONTENTS PROPERTIES button (top one on the left). Type **main** as the DEFAULT WINDOW, then click **OK.**

3. Right-click in the blank window on the left of the HTML Help Workshop and select INSERT HEADING from the shortcut menu. On the GENERAL tab, type *Introduction* as the ENTRY TITLE, then click ADD. Use the BROWSE button to locate and select Main.htm. Click **OK** twice to exit.

4.  Back in the main workshop window, right-click in the left pane and select Insert Heading from the shortcut menu again. Answer No when asked if you want to insert the entry at the beginning of the table of contents. This time, type **Choosing a Tree** as your Entry Title, and use the Add and Browse buttons to select Choose.htm. Click OK twice to exit.

5.  To use a book icon to set off the heading topics, click on your new **Introduction** entry, then click the Edit selection button (fourth from the top on the left). Choose its Advanced tab, then use the Index Image spin controls to change to 1 (a book). Click OK to save your changes.

6.  Right-click again in left pane of the workshop window, but this time choose Insert topic from the shortcut menu. Add the following entry titles and associated files:

    - Identifying your planting zone (Ch_zone.htm)

    - Selecting and assessing your site (Ch_site.htm)

    - Choosing appropriate species (Ch_species.htm)

    - Oak (Oak.htm)

    - Santa Cruz redwood (SantaCruz.htm)

7.  When you have added the above files, right-click on the entry for **Oak** and choose Move Right from the shortcut menu. Answer Yes to the prompt asking if you're sure you want to do this. Both the **Oak** and the **Santa Cruz redwood** entry beneath it should move to the right, appearing as subtopics of the **Choosing appropriate species** entry.

8.  With the **Santa Cruz redwood** entry selected, right-click and select Insert Heading from the shortcut menu. Add a heading titled **Preparing to Plant the Tree** that points to

the `prepare.htm` file. Select the new heading, click the
EDIT SELECTION button, and use the ADVANCED tab to change
its image to a book (1). Right-click this new entry and
choose MOVE LEFT from the shortcut menu. Move the
entry to the left one more time, so that it appears as a top-
level heading.

9.   Add the following files as sub-topics of the **Preparing to
Plant the Tree** heading.

   ▪   **Preparing the site** (`prep_site.htm`)

   ▪   **Preparing the tree** (`prep_tree.htm`)

10.   Add the following files as top-level headings with the book
icon.

   ▪   **Planting the tree** (`plant.htm`)

   ▪   **Caring for the new tree** (`care.htm`)

11.   From the FILE menu, choose SAVE ALL FILES.

## Index

Indexing is another complicated topic in the HTML Help Workshop.
Beyond the normal indexing questions of choosing terms and organizing
synonyms, you must also choose whether to insert the index entries in
the individual HTML files or directly in an index (`*.hhk`) file and whether
or not to use a binary index. There are also questions of ALINKS and
KLINKS. The more complex issues are covered in a later chapter. For the
tree-planting project, we'll simply add a few sample index entries to an
index file created within the HTML Help Workshop.

## Tree Project 9: Create the index

1. To create a new, blank index file, select the INDEX tab of the HTML Help Workshop. When a dialog labeled INDEX NOT SPECIFIED appears, choose CREATE A NEW INDEX FILE and click OK. In the SAVE AS dialog that appears, navigate to the Tree directory and type Tree as the FILE NAME, then click SAVE.

2. To tie the contents to your default window, click the INDEX PROPERTIES button (top one on the left). Type main as the DEFAULT WINDOW, then click OK.

3. Right-click in the blank window on the left of the HTML Help Workshop and select INSERT KEYWORD from the shortcut menu. On the GENERAL tab, type pine as the KEYWORD, then click ADD. Use the BROWSE button to locate and select SantaCruz.htm. Click OK twice to exit.

4. Repeat the previous step to add the following keywords and their associated files. You may add as many additional entries as you wish.

   - redwood (SantaCruz.htm)

   - evergreen (SantaCruz.htm)

   - deciduous (oak.htm)

   - soil (ch_site.htm and prep_site.htm). You can add multiple topic files to a single keyword by repeatedly choosing the ADD button in the INDEX ENTRY dialog.

5. When you finish adding entries, click the SORT KEYWORDS ALPHABETICALLY button (third from the bottom on the left). The HTML Help Workshop automatically alphabetizes your index.

# Compiling & testing the project

In general, compiling is the most automatic part of the process. And, if it works when you test it, you're done! (Troubleshooting will be covered in a later chapter.)

---

### Tree Project 10: Compile & test

1. Click the PROJECT tab of the HTML Help Workshop. In the project file pane on the left, verify that the project contains the following two lines:
   **Contents file=Tree.hhc**
   **Index file=Tree.hhk**
   If you don't see these lines, click the CHANGE PROJECT OPTIONS button (top on the left) and choose its FILES tab. Type `Tree.hhc` as the CONTENTS FILE and `Tree.hhk` as the INDEX FILE. Click **OK** to save your changes.

2. Click the ADD/MODIFY WINDOW DEFINITIONS (third button on the left) and click on its FILES tab. Use the drop-down lists to set `Tree.hhc` as the TOC and `Tree.hhk` as the INDEX. Click **OK** to save your changes.

3. Select the COMPILE HTML FILE button (third from the left on the top). Select both the SAVE ALL FILES BEFORE COMPILING and AUTOMATICALLY DISPLAY COMPILED HELP FILE WHEN DONE options.

4. Click COMPILE and watch the compiler's progress in the right pane of the workshop.

5. If the compiled file does not display automatically, click the VIEW COMPILED FILE button (fourth from the left on the top). Verify that the correct file is listed and click VIEW.

---

Enjoy your first compiled HTML Help file!

# Merging modular projects

Merging HTML Help modules allows you to customize online Help systems by quickly adding and removing a "chapter" of information from the project. When merged modules are present on the user's machine, they appear seamlessly in the table of contents, index, and full-text search; when the modules are deleted, they disappear just as seamlessly.

For example, the ManageX project was designed to support the addition of Smart Plug-Ins (SPIs)—special modules that add extra functionality in key areas. Not all SPIs were available when the main ManageX application was released and not all users would buy all SPIs. So I created the project with "stubs" for any SPI Help modules that would be created and/or purchased later on. The tree-planting project could use the same approach to allow for the creation of specialized zone planting guides.

Note that the actual merging process occurs when the user opens the HTML Help file, *not* when the Help author compiles the files. Because of this, merging occurs only for those files that are actually present on the user's system. This procedure lets you plan for expansion since the merged files do not need to exist when the master file is compiled.

## Efficiency

Planning and creating templates, style sheets, and script files saves a great deal of time during the production of the Help system's topic files (`*.htm`). If you're merging multiple modules, additional time savings accrue from the creation of a template for the project files (`*.hhp`, `*.hhc`, `*.hhk`) used in each module. When the first ManageX module became available, I used my HTML templates to create the documentation topics. Then I assembled the HTML files into a project in the HTML Help workshop. This project file became a template for the other modules. In fact, I discovered that the easiest way to create new modules was to copy the first module's project files, remove all the topic files and TOC/index entries, and then add the topic files and contents/index entries for the new module.

# CHAPTER 2

# Merging requirements

The actual merging requires you to perform the following tasks:

1. Set up project options:

   - Insure that compatibility is set for version 1.1 or later.

   - Insure that a binary index is used.

   - Specify merge files in the **Project Options.**

   - Define a consistent default window for all modules.

2. Create cross-references among modules:

   - Prepare for merged tables of contents.

   - Use proper syntax for cross-module links.

All tasks must be performed in the master module (in this case, `Tree.chm`). The merged modules (here, `Zone01.chm`, `Zone02.chm`, etc.) only need to use the consistent default window and the appropriate syntax for cross-module links.

# Setup options

## Ensuring compatibility & binary index options

These options are defined in the HTML Help Workshop's PROJECT tab. To set them up, go into the PROJECT OPTIONS and select the COMPILER tab. Set the COMPATIBILITY to 1.1 OR LATER and select the CREATE A BINARY INDEX option.

## Specifying merge files

If you're creating a modular merged project, you must specify the files to be merged in the PROJECT tab's OPTIONS > MERGE FILES dialog. You can specify dummy merge files (`Zone01.chm`, `Zone02.chm`, etc.) to take care of future additions. Just don't forget to use these same names in your table of contents and as the name of the final merged files.

## Window definitions

If you're merging modules, make sure you specify the same window name (for example, "**main**") as the default window for the project, contents, and index. (Each tab has a PROPERTIES page which allows you to specify its default window.)

# Merging references

## Preparing merged tables of contents

Under 1.1 and earlier versions of the HTML Help Workshop, merging files in the table of contents was definitely "bleeding edge." Sometimes they'd show up; most times they wouldn't. The pages were in the .chm; you could find them through the index or search facilities, but they wouldn't show up in the contents. Since the ManageX project wanted to preserve the appearance of merged modules, I used a complicated workaround with duplicates of the introductory pages included as part of the master file with links to the rest of the file. Unfortunately, this had unexpected side effects, including a situation where users who updated an individual module lost all the rest of the HTML Help system.

Fortunately, versions 1.2 and later of the HTML Help Workshop seem to have fixed most of the problems. When the merged file is present, it appears in the table of contents; when the merged file is not available, no entry appears.

This procedure adds an "Include" statement for the contents of your merged file. When the specified merge files are present on the user's system, they will appear in the contents; if the files are not present, no entry appears.

## Using proper cross-file link syntax

This syntax works with all versions of Internet Explorer. If you know users have IE 4.0 or later installed, you can replace `mk:@MSITStore` with `ms-its`.

HTML Help requires a special protocol for linking to pages within a compiled file. Links between pages in a single compiled HTML Help file (`*.chm`) use the standard format, with a relative path:

```
<A HREF="directory\page.htm">
```

In order to link to a page in another compiled HTML file, use this format:

```
<A HREF="ms-its:CompiledFile.chm::\page.htm">
```

where `page.htm` is the name of the specific topic you want to link to and `CompiledFile.chm` is the name of the merged compiled help file containing it.

---

### Tree Project Appendix: Creating a merged project

The following steps summarize the procedures necessary to set up a Master module for a merged Help project. We'll perform these steps on the Tree-Planting project; however, since we do not have the additional Zone modules, we will not be able to test the results.

1. In the left window of the HTML Help Workshop's PROJECT tab, double-click [OPTIONS].

2. Click the COMPILER tab. Use the drop-down list to set the COMPATIBILITY option to **1.1 or later** and click to select the CREATE A BINARY INDEX option.

3. Click the MERGE FILES tab. Click the ADD button. In the ADD MERGE FILE dialog that appears, type `Zone01.chm` in the text box titled SPECIFY THE NAME OF THE FILE TO MERGE. Merged projects work best if all merged modules are in the same directory, so you do not need to specify a path. Click **OK**. (In a real merged project, you would repeat this step for each merged module.)

4. Click **OK** again to close the Options dialog.

5. Since the tree-planting project already uses "Main" as the default window everywhere, you need make no more changes in this file. However, as you would create the "Zone" modules, you would need to make sure that all the window definitions were specified as **main** and used the same parameters as this master file.

6. To prepare for the merging of modules into the table of contents, go to the HTML Help Workshop's Contents tab, right-click the entry named **Choosing appropriate species,** and choose Insert file from the shortcut menu.

7. In the resulting dialog, type Zone01.chm::\Zone01.hhc as the File to include and answer **Yes** to the prompt asking if you want to include the file even though it can't be found. (In a real merged project, you would repeat this step and the preceding one for each additional merged file.)

8. On the Project tab, select the Compile HTML file button (third from the left on the top). Select the Save all files before compiling option, then click Compile.

# 3

# Bringing It Together:
## HTML Topics & Templates

The items covered in this chapter—HTML topics and templates—comprise both the beginning and the end of the main writing process. You will use the information in this chapter to create the content of your HTML Help system, creating templates for the elements you think you'll need, adding content to the templates to create the individual topics, and then refining the templates before creating more topics. In between, you'll add in your style sheets and script files (which may also be continually refined).

HTML is, of course, the basic language of HTML Help systems. While this chapter does not constitute a complete course in writing HTML, it does include many of the basic tags and HTML coding required to create HTML Help files and templates. Much of this material can be used in a "cookbook" fashion by simply copying the code and changing the content to suit your own needs. If you have any background at all in HTML or coding, you should be able to use this chapter to create all the files necessary for an HTML Help system.

Templates, in the sense used here, are exemplary HTML files that combine reusable elements (graphics, CSS, DHTML) with boilerplate text for common tasks and placeholders for text and graphics that changes in substance but not in style. Rapid development can occur once the templates are complete and the application is ready for documentation: simply open the appropriate template, save it under another name, and make edits as necessary to reflect the individual concepts and procedures for that topic.

Templates bring your content together with cascading style sheets, JavaScript files, and with other reusable elements so that you can quickly and consistently create the actual HTML Help topics. Templates serve the author's need for automating the process without compromising quality; they serve the user's need for a consistent presentation that aids comprehension without being distracting. The topics themselves contain the substance of the online system, the actual information that users want and need.

More complex templates are possible in HTML editors that explicitly support templates as a feature. But, with a little forethought and creativity, all you really need to create a serviceable template for your topics is the HTML Help Workshop or a basic text editor such as the Windows Notepad.

# Where to author

When deciding where to create your topics and templates, first consider your own experience and preferences. Do you want to work in a WYSIWYG environment, to dig directly into the code, or to swap between the two approaches? Similarly, do you want the application to do lots of "hand-holding" with built-in formats, scripts, etc.? Or would you prefer that the application keep its hands off of your code changes? Do you tend to customize everything you can about the application or use it out of the box?

When you're assessing authoring environments, consider the following specifics that will help insure the product works with HTML Help:

- HTML markup consistent with the HTML 3.2 or higher specifications. Ideally, the markup should not rely heavily on local formatting (such as <FONT> tags on every paragraph) or <DIV> tags (except when creating DHTML effects).

- Ability to access and edit directly in the code.

- Support for cascading style sheets (CSS). Some HTML editors include CSS editors directly within the product.

- Support for dynamic HTML (DHTML). Most HTML editors are limited to bundling a few scripts, but some include more extensive DHTML support.

- Site management tools, especially global search/replace and automated link testing/updates.

- Asset storage or libraries (ways to easily access reusable text and your own custom code).

- Template creation and implementation.

With the current range of available HTML editors, you should be able to find one (or more) to meet almost any set of requirements. As you work on HTML Help, you're almost guaranteed to do some hands-on editing in the Windows Notepad or in the HTML Help Editor itself. Serious developer types may want to use Microsoft's Visual InterDev, but that's overkill for most HTML Help authors. If you already have an HTML editor you love, that's probably what you should use. If you're looking for new tools, check out the many downloadable demos available on the Web to find what's right for you. Visit their Web sites (table 3.1) for demos of their tools.

**Table 3.1 Tools for HTML Help authoring**

| APPLICATION & MANUFACTURER | DEMO/DOWNLOAD URL | COMMENTS |
|---|---|---|
| HoTMetaL Pro® from Softquad | `www.hotmetalpro.com` | Overall HTML editing, with site management tools, CSS editor, & a few DHTML scripts |
| HomeSite® from Allaire | `www.allaire.com` or `commerce.allaire.com/download/` | For overall HTML editing; integrates well with Dreamweaver |
| Dreamweaver® from Macromedia | `www.macromedia.com/software/dreamweaver/` | Focused on DHTML; also a graphics-oriented HTML editor & site management tools. Even does straight HTML! |
| ForeHTML Pro® from ForeFront | `www.ff.com/indexDown.html` | Specifically designed for HTML Help & other online Help systems |
| Doc-to-Help 2000® | `www.wextech.com/pr4downloadsu.htm` | Specifically designed for HTML Help & other online Help systems |
| RoboHelp HTML® from eHelp, (formerly Blue Sky Software) | `www.ehelp.com/resources/downloads/ehelp.htm` | Specifically designed for HTML Help & other online Help systems |

For updates on downloadable demos, check the companion Web site, `www.jmek.net/html_help`.

| Application & Manufacturer | Demo/Download URL | Comments |
| --- | --- | --- |
| HotDog® from Sausage Software | www.sausage.com | For HTML editing; primarily focused on tags |
| Front Page 2000® from Microsoft | Demo must be ordered, downloaded, from: www.microsoft.com/ frontpage/trial/ default.htm | Consider only FP 2000; earlier versions add proprietary code and "extensions" |
| CoffeeCup® from Coffee Cup Software | www.coffeecup.com | Primarily for CSS creation & editing |
| Paint Shop Pro® from JASC | www.jasc.com | De facto standard for screen captures; also general graphics tools including conversions, color replacement, layers |
| GIF Animator®, SmartSaver Pro®, & PhotoImpact® from Ulead | www.ulead.com | Three specialized Web graphics tools to create animated GIFs; save Web graphics in small files; & create DHTML such as image rollovers; respectively |

# HTML Help Editor

The HTML Help Workshop itself includes a barebones editor that lets you modify an existing HTML file by double-clicking its filename in the Project tab window. You can also use the editor to create a new HTML file by using the Workshop's File > New > HTML File menus and commands, which provide only a few features beyond the Windows Notepad.. This Workshop's editor is limited to the standard Cut/Paste/Copy/Find & Replace types of commands on the Edit menu and a few HTML-specific commands on the Tags menu,

Specifically, the Tags menu supports:

A bug in Find/Replace: these commands do not return a "not found" message when there are no more occurrences of the search string. The commands remain silent, leaving you to guess if the program has finished or crashed.

- Insert Text Block or Edit Text Block (figure 3.1) : Text blocks are straight, unformatted snippets that you type in an empty window. Despite their name, text blocks can include HTML coding (which is, after all, straight text) so you could create text blocks for frequently used formatting (such as numbered lists) to speed up HTML creation/ editing. Choose your text blocks with care, as they are global for a particular computer (that is, they are shared by all projects you edit with a single installation of the Workshop), but they are not available across multiple computers. Also, you are limited to a total of nine text blocks. (The blocks are stored in the Windows Registry, so there's no safe and effective way around this limitation.)

**Figure 3.1 Text blocks.** *The HTML Help Workshop's editor lets you store up to nine collections of reusable code as* text blocks. *These text blocks may contain HTML code as well as boilerplate text.*

- **CHARACTER FORMATTING:** Surrounds the currently selected text with codes for the basics: bold, italics, emphasis, strike, strong, underline. (If no text is currently selected, this command inserts start and end tags for the selected format.)

- **HEADING...:** Inserts headings from levels 1 to 6, and aligns the headings left, right, or center. That's all folks.

- **COMMENT:** Type some text in this window, and the Workshop inserts it into the HTML file with `< ! - -` and `—>` comment tags to keep your remarks from displaying in the browser window.

- **TITLE:** Inserts the text you type here into the HTML file's `<HEAD>` section, surrounded by `<TITLE>` tags.

- **HTML HELP CONTROL...:** The one really useful feature. This command allows you to insert an ActiveX control to perform HTML Help specific items such as related topics, table of contents, training cards, or keyword search. (For more information about these controls, see Chapter 9, "Accelerating Links: Cross-Referencing Options.")

Unless you normally code HTML in a text editor, the Workshop's editing features are really only useful for quick modifications or for adding HTML Help Controls. The HTML Help Image Editor, however, is quite a useful tool for the most common graphics tasks in online Help: screen captures and file format conversions.

# HTML Help Image Editor

The HTML Help Workshop ships with the standalone HTML Help Image Editor (`flash.exe`), which is integrated into the Workshop on the Tools menu. It's definitely no substitute for an image editor: you cannot draw or paint anything, even a straight line. It primarily focuses on the two main elements of HTML Help graphics: screen captures and file/format management.

The file/format management capabilities, such as the Art Manuscript and image project functions, are useful for HTML Help systems with large numbers of images. Art Manuscripts are simple HTML files containing a table of thumbnail images linked to the original images, allowing you to preview and catalog your HTML Help system's image files

Image projects can list all the files contained in multiple folders on your local or network drive (figure 3.2), providing quick access to and information about each image file. Projects are created in the Browse window (accessed with the BROWSE WINDOW button on the toolbar). Once in the BROWSE window, click the CHANGE button and then (in the standard file browsing dialog that opens) click the PROJECT button.

Browse Window
button

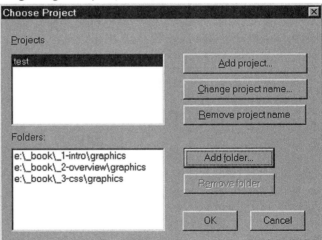

*Figure 3.2* *Image projects.* *The* Choose Project *dialog in the* HTML Help Image Editor *lets you collect images from various locations into a single project for easy access.*

From this point, you can name the project and define its contents by choosing folders on a local or network drive. Once files are added to a project, you can also export a file list. Or, if you want more information about a single file, right-click its file name in the BROWSE window to access a variety of information about the file (figure 3.3).

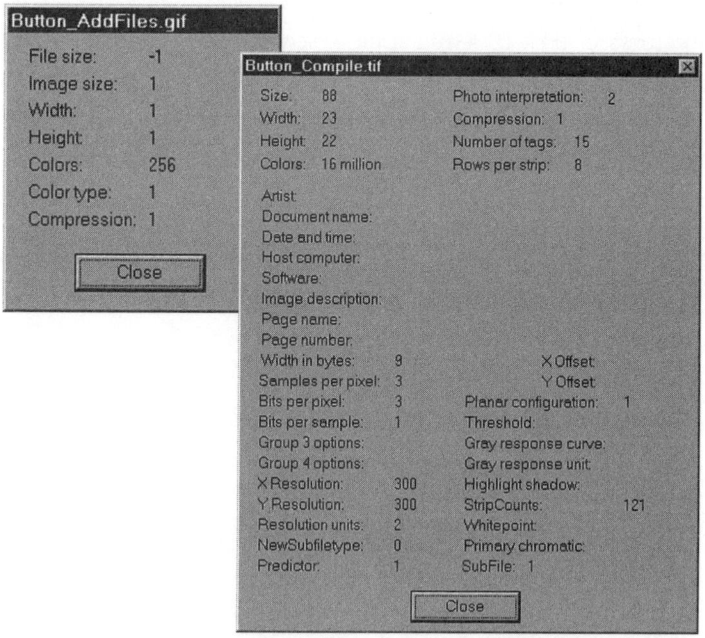

**Button_AddFiles.gif**

| | |
|---|---|
| File size: | -1 |
| Image size: | 1 |
| Width: | 1 |
| Height: | 1 |
| Colors: | 256 |
| Color type: | 1 |
| Compression: | 1 |

Close

**Button_Compile.tif**

| | | | |
|---|---|---|---|
| Size: | 88 | Photo interpretation: | 2 |
| Width: | 23 | Compression: | 1 |
| Height: | 22 | Number of tags: | 15 |
| Colors: | 16 million | Rows per strip: | 8 |

Artist:
Document name:
Date and time:
Host computer:
Software:
Image description:
Page name:
Page number:

| | | | |
|---|---|---|---|
| Width in bytes: | 9 | X Offset: | |
| Samples per pixel: | 3 | Y Offset: | |
| Bits per pixel: | 3 | Planar configuration: | 1 |
| Bits per sample: | 1 | Threshold: | |
| Group 3 options: | | Gray response curve: | |
| Group 4 options: | | Gray response unit: | |
| X Resolution: | 300 | Highlight shadow: | |
| Y Resolution: | 300 | StripCounts: | 121 |
| Resolution units: | 2 | Whitepoint: | |
| NewSubfiletype: | 0 | Primary chromatic: | |
| Predictor: | 1 | SubFile: 1 | |

Close

*Figure 3.3 Image properties. For each image, the project stores the standard information shown in the smaller dialog (on the left, above) and the extended information shown in the larger dialog (on the right, above).*

The Image Editor's screen capture features allow you to "grab" the current contents of your screen using the mouse, function keys, or a timer. With the mouse, you can define the section of the screen you want to capture; with the keyboard or timer options, you are limited to capturing a single window or the entire desktop. You also have the option to include the cursor, if desired. Once captured, the image can be sized, cropped, and converted to various formats and color depths.

Once the screen shots are captured, you can use the Image Editor's batch conversion feature to manipulate screen captures and other existing files between various image formats and color depths. As a variation on standard HTML, HTML Help displays primarily JPG and GIF graphic files. (It also supports some less common formats such as PNG.) The Image Editor supports conversions to 24-bit color JPGs and 16- or 256-color GIFs—the standard imagery for the Web. It also allows conversions to BMP, EPS, PCX, TGA, and TIF formats (none of which will display in HTML pages) for single-source documenters who may want to convert images from their HTML Help files for use in printed pieces. In addition, the conversion feature lets you set one or more images to a standard color depth of 16 colors, 256 colors, or 24-bit (16 million) color. (For most Help files, you'll want to use 256 colors.)

# Designing the templates

Most users of word processing and desktop publishing programs have at least a passing familiarity with the concept of templates: pre-built files that can store anything from a few simple bits of boilerplate text to complete documents with formatting, styles, graphics, and custom macros. Recently, the more sophisticated HTML editors have also begun to implement the concept, although they tend to focus on style rather than on content. For example, Macromedia's Dreamweaver (versions 2 and above) lets you define editable and non-editable regions of your templates and will propagate template changes to all site documents stored locally. Similarly, SoftQuad's HoTMetaL Pro 6.0 supports templates with read-only and replaceable text sections, as well as shipping with a series of templates for creating frequently used frameset designs and "decors" that can automate stylistic and graphic changes. Some HTML Help editors (such as ForeHTML Pro) also offer templates, including content-based templates (for example, Doc-to-Help's topic types).

In this chapter, however, the focus is on templates you can create in even the simplest of text editors, and which address content as well as format. In this context, an HTML Help system template is a single Web page with generic or placeholder text, standard graphics and formats (such as procedural lists), as well as links to CSS and DHTML files. These templates allow the rapid creation of structured content for an HTML Help system, while automating the production of a consistent look-and-feel. With templates, you don't have to remember whether you wanted to use an introductory paragraph before procedural steps. If you include boilerplate text, you won't even have to remember whether that pesky dialog box is called OPEN or BROWSE and how you explained its functionality and the procedures used with it..

# Identifying the necessary templates types

The first step in creating your templates is to identify the types of topics you'll require in your HTML Help system. All the templates in a system should work together, containing some consistent elements (especially in formatting choices such as overall colors and placement); but each template type has its own character.

The two classic Help topic types address conceptual and procedural information; many online Help systems also use section or chapter overviews, while others include appendices for reference information. If you plan to create intensely visual or dynamic content for task descriptions or other uses, you may also want a template for these pages. Although the types often overlap, it's easiest to identify your needs by considering the purpose and requirements of each type separately:

1. **Conceptual information.** Conceptual topics present the context for individual elements. They provide "behind the scenes" information: what something is and how it works, why the user might want to use that particular process or item, what other elements of the system are involved. The purpose of a successful conceptual information topic is to create understanding: the user understands the context of the process, module, or other item.

Many of the Microsoft Home products provide examples of branching interactive help

Conceptual information can fulfill the user's need for basic or advanced technical information, using presentation methods from simple text paragraphs to branching interactive demonstrations that let the user specify every aspect of the situation before launching the appropriate explanation. The type of conceptual information provided dictates many of the template design requirements. Textual descriptions will probably appear in the main HTML Help content pane; dynamic demonstrations usually launch a secondary window (and will probably use a separate visual/dynamic information template). Simple textual descriptions may require pop-up definitions or rich graphics to help novice users understand a new concept; more complex technical information may require expanding and collapsing paragraphs to keep the topic from being overwhelming. Consider your audience and your product before deciding how to design one or more conceptual templates.

2.  **Overview information.** Chapters or online Help sections often begin with a variant of the conceptual information type: an overview that provides a sort of "abstract" for the section. The purpose of an overview topic is to locate the user, either within the overall subject or within the online Help system itself. These overviews are designed to let a user know they are in the right section; present a "birds-eye view" of the section; or direct them to another, more appropriate section.

    Overview topics often require expanding/contracting lists of their subsections, or links to alternate sources of information. They are usually not heavily visual, unless they have been co-opted by the marketing department. They almost always appear in the main HTML Help content pane (although the table of contents pane should be "auto-synced" with the topic, contributing to the sense of "locating" the user within the system).

3.  **Procedural information.** Procedural topics form the nuts and bolts of most online Help and are included in even the most minimalist systems. At the very least, they provide numbered steps describing the sequence of actions necessary to complete a task. Ideally, they should also include a brief description of the procedure to assure users they've got the right procedure.

    The purpose of a procedural topic is simply to help the user accomplish the task. As such, the basic requirement is a list of numbered steps, perhaps with definitions of individual fields and a list of the choices available for each step of the task. More complex procedures may require branching procedures and shortcuts to particular programs or dialogs within the program. Although documentation theorists often suggest that screen captures are unnecessary since the Help and the application can be side-by-side onscreen, users sometimes like and need the reassurance of seeing that their screen matches the one in the procedure. For this reason, procedural topics should at least make provision for the possibility of a graphic.

4.  **Visual/dynamic information.** Pictures, pictures, and more pictures! On the Web, as well as in traditional documentation, users always seem to want more pictures. The purpose of a graphic topic can be to identify a component of the system, verify the results of a procedure, provide the context in which actions occur, or just catch and hold the user's attention.

    The main requirement for this kind of template is usually a separate blank canvas (secondary window) with navigational "hooks" that allow the user to access the visual information from within the textual material and move back to the text, either at the same point or in a location that logically follows from the graphic. Because graphics are often larger than the textual description, your graphic template's secondary window should resize dynamically to fit the contents (most text-based templates scroll to accommodate larger topics).

5.  **Reference information.** Reference topics provide information that users need only occasionally or data that is needed by only a few users (generally, the most technical users). Typical types of reference information include glossaries and programming APIs. The purpose of a reference topic is to educate the user quickly on a very specific, discrete piece of information.

    The requirements for these topics are generally quite simple and text-heavy, although some programming references require diagrams. Definition lists (created with the <DL> tag) are central to many reference types. If you have a type of reference information which occurs only in small chunks, consider pop-ups instead of a full-blown page template.

# Creating reusable elements

Once you've identified the necessary template types, you're ready to begin creating project-wide reusable components. These are aspects of your HTML Help system that should be consistent throughout the project, with appropriate variations for particular template types and project sections. For example, if you use a header graphic to identify the overall application or subject of the HTML Help system, different sections might insert different "subhead" text within the graphic, and different template types might use different color schemes Once you've mapped out your system and its template types, you're ready to identify the required components, create each item, and store them in a central location.

Some of the project-specific components (with template-type variations) to consider include:

- **"Branding" elements** such as graphic or textual headers and any special treatment of the product name.

- **Navigation aids** such as FORWARD and BACK buttons to implement a Windows help-style browse sequence or other forced-sequence information.

- **Reusable graphics** such as frequently referenced screen captures or a blank button. (You can then layer different text on the button to allow users access to animated procedures, glossary definitions, or other items.)

- **Reusable text** such as frequently repeated tasks, definitions, and other items.

## Fashioning the graphic elements

Reusable graphic elements for an HTML Help system can include branding elements, navigation aids, and other frequently referenced visual items. Creating the right components for a successful HTML Help system requires you to pull together classical design and Help principles as well as exploiting the possibilities and sensibilities of the Web. Sometimes your company will have corporate standards that constrain/liberate your design choices; sometimes you may have access to the services of a graphic artist or Web designer. But most often, Help authors seem to exist in isolation. In these cases, scout the Web for sites you admire and designs that complement your system's needs. You may even wish to consult actual printed books for inspiration. Read the books; consult your own design resources; and then create your design and supporting graphics.

## Assembling a screen capture library

For software documentation projects, you may also want to begin generating a library of screen captures at this point. You can get a jump start on the project even if the interface isn't completely frozen, as long as you have an easy-to-understand system for naming and storing graphics. Then you'll know exactly where to go to update screen captures as the user interface changes.

When naming screen captures, don't forget to avoid spaces in the filenames; underscores (for example, `button_print.gif`) usually work, but midstream caps (for example, `buttonPrint.gif`) are even safer. If possible, store your screen captures in a single common directory for the entire project; if not, at least use a special subdirectory for graphics that is separate from the topic files. (For more suggestions on setting up the project directory structure, refer to the *Directory structure* section in Chapter 6, "Creating Magic; The HTML Help Project File.") Also, don't forget to save screen captures in a Web-friendly format. Generally, that means the `.gif` format, although elaborate screens with photo-style graphics may work better in `.jpg` format. Since most HTML Help systems reside locally (that is, on the user's hard drive or LAN), small graphic file sizes are not as crucial in HTML Help as they are with Web-delivered content. However, you'll still want them relatively small (say, below 75k) to keep the size of the overall system within reasonable bounds.

The two most common tools for HTML Help project screen captures are the HTML Help Image Editor and JASC's Paint Shop Pro™. The directions refer specifically to the HTML Help Image Editor, but Paint Shop Pro commands are similar.

1.  Open the application you're documenting and set up the windows and dialogs as desired for the screen capture. In general, it's best to set your screen to the Windows default colors before capturing the image.

2.  Open the HTML Help Image Editor. (If you're in the HTML Help Workshop, go to the Tools menu and select HTML Help Image Editor.)

3.  Set up your approach from the Capture menu's Preferences dialog.

    - To include the cursor in the screen capture, click the General tab. Select the Include cursor in the capture option.

    - To control the file naming of your captures, click the Filename tab. Type in a meaningful File prefix and set the file extension to `.gif` (unless you're capturing photographic-style images). Type the name of your graphics directory in the Save in field.

    - Click OK to close the dialog.

4.  To start the process, go to the Capture menu and choose Using the keyboard or Using a timer. (Using the mouse is not recommended. It has some odd quirks, such as capturing a window frame without its contents!)

    - If you're using the keyboard, the HTML Help Image Editor automatically disappears. Press F11 to capture the specific window that is in focus or F12 to capture the entire desktop. (You can change these settings in Capture > Preferences > Hotkeys.)

Avoid using the mouse to capture screens with the HTML Help Image Editor—its captures are unpredictable.

- If you're using a timer, set the DELAY for the number of seconds it will take you to get the appropriate elements in focus, then use the radio buttons to select whether you want to capture the entire DESKTOP or just the WINDOW UNDER CURSOR. Click OK to hide the HTML Help Image Editor and make the capture.

5. After the screen is captured, you can make a few minor changes.

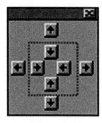

ADJUST SELECTION
WINDOW

- To crop the image (that is, remove unnecessary elements at the edges of the image), click and drag to select the area you want to retain. You can use the arrows in the small ADJUST SELECTION WINDOW to change the selected area pixel by pixel. (If you do not see the ADJUST SELECTION WINDOW, use the VIEW menu and make sure the window is selected for display.) When the correct area is selected, go to the EDIT menu and choose CLIP. (You can also use AUTO-CLIP to remove unwanted areas of solid color at the edges of the capture. The color selected is the one at the upper left corner of the selected area.)

- To size the image to a particular number of pixels or by a specific percentage, select EDIT > SCALE and use the IMAGE SCALING dialog.

- To change the size of the canvas (the overall "blank sheet" on which the image resides), select EDIT > EXPAND/CONTRACT and use the resulting dialog to add or remove pixels from the canvas edges without resizing the actual captured image.

- To help guard against unexpected shifts in the way the screen capture's colors display on the user's system, reduce the number of colors in the screen capture. Go to the COLORS menu and choose CONVERT TO 256-COLOR. For screen captures, choose the WINDOWS option and click OK.

6. To save the screen capture, choose FILE> SAVE. If you set up to capture in .jpg format, set the compression and other settings. (Remember that lower compressions provide a sharper image but a larger file.)

## Writing reusable text

The non-sequential nature of user-assistance systems (the main product of HTML Help) inevitably leads to repetitious descriptions of common tasks and elements. Despite the ability to hyperlink to frequently used components, online help authors inevitably find themselves writing the same thing many times. Sometimes each description should be slightly different, to accommodate different purposes, audiences, and learning styles. But many times you simply need to repeat the same information in different locations. For these situations, reusable text snippets can be invaluable.

Although you can create these text snippets anywhere, be sure to store them in plain text format. The HTML Help Workshop's text editor allows you to store nine text blocks; more sophisticated HTML editors provide more complex systems. At the least, you can store text snippets in a Notepad file.

For the most efficient system of reusable text snippets, be sure to include at least the following basic HTML tags with the text:

- Paragraphs should begin with `<P>` and end with `</P>`

- Bold-faced text should begin with `<B>` and end with `</B>`

- Italicized text should begin with `<I>` and end with `</I>`

For more information about these and other HTML tags, see the following sections.

# Creating the templates

With all the planning decisions made and your standard graphic and textual elements stored away, you're ready to begin writing the actual templates. Using an HTML editor or Notepad, assemble the HTML code together with your available graphics and boilerplate text. (Most of the rest of this chapter provides assistance in using the basic HTML tags.) Each template should be an HTML (plain text) file and should be stored in read-only format.

## What it looks like

This section examines a basic procedural template (simplified from the one in the overview chapter), pairing its HTML code with the resulting HTML page (figure 3.4). The template could also include boilerplate text, nested lists, or shortcuts to dialog boxes; in other words, it can be as simple or as complex as you like. The code looks like this:

The line spacing and indentations in this sample are for readability only; they do not affect the HTML code.

```
<HTML>
 <HEAD>
  <TITLE>ModuleTitle</TITLE>
  <LINK REL="STYLESHEET" REF="..\Common\project.css">
  <!- Comment hide script from older browsers
   <SCRIPT
    LANGUAGE="javascript" SRC="..\Common\project.js">
   </SCRIPT>
  ->
 </HEAD>

 <BODY>
  <H1>Main Topic Heading</H1>
  <P>Introductory descriptive text about the
procedure.</P>

  <IMG SRC="..\Graphics\open.gif" ALT="Alt Text">
```

```
<H2>Performing the task (sub-title)</H2>

  <OL>
   <LI>Step1</LI>
   <LI>Step2</LI>
   <LI>Step3</LI>
   <LI>Step4</LI>
  </OL>

 </BODY>
</HTML>
```

And the resulting topic template looks like this (figure 3.4):

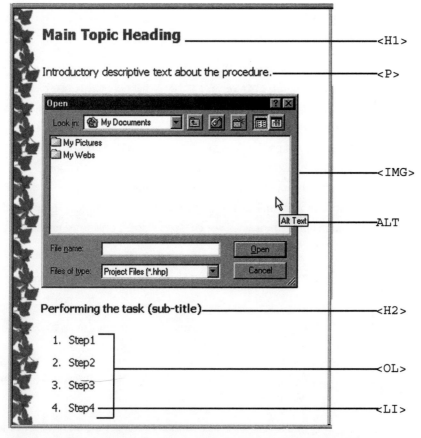

*Figure 3.4 Procedural template. The HTML code for the procedural topic produces this HTML topic page.*

# How it's done

When you begin writing your HTML template, enter the following lines, which make up the absolute minimum requirements for any HTML page:

```
<HTML>
    <HEAD>
    </HEAD>

    <BODY>
    </BODY>
</HTML>
```

These three pairs of start and end tags signify that this is an HTML page with a heading section and a body section.

Check out *Titling tricks* at the end of this chapter for information on how HTML Help treats the `<TITLE>` tag.

The `<HEAD>` section in this template also contains a title (shown here as `<TITLE> ModuleTitle </TITLE>`) that defines the text displayed in the page's title bar as well as links to a cascading style sheet (`project.css`) and to an external script file (`project.js`). Notice that the links are specified with paths relative to the location of the final topic file. (This is one of the reasons for using a standardized directory structure.) The external style sheet defines the leaf border on the left of the page as well as the color, size, and family of the fonts used to display the text. (For more information about these lines, see chapters 4 and 5 on cascading style sheets and DHTML.)

The `<BODY>` section of the template contains the displayed content.

1.  `<H1>` denotes a level 1 heading element, the highest-level heading, used here for the topic title. You may use up to six levels of headings, designated as `<H1>` through `<H6>`.

2.  All paragraph elements should have their textual content enclosed within `<P>` tags.

3.  `<H2>` denotes a second-level heading, here used for a heading leading in to the procedural steps.

4. The < IMG> element links to a graphic (here, a picture of an HTML Help dialog box). This element has two attributes: SRC specifies the source of the image file (its path relative to the final HTML topic file); ALT specifies alternate text that displays when the browser has images turned off and that pops up when the user mouses over the image. This is a quick way to add tool tips to images. Note that each attribute is followed by an equals sign and that its values are enclosed in quotation marks. There is no punctuation between attributes within an element.

5. The <OL> tag creates an ordered (automatically numbered) list. Note that the individual list items <LI> fall between the start and end tags for the list.

6. The body section closes </BODY> after all the content tags have closed.

7. The last line of the HTML file is an end tag </HTML>.

Each line in the template is composed of an HTML tag and/or specific content. The HTML tags may include HTML elements (such as < IMG> for the image) and/or HTML attributes (such as SRC for the image source). The next section describes some of the HTML elements and attributes most commonly used in HTML Help systems.

# Recipes for common HTML

The entire range of HTML tags specified by the World Wide Web Consortium (W3C) and supported by the major Web browsers opens up enormous possibilities; by the same token, learning all the tags at once would present an almost impossible learning curve. On the other hand, a quick look at the editor included in the HTML Help Workshop might lead one to believe that an entire HTML Help system can be built with only the tags for headings, the page title, and local formatting (bold, italics, etc.). The reality lies somewhere between the two extremes.

In general, a good solid HTML Help system can be built with the roughly two dozen different tags described in this chapter. (The previously examined template uses 12 tags, including those for linking to cascading style sheets and external scripts.) The syntax and examples can be used as "recipes" for creating your own HTML page templates. For additional information about HTML, consult one of the many excellent books and Web sites that teach HTML, or check the HTML Help Workshop's online help.

## Basic syntax

The basic format used for each of the described HTML elements consists of a start tag (such as `<H1>` for level 1 headings or `<P>` for paragraphs), the text affected by that element, and then an end (such as `</H1>` or `</P>` in the previous examples). Some of the tags (such as `<P>` for paragraphs) also take attributes with formatting values (such as the `ALIGN` attribute, which can be set to equal `LEFT`, `RIGHT`, or `CENTER`). The basic syntax of an HTML element, then looks like this:

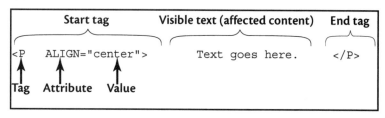

HTML is case-insensitive, so the capitalization shown above is important only for human readability. If an element tag has more than one attribute, the individual attributes are separated only by a space (no commas or semicolons).

# Document setup elements

Every HTML document requires three pairs or element tags, designating that it is an HTML document and marking the head and body sections within the document. In addition, it is good form to include a title for the page. The `<HTML>`, `<HEAD>`, and `<BODY>` tags describe these basic elements. Other elements may be nested within each of these tags.

## HTML

| **Syntax:** | `<HTML>`<br>`entire document text`<br>`</HTML>` |
|---|---|

The `<HTML>` tag identifies the document as using HTML elements and conventions. The start tag is the first item in the page; the end tag is the last item.

## HEAD

| **Syntax:** | `<HEAD>`<br>`Head elements such as TITLE,`<br>`LINK, SCRIPT`<br>`</HEAD>` |
|---|---|

The `<HEAD>` tag defines the section of the document that stores overall information about the page, such as the page title, local styles and scripts, and links to external style sheets and script files.

## Title

| Syntax: | `<TITLE>Page name</TITLE>` |
|---|---|

The `<TITLE>` element tags must appear between the `<HEAD>` `</HEAD>` tags of the HTML page. The title specifies the text that will appear on the title page of an HTML document. Unfortunately, this does not work quite so cleanly in HTML Help. For specific information, see the section on *Titling tricks* at the end of this chapter.

## Body

| Syntax: | `<BODY>` |
|---|---|
| | `All the displayed` |
| | `information on the page` |
| | `</BODY>` |

The `<BODY>` `</BODY>` tags enclose the bulk of the HTML page. They simply mark the start and end of the information that will be displayed in the browser or HTML Viewer window.

# Local formatting tags

Local formatting tags allow you to apply specific formatting to sections of text, from a single letter to the entire document. Except for `<BR>`, all the elements below require both starting and ending tags.

## Bold & Italic

| Syntax: | `<B>text</B>` or |
|---|---|
| | `<I>text</I>` |
| **Example:** | `Only the word <B>bold</B> is` |
| | `bold; only the word` |
| | `<I>italics</I> italicized.` |
| | `or <I><B> This entire` |
| | `sentence is bold and` |
| | `italicized.</B></I>` |

The tags for bold and italics work just like old word processing codes: insert the start tag at the beginning of the section you want to format, then insert the end tag when you want to stop the formatting. The tags can affect a single letter or an entire HTML page.

These tags can be nested, as shown above. Note that end tags follow the reverse order of the start tags: that is, if you open the italics tag and then the bold tag, you should close the bold tag before you close the italics tag.

## Code

| | |
|---|---|
| **Syntax:** | `<CODE>text</CODE>` |
| **Example:** | `Use the <CODE>code format tags</CODE> formatting to create monospaced code or HTML samples.` |

The `<CODE>` tag works like bold or italics, except that it formats the text in a monspaced font so that it looks like computer code.

## Font

| | |
|---|---|
| **Syntax:** | `<FONT FACE="Arial" COLOR="blue" SIZE="4">text</FONT>` |
| **Attributes & Values:** | `FACE="font face name" COLOR="RGB, Hex, or Name" SIZE="1 (smallest) to 7(largest)"` |
| **Example:** | `This <FACE="Arial" COLOR="red" SIZE="7"> WORD </FONT> will be big and red.` |

The `<FONT>` tag specifies the face, color, and size of a text, from a letter to the entire page. For information about the allowable values, consult Chapter 4, "Doing It in Styles: CSS (Cascading Style Sheets).

## Center

| | |
|---|---|
| **Syntax:** | `<CENTER>text</CENTER>` |
| **Example:** | `<P>This line will probably be` |
| | `left-justified, but </P>` |
| | `<CENTER>these words</CENTER>` |
| | `<P>will be centered</P>` |

Anything between `<CENTER>` `</CENTER>` tags will be centered, from a word to a page. No similar tags exist for left and right justification.

## Break

| | |
|---|---|
| **Syntax:** | `text<BR>text` |
| **Example:** | `This appears on one line,` |
| | `<BR>` |
| | `this on the next. Or use` |
| | `<BR></BR>` |
| | `for XML compliance.` |

The `<BR>` tag forces a line break (carriage return) at the point where it is inserted. It is one of the few tags that does not require an end tag. If you do use an end tag, nothing can appear between the start and end tags.

## No Break

| | |
|---|---|
| **Syntax:** | `<NOBR>coherent text</NOBR>` |
| **Example:** | `Use this tag to be sure that` |
| | `<NOBR>Names</NOBR> or` |
| | `<NOBR>Code</NOBR> appears` |
| | `all on the same line.` |

The `<NOBR>` tag provides some control over hyphenation and line breaks in HTML. Anything within a pair of these tags appears on the same line. But be careful: a long text string within `<NOBR>` tags can resize your window or have other unpredictable results.

# Body element tags

These elements can stand on their own within the <BODY> of an HTML document. This section presents the elements with their most commonly used attributes. For more robust formatting and design approaches to these elements, you should use a cascading style sheet as described in Chapter 4, "Doing It in Style: CSS (Cascading Style Sheets).

## Headings

| | |
|---|---|
| **Syntax:** | `<H1>Heading Text</H1>` |
| **Attributes & Values:** | `<H1>` to `<H6>` |
| | `ALIGN="center or left or right"` |
| | `CLASS="style sheet class"` |
| | `STYLE="in-line styles"` |
| **Example:** | `<H1 ALIGN="right"> top-level right-aligned heading </H1>` |

HTML supports six levels of headings, from `<H1>` as the highest level heading to `<H6>` as the lowest level heading. No matter what the level, all headings are considered block elements; that is, HTML automatically inserts a break before and after the element.

Headings support alignment (justification) values included inside their start tag. Beyond this alignment, most other stylistic attributes of headings can be specified with the use of a `STYLE` attribute. However, since headings *should* be formatted consistently, it's best to use your cascading style sheet to define each heading level's formatting options. If you really must have multiple types of `<H3>` in your system, use a style sheet to define the appropriate classes and then reference the desired class (for example, `CLASS="procedure3")`.

## Paragraphs

| | |
|---|---|
| **Syntax:** | `<P>Paragraph Text</P>` |
| **Attributes & Values:** | `ALIGN="center or left or right"` |
| | `CLASS="style sheet class"` |
| | `STYLE="in-line styles"` |
| **Example:** | `<P CLASS="quote"> This` |
| | `paragraph will be indented` |
| | `1/2 inch from the normal` |
| | `left paragraph margin.` |
| | `Useful for quoted material` |
| | `</P>` |

Paragraphs function much like headings: they are block-level elements with a break before and after each paragraph; they support the three basic alignment tags; and they are best formatted from a style sheet. However, since HTML only supplies a single paragraph tag and HTML Help systems are likely to require multiple approaches to paragraph formatting, the CLASS attribute is frequently used with paragraph tags.

Paragraphs do not absolutely require an end tag. It is, however, good form to include one (and will be required if you move to XML). It will also keep you out of trouble with overlapping tags and confused scripting.

# Images

| Syntax: | `<IMG SRC="url.htm">` |
|---|---|
| **Attributes & Values:** | `SRC="URL/path to image file"` |
| | `ALIGN="absbottom"` *or* |
| | `"absmiddle"` *or* `"baseline"` *or* |
| | `"bottom"` *or* `"left"` *or* `"middle"` |
| | *or* `"right"` *or* `"texttop"` *or* |
| | `"top"` |
| | `ALT="alternate text"` |
| | `BORDER="pixel width of` |
| | `border"` |
| | `CLASS="style sheet class"` |
| | `HEIGHT="height in pixels"` |
| | `WIDTH="width in pixels"` |
| | `STYLE="in-line styles"` |
| **Example:** | `<IMG` |
| | `SRC="\common\graphics\myPix.gif"` |
| | `ALT="My Text" BORDER="0">` |

The `<IMG>` tag allows you to insert an image into your HTML Help file. This tag rarely takes an end tag. It does, however, take more than the usual number of attributes within its single tag.

The only required attribute is the `SRC` (source) attribute which specifies where the image file can be found. This should be specified as an absolute path or URL, or in relative terms (relative to the final HTML topic file).

`ALIGN` specifies the alignment of the image relative to the text surrounding it.

`ALT` is a very useful attribute. By specifying alternate text, you insure that users will see some information even if they have image viewing turned off or if the link to the image is broken. It also lets you create a quick bit of "tool-tip" style information without additional programming. This text appears whenever the user's mouse pauses over the image.

The IMAGE tag's BORDER attribute lets you set the width of the border that HTML places around all images. Probably the most commonly used setting is "0," which turns the border off. If you want a border around your image, it's best to create in your image editing program.

The HEIGHT and WIDTH attributes allow you to pre-specify the size at which the image will display. This has several advantages. First, it allows for faster loading of the HTML page, since the browser knows how much space to allot to the image. Second, it allows you to scale the image without returning to your image editing program. Just be sure that the sizes you specify are proportional to the original image sizes, or you'll distort the graphic.

The STYLE and CLASS attributes work as described in the section on paragraph <P> tags.

## Anchors

| | |
|---|---|
| **Syntax:** | `<A HREF="url.htm">Click Here</A>` |
| **Attributes & Values:** | `HREF="URL or path to the target"` `CLASS="style sheet class"` `STYLE="in-line styles"` |
| **Example:** | `For more info, click <A HREF="file.htm">Here</A>` |

Anchors are also known as "jumps" or links; they are the tags that allow the user to click in one document and access information on another page or elsewhere on the Internet.

The <A> tag requires the HREF attribute to specify what the browser will display when the user clicks on the text between the anchor's start and end tags. The CLASS and STYLE tags let you specify the formatting of the text the user clicks on. Most often, these tags are used to change the blue underlining that is the browser default for anchor tag text.

# Lists

It has been said that hard-core Help authors dream in bulleted lists. While that may be an exaggeration, it is certainly true that lists (bulleted or otherwise) are the foundation of online Help systems. This section provides a cookbook approach to lists, with the code snippet recipes below designed to offer cut-and-paste solutions for the most common list situations.

## Bulleted (unordered) lists

| | |
|---|---|
| **Syntax:** | ```<UL>```<br>```<LI>Item 1 text</LI>```<br>```<LI>Item 2 text</LI>```<br>```</UL>``` |
| **Attributes & Values:** | ```CLASS="style sheet class"```<br>```STYLE="in-line styles"``` |
| **Example:** | *see below* |

The HTML tag `<UL>` produces an unordered list; or, in more common language, a bulleted list. It uses class and style attributes in the same way as paragraphs do; it does not, however, support an alignment tag. Note also that the class and style attributes can be applied either to the list as a whole (by placing them within the `<UL>` tag) or to individual list items (by placing the attributes within the `<LI>` tag).

Bulleted lists are frequently used to list features, options, and other non-sequential bits of information. For example, the following descriptive paragraph and bulleted list might appear in an overview topic:

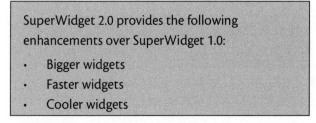

SuperWidget 2.0 provides the following enhancements over SuperWidget 1.0:

- Bigger widgets
- Faster widgets
- Cooler widgets

The following "recipe" produces the bulleted list example, but uses place-holder text instead of the SuperWidget text. Note that `leadinText` reminds you that the paragraph introduces the list. Also, each bit of place-holder text is a single word so that you can use a simple double-click to select it for replacement with meaningful text.

```
<P>leadInText</P>
<UL>
    <LI>Item1</LI>
    <LI>Item2</LI>
    <LI>Item3</LI>
</UL>
```

### Numbered (ordered) lists

| | |
|---|---|
| **Syntax:** | `<OL>`<br>`<LI>Item 1 text</LI>`<br>`<LI>Item 2 text</LI>`<br>`</OL>` |
| **Attributes & Values:** | `CLASS="style sheet class"`<br>`STYLE="in-line styles"` |
| **Example:** | *see below* |

The HTML tag `<OL>` produces an ordered or numbered list, the primary format used for procedural instructions. Like unordered lists, ordered lists can take style and class attributes applied either to the list as a whole (by placing them within the `<OL>` tag) or to individual list items (by placing the attributes within the `<LI>` tag).

The following example might appear in a procedural topic:

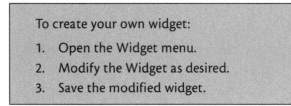

To create your own widget:

1. Open the Widget menu.
2. Modify the Widget as desired.
3. Save the modified widget.

The numbered list example can be created with the following recipe. Note that the placeholder `toDoIttext` reminds you to use an infinitive for this type of list:

```
<H3>toDoItText</H3>
<OL>
    <LI>Item1</LI>
    <LI>Item2</LI>
    <LI>Item3</LI>
</OL>
```

### Numbered list with bullet sub-items

Procedures are often more complex than simple 1-2-3 steps, necessitating nested lists. The following example might appear in a procedure involving multi-tabbed dialog boxes.

> To modify an existing widget:
>
> 1. Open the previously created Widget.
>
> 2. Choose Widgets > Modify, then:
>    - To change the color, choose a color.
>    - To change the size, type in a number of pixels.
>
> 3. When you finish modifying your Widget, close the Modify dialog box.

This combination list can be created with the the following recipe. Note that the end tag `</LI>` tag for the numbered list's `Item2` does not appear until *after* the end `</UL>` tag for the subordinate bulleted list.

```
<H3>toDoItText</H3>
<OL>
    <LI>Item1</LI>
    <LI>Item2
        <UL>
            <LI>subItem1</LI>
            <LI>subItem2</LI>
        </UL>
    </LI>
    <LI>Item3</LI>
</OL>
```

## Definition list

| | |
|---|---|
| **Syntax:** | `<DL>`<br>`<DT>Term to be defined</DT>`<br>`<DD>Definition of the term</DD>`<br>`</DT>` |
| **Attributes & Values:** | `CLASS="style sheet class"`<br>`STYLE="in-line styles"` |
| **Example:** | *see below* |

Definition lists, orginally designed for glossary-type information, are most often used for reference material. However, they can also be useful when you need a very low level sort of heading associated with a discrete chunk of information. Definition lists can take the style and class attributes applied to the list as a whole (within the <DL> tag), only to the definition terms (within the <DT> tag), or only to the actual definitions (within the <DD> tag).

The following example could be used in a glossary topic.

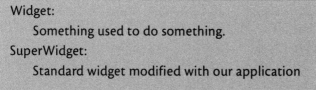

Widget:
   Something used to do something.
SuperWidget:
   Standard widget modified with our application

This glossary topic example can be created with the following recipe:

```
<DL>
    <DT>definitionTerm1</DT>
        <DD>definition1</DD>
    <DT>definitionTerm2</DT>
        <DD>definition2</DD>
</DL>
```

## Tables

Although HTML tables can become complicated, it's not really that difficult to create a simple table. Only three tags are required, setting off the table itself, individual table rows, and individual table cells (data), with a fourth tag available to separately format the table's heading row. For example, consider the following table of two equally wide columns, with a header row and three data rows, and its HTML code:

| ITEM | VALUES |
|---|---|
| ALIGN | center, left, right |
| WIDTH | percentage or pixels |
| BORDER | width in pixels |

```
<TABLE WIDTH="90%" BORDER="1">

  <TR>
    <TH WIDTH="50%"> Item</TH>
    <TH WIDTH="50%">Values</TH>
  </TR>

  <TR>
    <TD WIDTH="50%">ALIGN</TD>
    <TD WIDTH="50%">left, right, center</TD>
  </TR>

  <TR>
    <TD WIDTH="50%">WIDTH</TD>
    <TD WIDTH="50%">percentage or pixels</TD>
  </TR>

  <TR>
    <TD WIDTH="50%">BORDER</TD>
    <TD WIDTH="50%">width in pixels</TD>
  </TR>
</TABLE>
```

The first line of code uses a starting tag <TABLE> for the table element, specifying that the <WIDTH> of the entire table is 90% of the entire HTML page and that each cell is drawn with a 1-pixel wide <BORDER>. The next code "paragraph" describes the first row of the table. The row begins and ends with a table row tag <TR> and each cell of the row is opened and closed with a table header tag <TH> (which, by default, makes the content of the cell centered and bold). The <WIDTH> attribute for each cell in the table header (as well as in the subsequent table data cells) is 50% of the table width (in this case, 45% of the entire HTML page width). Each subsequent row also opens and closes with a table row tag <TR> and its component cells open and close with table data tags <TD> using a <WIDTH> attribute with a value of 50%. The entire code closes with an end table tag </TABLE>.

## Table

| | |
|---|---|
| **Syntax:** | `<TABLE>table text</TABLE>` |
| **Attributes & Values:** | `ALIGN="left or center or right"` |
| | `BGCOLOR="RGB" or "color name for table background"` |
| | `BORDER="pixel width of borders; 0=none"` |
| | `HEIGHT="height of entire table in pixels or as a percentage of the browser window width"` |
| | `WIDTH="width of entire table in pixels or as a percentage of the browser window width"` |
| **Example:** | *see above* |

Each table begins and ends with a table tag. Note that attributes specified as part of the opening table tag apply to the table as a whole. Most of the same attributes can also be specified for individual rows and cells (header or data). For example, the table as a whole might specify center alignment, so that the table is centered within the browser window. The table header cells might also be centered, but the table data cells are most often left aligned.

## Table row

| | |
|---|---|
| **Syntax:** | `<TR>row text</TR>` |
| **Attributes & Values:** | `ALIGN="left or center or right"`<br>`BGCOLOR="RGB" or "color name for row background"`<br>`BORDER="pixel width of borders; 0=none"`<br>`HEIGHT="height of table row in pixels or as a percentage of the width of the entire table"`<br>`WIDTH="width of table row in pixels or as a percentage of the width of the entire table"` |
| **Example:** | *see above* |

Each row in the table must be enclosed within table row tags `<TR></TR>`. These tags take most of the attributes available to the table as a whole, but apply them only to the particular row.

## Table header/table data

| | |
|---|---|
| **Syntax:** | `<TH>header text</TH>`<br>or<br>`<TD>header text</TD>` |
| **Attributes & Values:** | `ALIGN="left` or `center` or `right"`<br>`BGCOLOR="RGB"` or `"color name`<br>`for cell background"`<br>`BORDER="pixel width of`<br>`borders; 0=none"`<br>`WIDTH="width of table row in`<br>`pixels or as a percentage of`<br>`the width of the entire`<br>`table"` |
| **Example:** | *see above* |

Each cell in the table must be enclosed within table header `<TH></TH>` or table data `<TD></TD>` tags. The basic difference between the two tag sets is that the table header tags center and boldface the cell contents; table data tags default to left justification and no particular local formatting. These tags take most of the attributes available to the table and table row, but apply them only to the particular cell. In general, they do NOT take the height attribute, since each row should be a consistent height.

# Writing the HTML topic pages

Once you've created your templates, writing the topic is, if not exactly easy, at least no harder than writing usually is. In order to turn your templates into topics, you should:

1. Classify the topic according to the most appropriate template.

2. Open the selected template and use SAVE AS to create a new copy of the template in the appropriate directory location.

3. Edit the template, adding new text and changing existing boilerplate text. If you've created a text file of standardized text and formatting, cut and paste to further speed your writing.

4. Add graphics as needed and, if appropriate, use DHTML snippets from your script file.

5. Save your topic; test in the Internet Explorer browser; make adjustments as required and retest.

6. Save your final topic file in the appropriate directory and add it to your HTML Help project file.

Using the HTML Help project file is the subject of a later chapter.

# How HTML works with HTML Help— and how it doesn't

While you might think that HTML Help would support standard HTML in much the same way as its viewer engine (Microsoft's Internet Explorer) does, that's not the case. Some of the most interesting disconnects involve using the HTML <TITLE> tag, linking to other HTML files, and, as always, the use of the HTML Help Workshop's SPLIT FILE command.

As described in other chapters, the HTML Help Workshop's SPLIT FILE command is designed for Help authors who want to write all the topics in their entire HTML Help system in a single, long HTML file. The command inserts an ActiveX control that works as a sort of "break" tag, defining a new filename and title. It doesn't pick up any other information from the HTML document's <HEAD> section, so all topics after the first lose their links to style sheets, script files, etc. Nor can users search for topic titles in topics created with SPLIT FILE. For these reasons, it's best to just avoid the SPLIT FILE command.

## Titling tricks

As you're writing your templates and topics, notice the <TITLE></TITLE> tags within the <HEAD> element of each page. If you're creating an HTML page in a text editor, you'll simply type the desired title between the <TITLE> tags. Within the HTML Help Workshop, you can also use the TITLE command on the TAGS menu. Various dedicated HTML editors implement other approaches.

The page title also works differently in a standard Web browser than it does in the HTML Help Viewer. Web browsers do little with the title beyond placing it in the colored bar at the top of the page and passing it on to bookmarks and some search engines. In the HTML Help system, the simple

`<TITLE>` tag takes on new importance in line with the increased importance of targeted searches and indexing in HTML Help. The title of an HTML Help topic appears in the list of topics that pops up when an index entry has links to multiple pages; in the topic list returned from a search on the SEARCH tab; and in the user's FAVORITES list. It does *not* appear in the title bar of the HTML Help Viewer (that title is specified for each WINDOW TYPE in the project file) and, oddly enough, the HTML Help compiler does *not* use the designated title when creating an automatically generated table of contents.

Because the title appears in so many places and because these appearances are often in lists, a consistent and helpful titling format becomes important. A *consistent* format (in both grammar and capitalization) makes for a neat, clear list; a *helpful* format clues users in to the type of information available in a particular topic.

Classic user assistance standards (such as JoAnn T. Hackos and Dawn M. Stevens, *Standards for Online Communication.* New York, NY: John T. Wiley and Sons, 1997) recommend noun strings for conceptual topics (*The Online Help System*) and gerunds for procedural topics (*Using the Online Help System*), although some prefer infinitives for procedural topics (*To Use the Online Help System*). The second edition of the *Microsoft Manual of Style for Technical Publications* (Microsoft Corporation. Redmond, WA: Microsoft Press, 1998) presents a more complex series of distinctions depending on the level of the title (chapter, section, topic, or procedure heading). Either system is valid, as long as you apply it consistently. And don't forget to be consistent in capitalization as well, settling on the appropriate use of title case (*Using the Online Help System*) or sentence case (*Using the online help system*).

In case you've forgotten the terminology from high school grammar classes, a gerund is an *-ing* verb *(printing)* while an infinitive combines *to* with a verb *(to print).*

To aid users in understanding your topic titles, you may also want to consider a two-part title format that keys into the modules or interface elements of the application. For example, the HTML Help system for a financial program might preface topics with *Accounts Receivable* and *Accounts Payable;* a program with tabbed dialog boxes might use the tab names as prefaces. But do limit titles to a reasonable length (the HTML Help Workshop recommends no more than 60 characters) so that the title is not cut off by a non-resizeable window. (For example, you might want to shorten your financial program's *Accounts Receivable* preface to *AR.)*

## Author beware

HTML titles are also used for navigation within the HTML Help Workshop itself, althrough with notoriously unreliable results. When you're adding entries on either the CONTENTS or INDEX tabs, the Workshop's ADD dialogs list the HTML titles of topics available for linking to a contents entry or index keyword. The actual filename or URL appears in the dialog only after you've selected an HTML title.

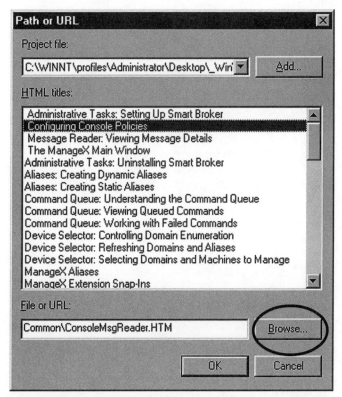

**Figure 3.5 Mismatched title.** *The file in the* File or URL *text box actually matches the* HTML title *below the one selected. Solve the problem with the* Browse *button (circled).*

Unfortunately, the filename or URL display often matches the title above or below the title that is actually selected in the list (figure 3.5). Even worse, the HTML Help compiler uses the filename or URL to determine which topic the given contents or index entry points to. This puts the Help author in the uncomfortable position of choosing the topic by its HTML title while the compiler focuses on the potentially mismatched filename.

The solution is to breeze through the PATH OR URL dialog by clicking its BROWSE button (next to FILE OR URL) and use the resulting OPEN dialog to choose the desired HTML file. Click OPEN and then OK to move right on back to the CONTENTS ENTRY or INDEX ENTRY dialog and continue your work.

# Linkages

The anchor element or <A> is one of the fundamental HTML tags; after all, it puts the *hyper* in *hyper*text by providing the simplest way to jump through topics, Web sites, and the entire World Wide Web. Unfortunately, it has some quirks in HTML Help, and the exact form of the link reference will depend on the location of your source and target files. The variety of possible relationships between source and target is nearly endless; this section covers the following permutations:

- Links within a single compiled HTML Help file (CHM)
  - Topics within the same directory of the CHM
  - Topics in different directories of the CHM
- Links between topics in different CHMs
  - CHMs within the same local directory
  - CHMs in different directories of the same local drive
  - CHMs on different (shared) drives
- External links from the CHM
  - To a Web page
  - To a file type other than .htm

- External links to the CHM

  - With a simple <A> tag

  - With a simple script

## Background basics

An anchor tag takes the following basic form:

```
<A HREF="protocol://location/filename"> Text </A>
```

The `protocol` that opens the `HREF` section varies. Probably the most common is the familiar `HTTP` that prefaces most Web pages on the Internet (for example, `http://www.company.com`). The `File` protocol refers to pages on the local system (such as `file://c:\mydrive\`)

The standard protocol for compiled HTML Help files is `ms-its`. Occasionally you may also see the non-standard shortened form (`its`) or the obsolete `mk@MSITStore` used for Internet Explorer 3.x. In general, you should use `ms-its`, unless you know viewers will be using IE 3.

The `location` in the anchor tag is usually a URL (uniform resource locator or Web address, such as `www.company.com`) or path (such as `C:\help\online`), and is followed by the filename for the specific file at that location (such as `index.htm`).

The anchor closes with the `Text` that actually appears on the Web page, followed by an end tag. By default, this anchor text is blue and underlined (until you change it with a style or cascading style sheet). The user clicks on the `Text` to jump to the new location.

In general, when writing the anchor tag's path, use *forward* slashes for Web-based information (URLs, htm files within the chm) but *back slashes* for Windows-based information (local files, including the `.chm` itself). However, these rules are flexibly implemented by Internet Explorer and the HTML Help Viewer, so experiment with slash direction when you're trouble-shooting links.

## Links within a single CHM

Starting from the simplest possibility, jumps between topic files within the same compiled HTML Help file take the basic form:

```
<A HREF="targetFile.htm">
```

This very simple form works if both topic files are not only compiled into the same HTML Help file, but also exist in the same directory within the HTML Help file. If you have created multiple subdirectories for your topic files, links from a topic file in one directory to a topic file (or graphic) in another directory must include the relative path from the file containing the anchor source to the file containing the anchor target. The anchor tag takes this form:

```
<A HREF="targetDirectory\targetFile.htm">
```

For example, consider the directory structure for a word processing help file shown below, based on the structure recommended in Chapter 6, "Creating Magic: The HTML Help Project File":

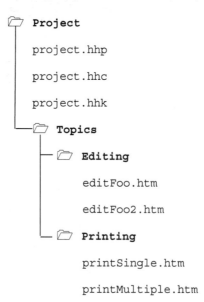

```
📁 Project
    project.hhp
    project.hhc
    project.hhk
    📁 Topics
        📁 Editing
            editFoo.htm
            editFoo2.htm
        📁 Printing
            printSingle.htm
            printMultiple.htm
```

A jump from `editFoo.htm` to `printSingle.htm` looks like:

```
<A HREF="../Printing/printSingle.htm">
```

## Links between CHMs

The anchor tags become more complicated when linking to locations outside the compiled HTML Help file.  Again starting from the simplest case, use the following form to jump between topics in different compiled HTML Help files stored when the CHMs are stored in the same directory:

```
<A HREF="ms-its:Project.chm::/directory/
topic.htm">
```

where `topic.htm` is the name of the specific topic you want to link to and `Project.chm` is the name of the compiled Help file containing it. Note that you can also use an absolute path to the target compiled HTML Help file (for example, replace `Project.chm` above with `C:\help\HTML\Project.chm`). However, this approach actually slows down display since it forces the HTML Help Viewer to download the entire CHM file before opening the desired topic page.  With a large file, this can take quite a few minutes the first time the link is clicked; subsequent clicks progress more quickly since the CHM file loads from a cache.

If both compiled HTML Help files are stored locally but in different directories, use a relative path in the link (again, you can use an absolute link, but it slows the first access to the link):

```
<A HREF="ms-its:path\project.chm::/directory/
topic.htm">
```

Intranets present yet another situation.  If the compiled HTML Help files are stored on different shared network drives, within the corporate LAN for example, use this format:

```
<A HREF="ms-its:\\sharedDrive\sharedDirectory\
Project.chm::/directory/topic.htm">
```

This situation requires double slashes following the `ms-its` protocol.

For a headstart on complex paths, open the CHM and display the target topic. Right-click an open area in the topic and choose PROPERTIES from the shortcut menu. Select and copy the contents of the ADDRESS (URL) field, then paste it into the anchor tag of the source topic. Some editing may still be required.

## External links *from* the CHM

You can also link from a topic in a compiled HTML Help file to a specific HTML page on the Web, using a standard anchor tag in the format:

```
<A HREF="http://www.company.com/directory/
page.htm">
```

Unless you add a specific target window, the page opens in the content pane of the compiled HTML Help file. To open the page in a new Web browser window, use this format:

```
<A HREF="http://www.company.com/directory/
page.htm" target="new">
```

At the present time, you cannot open any other file types directly within the compiled HTML Help file, but you can create an anchor in this format:

```
<A HREF="filename.ext">
```

This anchor opens a FILE DOWNLOAD dialog permitting the user to download the file or to open the file from its current location. This dialog appears even if the file is stored in the same directory and is compiled into the HTML Help project. The user will be able to open the linked file only if the appropriate application is installed. For example, if the above link opened an Adobe™ Acrobat™ PDF file, the user could open it only if Adobe Acrobat Reader is installed on the local machine.

Microsoft offers one scripting solution to the problem of opening a different file type from a CHM within the Workshop's online Help. An even more robust scripting solution is available in the HTML Help section of MSDN's Online Web Workshop. (The information is currently located at msdn.microsoft.com/workshop/author/htmlhelp/hh_online_doc2/ocx_scripts_linkchm.asp.)

## External links *to* the CHM

With versions 1.x of HTML Help, you cannot actually run a compiled HTML Help file over the Internet. The situation is similar to that or opening a file type other than `.htm` from within a compiled HTML Help file. A link from an HTML page of the format

```
<A HREF="project.chm">
```

opens a File Download dialog asking whether to run the file from its current location or to save the file to disk, even if the CHM and the Web page are stored in the same location.

However, if the CHM and the Web page are stored locally (for example, in an intranet installation), you can bypass the awkwardness of the File Download dialog with a very simple script. To use this approach, include the following lines between the `<HEAD></HEAD>` tags of the HTML document that will link to the compiled HTML Help file:

```
<script language="VBScript">
sub accessTopic(url)
    window.ShowHelp("ms-its:"+url+">main")
end sub
</script>
```

Replace the reference to `"main"` with the name of the default window type in your compiled HTML Help file. (If you've followed the recommendations of this book, the name of the default Window Type will be `"main"`.)

In the location where you want to place the link, type code of the following format. Do not enter any line breaks within the code:

```
<a href="#"
onclick='accessTopic("directory\project.chm::/
directory/topic.htm")'>
```

When the user clicks the target link, the referenced CHM file opens in its own window, without questions about file downloads.

This scripting solution may not work if your users have high security settings in Internet Explorer.

# Doing It In Style: CSS
## [Cascading Style Sheets]

Cascading style sheets define the *look* of an HTML Help system's *look and feel*—and they do it more quickly and efficiently than would be otherwise possible. A good cascading style sheet can change the design of hundreds of HTML pages with the modification of a single line in a simple text file. This speed and efficiency is particularly important in online Help systems, where rapid change appears to be the most enduring fact of professional life. Ever-shortening product cycles, last-minute product changes, even the turnover in management—all contribute to the need to create online Help systems at an increasing pace.

In addition to the need for rapid development, HTML authors—whether designing for the Web or for online Help systems—are often frustrated by the lack of control over the finished product. CSS gives you that control. In very uncomplicated terms, cascading style sheets are simple text files that specify the formatting (font, line spacing, indents, etc.) for each element (such as level 1 headings or list items) on an HTML page.

Cascading style sheets are part of the standards promoted by the World Wide Web Consortium (W3C). As described by Håkon Lie, one of the creators of the cascading style sheet specifications, CSS was designed as a simple mechanism to allow you to add style specifications describing the *appearance* your users see when they view the information which is *structured* in an HTML document (Håkon Wium Lie & Bert Bos, *Cascading Style Sheets: Designing for the Web*. Harlow, England: Addison Wesley Longman, 1997).

Under the original standards (CSS Level 1, adopted in December, 1996, and now supported by most Web browsers), you could quickly define font, color, borders, shading, and other presentation aspects of your text. The newer CSS Level 2 (adopted May, 1998, and gaining rapid support) adds the capacity for attaching multiple style sheets to a page, creating designs specific to online viewing or printout, with control over such new elements as page breaks.

CSS has been widely hailed as a return to the basic HTML separation of structure and presentation, as well as a method promoting rapid content development. Both these claims are true and are eminently applicable to online Help. Help writers will appreciate the way CSS allows decisions about style and presentation to be defined once and used many times. This efficient approach not only speeds up development, it also allows the writer to focus on content as it reinforces the original HTML distinction between substance and style, structure and presentation, content and color.

This chapter discusses cascading style sheets: what they are, how to use them, and how to create them. Since CSS, like any computer-based standard, has many different implementations, this chapter focuses on how CSS standards apply to HTML Help and, even more specifically, to compiled HTML Help. In general, this means following Microsoft's implementation of CSS in Internet Explorer versions 4 and above. Fortunately, Microsoft and the major browsers seem to be moving towards ever greater adherence to the W3C recommendations, so that Help writers will find it ever easier to create a single cascading style sheet applicable to most user situations.

# What CSS is & what it does

At the beginning of the Web revolution, most HTML pages were bland (figure 4.1):

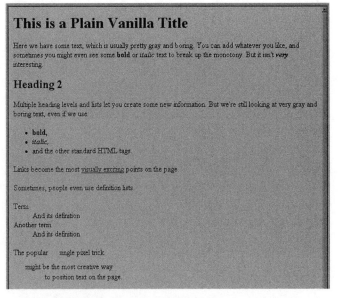

**Figure 4.1 Plain vanilla page.** *Without formatting or style sheets, Web pages tend to be bland and "plain vanilla."*

And basic Help text looked like figure 4.2:

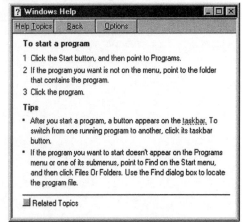

**Figure 4.2 Basic Windows Help.** *Standard Help pages are also visually unexciting.*

The Web browser and the Windows help layout engine determined the colors, fonts, and spacing of the text. The idea behind HTML was to create a language that described the *structure* of information and displayed it accordingly. However, as writers and designers followed scientists to the Web, these new users expected control over *style* as well as structure. They quickly got creative with table and the "single pixel trick" (formatting text blocks by inserting a 1-pixel transparent `gif` sized to provide the desired amount of white space). Font colors and page backgrounds became popular, but it was still a cumbersome process. Web designers often had to individually tag each paragraph, each table cell, with the desired changes. The process was definitely a step backward from the sophisticated word processing and desktop publishing tools available for print materials.

Cascading style sheets add the ability to control *style* as well as *structure*. In particular, CSS gives writers working with HTML (for the Web or for HTML Help) one of the most important design tools: automated styles.

The automated styles in word processors and desktop publishing programs allow writers to designate a level 1 heading as, for instance, red 24-point Arial type, centered, with 18 points before and 12 points after. After the original style definition, simply adding a "Level 1 Heading" style to text applies seven separate style attributes in a single command. The process is immeasurably more efficient and consistent—there's no need to remember whether it was 22-point or 24-point type, light red or dark red, etc. A spiced-up version of the previous HTML page (figure 4.3) takes just these lines of ASCII text, which we'll call our "cayenne" style sheet:

Don't worry; these lines are explained later in this chapter.

```
BODY        { background-color: black; font-family:
             "arial narrow"; font-size: 12pt; color:
             white; font-weight: bold; }

H1          { font-family: "arial black" ; font-
             size: 24pt;    text-align: center; color:
             red; margin-bottom: 12pt; }

H2          { color: yellow; font-weight: bold; }

DT          { color: #FDCB02; font-weight: bold;}

A           { color: #F40000;}

.visited    { color: #D20000; }
```

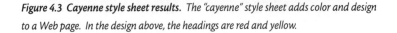

**This is a Plain Vanilla Title**

Here we have some text, which is usually pretty gray and boring. You can add whatever you like, and sometimes you might even see some bold or *italic* text to break up the monotony. But it isn't *very* interesting.

Heading 2

Multiple heading levels and lists let you create some new information. But we're still looking at very gray and boring text, even if we use:

- bold,
- *italic*,
- and the other standard HTML tags.

Links become the most <u>visually exciting</u> points on the page. Sometimes, people even use definition lists.

Term
    And its definition

The popular    single pixel trick

    might be the most creative way
            to position text on the page.

*Figure 4.3 Cayenne style sheet results. The "cayenne" style sheet adds color and design to a Web page. In the design above, the headings are red and yellow.*

With CSS, HTML gains the power of print-based style sheets and more. A single CSS file can control one page or an entire project comprising hundreds of pages. The CSS file can be reused for new projects or it can be quickly altered, changing a single line of CSS text so that the red Arial heading becomes blue Bodoni, and the changes in that one file flow to every linked page in the project. In addition, the "cascading" part of "cascading style sheets" means that an HTML page can deal with more than one style sheet. So a company-wide CSS file can control page background and major headings; a series of product-specific CSS files can add color coding that identifies each product in a line; and special CSS files can customize pages for special purposes (such as procedural topics vs. conceptual topics).

# How to do it

The most efficient way to use CSS in HTML Help requires three steps:

1.  In the <HEAD> of each HTML file, add a line linking to an external style sheet. (This line can be added before or after creating the CSS file; all it requires is the style sheet's filename and path relative to the HTML file.)

2.  Define the desired styles in a cascading style sheet, an ASCII text file with a .css extension.

3.  Explicitly add the cascading style sheet file to the [FILES] section of your HTML Help project file.

The first step adds a line to the individual topic file as described in the section *Types of cascading style sheets.* Step three is also a one-line process described in *Adding the style sheet to the project.* The second step involves the bulk of the work and is described in detail in the rest of this chapter.

## Browser-dependence

Like most "standards," CSS actually has many implementations. What works in Microsoft Internet Explorer doesn't work in Netscape Navigator™, and what works in version 3 may not work in versions 4 or 5. Browsing the World Wide Web Consortium CSS standards (http://www.w3.org/style/css or in Håkon Lie's book) provides great ideas—and frustration as you discover tags not implemented in Internet Explorer.

The first rule of CSS in HTML Help: use CSS as supported by Internet Explorer 4 and above..

The first rule of CSS in HTML Help: use only those CSS recommendations supported by Internet Explorer. With the 1.x versions of HTML Help, use the CSS for Internet Explorer version 4. And watch out for changes as the 2.x versions of HTML Help become dependent on IE 5 installations.

In its entirety, CSS recommendation and implementations are complex enough to fill a complete book. However, CSS for compiled HTML Help is relatively short and simple. This chapter describes CSS as it works with compiled HTML Help running with at least Internet Explorer 4 .

# Types of cascading style sheets

As the earlier sample shows, cascading style sheets are simply lines of ASCII text describing properties (such as font-family, text-align, color) of individual HTML elements (such as paragraphs <P>, headings <H1>, and anchoring links <A>). The lines of ASCII text can be stored in various locations, depending on the type of style sheet. HTML Help works best with the following three types of cascading style sheets:

- Linked style sheets, stored in separate text files, are the most efficient approach for HTML Help.

- Embedded style sheets are ASCII lines added to the <HEAD> section of each HTML file.

- Inline styles are lines placed within the HTML file next to the text they affect.

If a single HTML file contains multiple types of style sheets, the "cascading" aspect determines which style sheet type takes precedence. Simply stated, inline style sheets override all others, followed by embedded and then linked style sheets.

The CSS recommendations include a fourth type—imported style sheets— which are theoretically supported by IE 4 and above. However, in practice, imported style sheets are difficult to implement and don't really add any functionality not covered by linked style sheets. For these reasons, imported style sheets are not covered in this chapter.

The CSS "cascade" gives inline styles precedence, followed by embedded, and then linked style sheets.

## Linked style sheets

Linked style sheets are probably the most commonly used and certainly the most efficient type of cascading style sheet for HTML Help. A linked cascading style sheet is an ASCII text file composed of a list of rules (described in the next section) and named with a .css extension. Linked style sheets allow the efficiency of defining a style once and using it many times. Also, since the styles are stored in a single, central location, making a change to the style sheet (for example, setting body text to Arial instead of Times Roman) flows through all of the linked HTML files.

To link an external style sheet named `MyStyleSheet.css` to an HTML page, add the following line between the HTML page's `<HEAD>` and `</HEAD>` tags:

```
<LINK REL="stylesheet" HREF="MyStyleSheet.css"
TYPE="text/css">
```

If the style sheet is not in the same folder as the HTML page, be sure to include the relative path. For example, assume the directory structure:

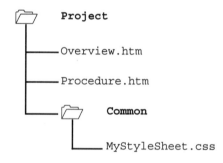

The linking code in the HTML page would be:

```
<LINK REL="stylesheet"
HREF="CommonMyStyleSheet.css" TYPE="text/css">
```

The W3C recommendation envisions linked style sheets as providing alternative style sheets, while imported style sheets allow the merging of multiple style sheets within one document. However, in practice, multiple linked style sheets in a single HTML file also function as merged style sheets, with later linked style sheets taking precedence over earlier ones. As an example, consider an HTML file with the following lines:

```
<LINK REL="stylesheet" HREF="1.css" TYPE="text/css">
<LINK REL="stylesheet" HREF="2.css" TYPE="text/css">
```

If style sheet 1 and 2 define an element in different ways, the definition in 2 prevails. So if 1 defines <H1> as red and 2 defines it as blue, all instances of <H1> in the document appear as blue. However, if 1 contained a style sheet rule for a particular element not defined in 2, then the definition from 1 would display. Again, if 1 defined <H1> as red and 2 did not define <H1>, all instances of <H1> in the document would appear red.

Linked style sheets take precedence over imported style sheets, but are themselves overridden by inline and embedded styles.

# Embedded style sheets

Embedded style sheets are just what their name says: *style sheets* (that is, lines of ASCII text defining style rules) *embedded* (that is, added) right into the HTML page. Use an embedded style sheet to apply styles to a single document (Web or HTML Help page). While embedded style sheets do not supply the one-to-many power of linked or imported style sheets, they are useful for setting up styles that don't travel throughout an entire HTML Help project, but are invoked many times within a single page.

To embed the cayenne style sheet at the beginning of this chapter, add the following lines between the HTML page's <HEAD> and </HEAD> tags:

```
<STYLE TYPE="text/css">
<!—

BODY        { background-color: black; font-family:
            "arial narrow"; font-size: 12pt;
            color: white; font-weight: bold; }

H1          { font-family: "arial black" ; font-
            size: 24pt;    text-align: center; color:
            red; margin-bottom: 12pt; }

H2          { color: yellow; font-weight: bold; }

DT          { color: #FDCB02; font-weight: bold;}
```

```
A           { color: #F40000;}
.visited   { color: #D20000; }
-->
</STYLE>
```

Note the `<!--` and `-->` enclosing the style sheet text. This identifies these lines as "comments" which will be ignored by older, non-CSS-compliant browsers. In practice, of course, replace the `BODY`, `H1`, `H2`, `DT`, `A`, and `.visited` lines by your own style sheet rules.

# Inline style sheets

Inline style sheets might more accurately be called inline styles, since they simply use the `<STYLE>` tag to format an individual element. For example, to make paragraph text bold and red, use the following lines:

```
<P STYLE="color: red; font-weight: bold;"> Paragraph
text here </P>
```

For many properties, the `<DIV>` and `<SPAN>` selectors take inline styles even further, allowing a style to be applied to any segment of text. Simply surround the desired text with `<DIV></DIV>` (for a block element separated from surrounding content with line breaks) or `<SPAN></SPAN>` (for inline elements which flow into surrounding content with no breaks). For example, a single word can turn become italicized and underlined with the following code:

```
<P>Any word group can change style and become
<SPAN STYLE="font-style: italic; text-decoration:
underline">italicized and underlined</SPAN> within
other text. </P>
```

The result in a Web page would be the following:

> Any word group can change style and become *italicized and underlined* within other text.

CSS works better if you use closing tags such as `</P>` even where not strictly required by HTML. (Besides, neatly closed tags help prepare you for XML!)

The <SPAN> and <DIV> selectors work with most, but not all, CSS properties (the exceptions are generally noted in the properties reference sections later in this chapter).

Inline styles override all other style sheet types.

Most of the example code in this chapter uses inline styles, simply because they are easier to see within the constraints of a few lines of code. However, in actual HTML Help systems, it's generally more efficient to use linked or embedded style sheets.

# Creating the style sheet

Creating a cascading style sheet is one of those times that the simplest tools may be the best. Many HTML editors include CSS editing and creation tools; there are even a few dedicated style sheet editors. While these tools are useful for drafting style sheets, most writers find themselves reverting to the basic Windows Notepad at some point. Fortunately, CSS was designed to be simple enough to be coded by hand and brief enough to promote rapid development and allow the finished product to load quickly in the Web browser window (Håkon Wium Lie & Bert Bos, *Cascading Style Sheets: Designing for the Web*. Harlow, England: Addison Wesley Longman, 1997).

One of the best CSS editing tools is included in Microsoft's Visual InterDev ... ask your developers if they have a copy you can take for a test drive.

## Style definition: the basics

Each style defined in a style sheet requires a *style sheet rule* consisting of the following parts:

- A selector identifying the element which the rule affects; usually this is a standard HTML element such as <P> or <LI>.

- One or more declarations describing the formatting for the specified selector. In turn, each declaration consists of:
    - a property, one of approximately 50 CSS-supported aspects of formatting, such as font-family, margin-top, or border-style; and
    - a value, a precise specification for the property, such as the name of the font-family or the size of the margin-top.

Figure 4.4 applies these parts to a typical style sheet rule.

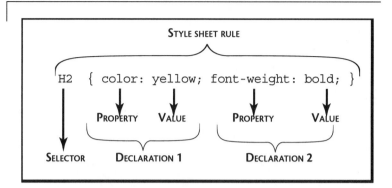

**Figure 4.4 Anatomy of a style sheet rule.** *CSS style sheets are composed of rules that follow a certain standardized syntax in defining selectors through the use of declarations which are, in turn, composed of properties and values.*

For some inexplicable reason, IE prefers a semicolon after the last declaration, although the standard does not require it.

In this rule (from the cayenne style sheet earlier in the chapter) all second-level headings are formatted with the following text (the *style sheet rule*):

```
H2   { color: yellow; font-weight: bold; }
```

This basic style sheet rule formats all second-level headings in bold yellow type. The rule identifies `<H2>` as the element to be formatted, so that this rule governs all text appearing between `<H2>` and `</H2>` tags. The rule uses two declarations `color: yellow;` and `font-weight: bold;` to specify that the `H2` text is bold and yellow. Each declaration consists of a *property* (in this example, *color* or *font-weight*) and its value (in this example, *yellow* and *bold*, respectively).

As with basic HTML code, the Web browser ignores most spaces and line breaks; adding spaces makes the code human-readable. The punctuation, however, is critical in allowing the browser to read the code. Each style sheet rule requires the following punctuation:

- **curly braces** surrounding the declaration (or list of declarations), separating it from the selector and from any other style sheet rules;

- **semicolons** separating the declarations in a list (a semicolon following the last declaration is recommended but not required);

- **colons** within each declaration, separating the property from its value.

One place where spaces do matter in HTML: do not put a space between a value and a unit of measurement (for example, 1in, not 1 in).

# The rules of inheritance

When creating style sheet rules using simple HTML elements as selectors, remember that CSS sees the elements in a tree structure (figure 4.5).

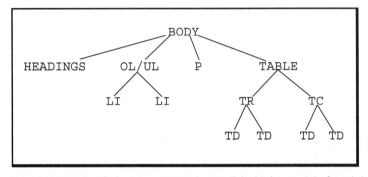

***Figure 4.5 CSS rules of inheritance.*** *HTML elements "inherit" characteristics from their "parents," the HTML elements above them on the CSS/HTML tree*

Even as CSS includes a "cascade" defining the relative importance of different style sheet types, the recommendation also provides "inheritance" as a means of defining common characteristics among elements in a style sheet. CSS-defined characteristics flow down the tree unless specifically overridden. In CSS terminology, the "children" of a "parent" element inherit most of its characteristics unless the style sheet specifically changes the values for a particular property.

For example, since `<BODY>` is the parent element for a page, a style sheet rule defining the body font as Arial Narrow dictates that all text in `<P>`, list, heading, and table tags appears as Arial Narrow unless specifically defined otherwise. Similarly, if the style sheet rule defines `<P>` text as being red, then `<B>` and `<I>` text within that paragraph will not only be bold or italicized, it will also be red. Inheritance, however, is not perfectly implemented and often seems mostly to account for unexpected results when a parent element's rule flows down to its children. Nor is it completely logical; for example, all heading levels inherit from the `<BODY>`, not from each other. So `<H3>` inherits from `<BODY>`, not from `<H1>` and `<H2>`.

Many style sheet properties are inherited; the W3C recommendations and the rest of this chapter note the specifics for each property.

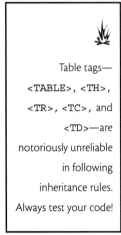

Table tags— `<TABLE>`, `<TH>`, `<TR>`, `<TC>`, and `<TD>`—are notoriously unreliable in following inheritance rules. Always test your code!

# Selectors

Although style sheet rules generally involve multiple declarations, they typically use a single selector to identify the element formatted by the rule's declaration(s). Most selectors are simple HTML elements such as H1, P, LI, or even BODY. However, the slightly more complex *class* and *contextual* selectors add flexibility to CSS and power to HTML Help systems.

## Class selectors

A *class selector* defines a specialized category that can be applied to any of the standard HTML elements. (In HTML's terminology, the class becomes an *attribute* of the HTML element.) In the style sheet, the rule for a class selector (figure 4.6) looks just like a rule for a standard HTML element except for a period before the class name.

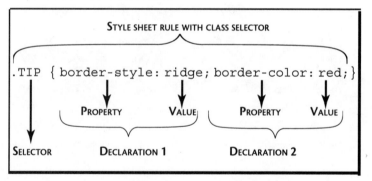

*Figure 4.6  Anatomy of a style sheet rule with a class selector. Class selector rules are written just like any other style sheet rule.*

Applying the class selector to the HTML element is as simple as adding "CLASS=" and the selector name to the basic HTML code.

As an example, online Help often uses special styles for tips meant to make the application function more efficiently. Creating a TIP class in a style sheet defines standard formatting used every time the TIP class is applied to an HTML element. To create a `TIP` class having a ridged red border, add the following line to the style sheet:

```
.TIP { border-style: ridge; border-color: red; }
```

In the HTML code, add the class selector to the text as follows:

```
<P CLASS="TIP"> Note that a class selector must
consist of a single word.  The word may contain
numerals or dashes, but not spaces or any other
punctuation marks. The class selector should not
begin with a numeral.  IE 4 allows class selectors
to begin with numerals, but the CSS recommendation
does not.  Why look for trouble?</P>
```

This code added to the cayenne style sheet used at the beginning of the chapter displays in Internet Explorer or an HTML Help system surrounded by a red ridge-type border (figure 4.7):

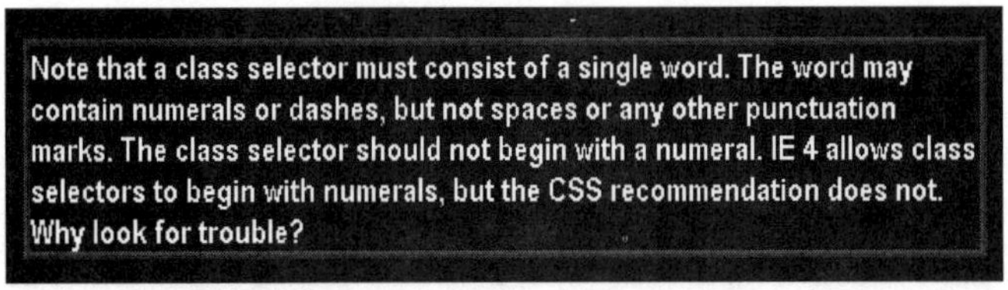

*Figure 4.7 Creating special formatting with class selectors. The* `.TIP` *class selector defined above and applied to an HTML paragraph produces a paragraph with a ridged red border. This paragraph also has a black background and white text, inherited from the underlying paragraph* `<P>` *style.*

(By the way, the "tip" is true.) Once defined, the class selector can be added to any appropriate HTML element. For example, the `.TIP` class with the red border would be logical with a paragraph, heading, or list item (that is, with tags such as `<P>`, `<H1>`, `<H2>`, or `<LI>`), but wouldn't make much sense with a `<B>` tag. On the other hand, a simple `.REDTEXT` class would work with `<B>` and `<I>` tags, creating red bold or italicized text.

# Pseudo-classes

CSS includes three useful *pseudo-classes* which apply to `<A>` links. The default pseudo-class is `A:link,` which transforms into `A:active` when the mouse hovers over the link, and then becomes `A:visited` once the link has been clicked. The following three lines would display links in blue by default, changing to red when clicked and then to navy after they've been visited:

```
A:link    { color: blue }
A:visited { color: red }
A:visited { color: navy }
```

Color and underlining work well with link pseudo-classes; other property changes are less reliable.

# Contextual selectors

*Contextual selectors* define formatting for elements appearing only in certain situations. Multiple selectors are used to precisely identify the element. For example, the selector `H2 B` refers to bold text within a level 2 heading. The selectors are read in reverse order (right to left), progressing from specific to general, such that the selector list XYZ signifies element Z appearing in element Y appearing in element X.

A typical example for a Help author would be the formatting of list items appearing in bulleted lists vs. those appearing in numbered lists, and the formatting of bulleted lists appearing on their own vs. those appearing as subtopics within a numbered list. The following style sheet rules might apply to such a situation:

```
UL LI      { list-style-type: disk; }
OL LI      { list-style-type: decimal; }
OL UL LI   { list-style-type: circle; }
```

Using these rules (see below), list items `<LI>` appearing in unordered lists `<UL>` are marked with black circles (● or "disk") unless the unordered list appears within an ordered list `<OL>`, when the list items are marked with an open circle (○). List items in ordered lists are numbered ("decimal").

# Anatomy of a value

In a style sheet rule, a *value* is a precise specification of a property. Most CSS values can be specified in many different ways. For example, color values may be specified according to standard color names, RGB values, or hexadecimal values. Most spacing values can be specified by numbers (in various units) or by percentages, in absolute or relative terms. Different ways of specifying values can be mixed within a single style sheet rule or HTML page; however, too much variety can lead to confusion for the Help author, if not for the HTML.

## Color values

CSS color values typically apply to text, backgrounds, and borders. (You cannot use CSS to specify colors in graphics.) The color values can be expressed using a set of 16 CSS-defined color names, RGB values, or hexadecimal notation.

### CSS color names

The CSS recommendation for colors lists 16 colors, taken from computer system palettes. These names are case insensitive. The color names, with their corresponding hexadecimal values, are as follows:

Be sure to spell "gray" with an "a," not an "e."

| black   | #000000 | green  | #008000 |
| silver  | #C0C0C0 | lime   | #00FF00 |
| gray    | #808080 | olive  | #808000 |
| white   | #FFFFFF | yellow | #FFFF00 |
| maroon  | #800000 | navy   | #000080 |
| red     | #FF0000 | blue   | #0000FF |
| purple  | #800080 | teal   | #008080 |
| fuchsia | #FF00FF | aqua   | #00FFFF |

# RGB color values

Computer monitors display color by combining red, green, and blue light (called the RGB color model). So computer colors are traditionally specified by the amount of red, green, and blue in a range from 0 (no light) to 255 (total light). Combining the three RGB values produces colors such as 0,0,0 (black), 255,0,0 (pure red), 0,255,0 (pure green), 0,0,255 (pure blue), or 255,255,255 (pure white). Various combinations in between produce most of the colors in the rainbow.

When specifying RGB colors in a style sheet rule, separate the three values with commas, enclose the list in parentheses, and preface the parenthetical list with the letters "rgb." So the rule for a pure blue level one heading would be:

```
H1 { color: rgb(0,0,255); }
```

# Hexadecimal values

Interestingly, HTML authors most frequently use the inscrutable hexadecimal system to specify colors. Hexadecimal (affectionately called "hex") is a base-16 number system that allows you to specify more than 16 million colors. (As you'll see in the section on *Browser-safe colors*, only 216 of them are useful in HTML.) In order to list all of the 16 allowable "digits," the hexadecimal uses letters as well as numerals, so counting from 0 to 15 in hexadecimal is:

```
0 1 2 3 4 5 6 7 8 9 a b c d e f
```

Like the RGB model, hex colors use three sets of "numbers" to specify the red, green, and blue values of the desired color. So black is similar in both systems—0,0,0 in RGB and #000000 in hex—but white is very different—255,255,255 in RGB and #FFFFFF in hex. Note the different presentation. Where RGB separates the three values with commas, hex puts a number sign (#) before the values and then runs them all together. The rule for blue heading 1 shown in RGB above translates to hex as

```
H1 { color: #0000FF; }
```

Confused by color values? Try one of the color lookup tables available on the Web, or make your color choices in one of the many graphics applications with a Web-based color palette.

If the RGB and hexadecimal color systems seem confusing, take heart. You really only need to use 216 of the colors, made up only of the values specified in the browser-safe color chart (table 4.1) that follows.

## Browser-safe colors

One of the joys of online design is that color is free and freely available, rather than an expensive add-on as it is in print media. However, this joy is countered by the limitations of the now-notorious Web browser palette of 216 colors. For technical reasons, you can only count on users' monitors displaying 256 colors at a time. In addition, the Windows system reserves certain colors for its own use and the two main Web browsers do not use the same colors. As a result, only 216 colors are "browser-safe," that is, relatively certain to display without dithering (the dot-pattern used to simulate a color not directly available onscreen).

In Adobe Photoshop, you can limit your choices to the Web-safe colors by converting to Indexed color mode and choosing the Web palette.

Fortunately, it's relatively simple to identify the browser-safe colors using RGB or hexadecimal values, as well as the CSS-specified color names. Safe RGB values contain only the following numbers: 0, 51, 102, 153, 204, and 255. Safe hex values use only 00, 33, 66, 99, CC, and FF. So rgb(51,204,0) and its hex equivalent (#33CC00) are browser-safe; but values such as rgb(26,204,0), rgb(222,111,03), #213467, or #012345 are not. Table 4.1 contains all browser-safe color values, together with their comparable percentage values.

TABLE 4.1 BROWSER-SAFE COLOR VALUES

| % OF COLOR | RGB VALUE | HEX VALUE |
|:---:|:---:|:---:|
| 0% | 00 | 00 |
| 20% | 51 | 33 |
| 40% | 102 | 66 |
| 60% | 153 | 99 |
| 80% | 204 | CC |
| 100% | 255 | FF |

# Spatial values

Spatial values are considerably simpler than color values—at least in terms of understanding the unit specification. How they actually display is another question, which is addressed within the specific properties. Spatial properties can be absolute or relative.

## Absolute: length values

Most absolute spatial values use familiar measurements of length. Within the style sheet rule, use two-letter abbreviations with no period at the end, and no space between the value and the unit. For example,

```
{ P font-size: 12pt; margin-left: 10px; }
```

Table 4.2 shows the standard spatial units, their abbreviations, and their size in relation to inches, organized from the smallest to the largest unit.

TABLE 4.2 ABSOLUTE LENGTH VALUES

| UNIT | ABBREVIATION | EQUIVALENCY TO 1″ |
|---|---|---|
| inch | in | 1.00 |
| pica | pc | 6.00 |
| centimeter | cm | 2.54 |
| millimeter | mm | 25.40 |
| point | pt | 72.00 |
| pixel | px | device-dependent* |

*Note: Pixel size depends on monitor resolution.*

Since many designers came to HTML from desktop publishing, points and picas are the most frequently used measurements. However, when specifying style sheet rules for elements that will be used with dynamic HTML (DHTML, see Chapter 5), pixels are a more reliable way to position elements that may need to align precisely onscreen.

## Relative: percentage values

Relative values are generally specified as a percentage, usually in relation to the parent element. For example, an <H2> element's font-size might be specified as 80%. If its parent <H1> element had 20-point type, then the <H2> element would use 16-point type (80% of 20-points).

## Keywords

CSS also supports the use of keywords for some values. For example, font size may be specified using the absolute keywords xx-small, x-small, small, medium, large, x-large, and xx-large, or the relative keywords smaller and larger. However, the results are difficult to predict, so it's best to stay with numerical values.

# Crucial properties for Help

The following sections describe the CSS Level 1 and Level 2 properties as implemented by Internet Explorer 4 and above. In each case, the property name is followed by a box showing the standard syntax, acceptable values for use in the syntax, and an example of the property and its values as they would be specified in a style sheet rule.

Because this book is designed for writers, not programmers, the syntax and values are described using words rather than mathematical symbols. Thus, when you can use only one of the acceptable values, the value list is separated by the word *or;* when you can use one or more of the acceptable values, the values are separated by the words *and/or.*

The sections below loosely reflect the W3C classification of CSS properties as governing fonts, text & typography, color & background, boxes, and classification (lists). At the end of most categories, you'll find a shorthand property that allows you to set multiple properties with a single style sheet rule. A final category, printing, introduces two new properties that govern page breaks when printing out online Help files.

# Font properties

Font properties govern the most basic aspects of the text presented on a Web page or HTML Help file: its font (Arial vs. Helvetica), size, weight, style, etc. Previous to the implementation of CSS-1, Web designers could only use proprietary tags (such as Netscape's <FONT> or Internet Explorer's <FONT FACE>) with limited flexibility (for example, <FONT SIZE> only allowed relative values of 1 to 7). But the CSS font properties provide almost total control, without resorting to the awkward workaround of a graphic "picture" of the text.

All font properties are inherited.

## font-family

| Syntax: | {font-family: value, value, value;} |
|---|---|
| **Acceptable values:** | family name *and/or* generic family name |
| **Example:** | {font-family: verdana, arial, sans serif} |

Want to know exactly how the system sees a font's name? Use the version found in the font drop-down menu of any Microsoft Office product.

The {font-family} property not only allows you to specify the desired type face, it also provides for gracefully degrading page design through the use of multiple values. Any font-family rule can specify a number of fonts in descending order of preference; you can even include a generic font-family for times when none of the preferred fonts are available on the user's system. For example, imagine an HTML Help system designed for optimum display with all headlines in Comic Sans. That's fine if all users are on Windows 98, which ships with Comic Sans as a system font. But what about those on other platforms? Or someone who's removed Comic Sans from the font folder? In those cases, prevent the system from reverting to the browser default (probably Times New Roman) by adding more fonts in a comma-separated list. The browser will work through the list until it finds an available font. For added safety, the last value should be a *generic font-family.* Acceptable generic font-families include `serif`, `sans-serif`, `cursive`, `fantasy`, and `monospace`.

It's also important to realize that the HTML Help display engine interprets font-family names literally; for example, it won't substitute *courier new* when *courier* is unavailable. It won't even apply the italic style to *courier* if it can't find *courier italic.* So the best `{font-family}` list may be the most redundant one; for example: `{font-family: "verdana bold", "arial bold", verdana, arial, sans-serif}`.

Two more points to be careful about when specifying `font-family` names: CSS specs and the HTML Help layout engine prefer lowercase names (`arial`, not `Arial`) and they prefer multi-word font-family names to be enclosed in single or double quotation marks (`"arial bold"` is better than `arial bold`). These points were critical in earlier versions of Web browsers; from IE 4 onwards, they're no longer essential but are still considered the "best practice" and the safest way to go.

## font-size

| | |
|---|---|
| **Syntax:** | `{ font-size: value; }` |
| **Acceptable values:** | length or percentage or keywords (points, pixels, or percentages recommended) |
| **Examples:** | `{ font-size: 10pt; }`<br>`{ font-size: 150%; }` |

For most Help authors, it's easiest to specify `{font-size}` in points, a familiar approach from printed documents as well as Windows Help. (Note that HTML isn't as flexible as most word processors: points must be specified in whole numbers; sorry, no 10.25-point type.)

However, pixels and percentages are useful in some situations. If you plan to use any DHTML or complex alignments of HTML elements, *pixels* provide the most reliably consistent measurements onscreen. In fact, some of the most popular DHTML tools use only absolute positioning set in pixels.

*Percentages* furnish a way to maintain stylistic relationships even if users set their systems to larger fonts (for example, to meet accessibility concerns). A font-size specified as a percentage is calculated relative to the font-size of the parent element; that is, if the CSS specifies the basic <BODY> font-size at 10pt and sets <H1> at 150%, all level one headings display at 15 points. (This is new in IE 4.0 and higher; previous versions computed percentages from the element's default size.) Remember that all heading levels inherit from the <BODY> tag, not from higher-level headings. So, if <BODY> is set to 10pt, <H1> is set to 200%, and <H2> is set to 200%, both levels display in 20 point type (200% times the body's 10pt type), rather than <H1> being 200% of body and <H2> being 200% of <H1>.

## font-style and font-weight

| | |
|---|---|
| **Syntax:** | {font-style: value;} |
| **Acceptable values:** | normal *or* italic |
| **Example:** | {font-style: italic;} |
| **Syntax:** | {font-weight: value;} |
| **Acceptable values:** | normal *or* bold |
| **Example:** | { font-weight: bold;} |

Confusingly enough, CSS uses separate properties to specify bold and italic fonts. {font-style} toggles between italic and normal, while {font-weight} toggles between bold and normal.

In theory, these two properties also support additional values, but Web browsers implement the additional values erratically. For example, the {font-style} can also be oblique, a variant of italic with little visible difference. {font-weight} can use relative values (bolder, lighter) and numeric weights (100, 200, 300, etc., up to 900, with 400 defined as "normal"), but there's not always a clearly visible difference and the addition of fonts such as "Arial Black" or "Arial Bold" further muddies the waters. Best to stick with the simple bold and italic values.

# font-variant

| | |
|---|---|
| **Syntax:** | { font-variant: value; } |
| **Acceptable values:** | normal *or* small-caps |
| **Example:** | { font-variant: small-caps; } |

The {font-variant} property, like {font-weight} and {font-style}, toggles between normal fonts and a single value; in this case, small-caps. Note that small-caps ignores internal capitalization; when applied to text such as "Small Caps," it displays as SMALL CAPS, not SMALL CAPS.

# font [shorthand property for font properties]

| | |
|---|---|
| **Syntax:** | { font: font-style and/or font-weight and/or font-variant then font-size/line-height then font-family; } |
| **Acceptable values:** | all values for individual properties |
| **Notes:** | • order is crucial (see details below)<br>• font-size and font-family are required<br>• line-height (if used) is specified as font-size/line-height |
| **Example:** | {font: bold small-caps 10pt/ 12pt Verdana; } |

The {font} property supplies a shorthand approach to CSS fonts, allowing you to set all font properties—plus line-height—in a single style sheet rule. The trickiest aspect is the order in which properties must be specified. It helps to think of the style sheet rule as having three sections:

- The first section may contain any of the following three properties: font-style (italic), font-weight (bold) and/or font-variant (small-caps). None are required. Within this section, the order of the properties doesn't matter, but these properties must be specified before the properties for any other section.

- The second section must contain the `font-size` and may contain a `line-height` value. First comes `font-size`; if `line-height` is specified, a slash (/) separates the two values.
- The third section must contain at least one `font-family` and may contain more than one `font-family` (in a comma-separated list).

Note the punctuation for the font property:

- a slash between the font-size and line-height
- commas between font-family names (if more than one is specified)
- a semicolon at the end of the values
- except for the three cases above, values are separated with spaces

# Text & typography properties

Text and typography properties generally govern the spacing of text rather than the formatting controlled by font properties.

`text-decoration` and `vertical-align` (which apply on a character-by-character basis) are not inherited; all other text & typography properties (which control spacing of character blocks) *are* inherited.

## text-decoration

| | |
|---|---|
| **Syntax:** | `{text-decoration: value;}` |
| **Acceptable values:** | `none, underline, overline, line-through` |
| **Example:** | `{text-decoration: none}` |

The `{text-decoration}` property fits awkwardly between its functional position with the font properties (which control formatting applied to letters and other characters) and the alignment its name suggests with text properties (which control spacing of letters and other characters).

In addition to allowing standard underlining, this property's `overline` value can serve as a decorative element while the `line-through` value might be useful in demonstrating changes (with the line-through designating characters that had been removed).

This property is most commonly used to remove underlining from links. Many HTML authors follow Edward Tufte's dictate to use "less ink" by designating links with color rather than underlining. For example, adding `text-decoration: none` to the style sheet rules in the earlier section on pseudo-classes provides a cleaner look while still signaling the links:

```
A:link { text-decoration: none; color: blue }
A:link { text-decoration: none; color: red }
A:link { text-decoration: none; color: green }
```

If you're using a great deal of superscripted and subscripted text, explore W3C's new MML (Mathematical Markup Language).

## vertical-align

| | |
|---|---|
| **Syntax:** | {vertical-align: value;} |
| **Acceptable values:** | sub *or* super |
| **Example:** | {vertical-align: sub} |

The {vertical-align} property, designed to create superscripts and subscripts, only became implemented in version 4.0 of Internet Explorer. In theory, the property can also be applied to any inline element (that is, a few characters or a small graphic). It works as designed with text; however, it works erratically, if at all, with graphics.

## text-align

| | |
|---|---|
| **Syntax:** | { text-align: value;} |
| **Acceptable values:** | left *or* right *or* center *or* justify |
| **Example:** | { text-align: center;} |

The {text-align} property brings simple control over justification (left, right, center, or fully justified) to HTML. Like the {text-indent} property, it applies only to block-level elements (i.e., those that begin and end with a line break, such as <P>, <H1>, <OL>, or <LI>. Unlike {text-indent}, this property is not lost when an element is broken by another element. So a {text-align} value applied to an ordered list <OL> or unordered list <UL>, will be inherited by all items in the list <LI>.

Unlike {font-size}, {line-height} is not limited to whole numbers.

The {text-align} property was also designed to be applicable to replaced elements (such as images). In practice, however, this works only if you apply the style to a block-level element (such as <P>) containing the image.

# line-height

| | |
|---|---|
| **Syntax:** | {line-height: value;} |
| **Acceptable values:** | normal *or* number *or* length *or* percentage |
| **Example:** | {line-height: 2} |

The CSS {line-height} property corresponds to the line spacing in word processing and the leading of desktop publishing. All three approaches are designed to control the spacing between lines of text. In particular, {line-height} measures the distance from the *baseline* of one text line to the baseline of the next. (The baseline is the line that text sits on; note that letters such as *y, z,* and *g* have tails, or *descenders,* that fall below the baseline.) In general, Internet Explorer adds all the line-height above the text, so that paragraphs tend to have an extra bit of "space before."

Absolute values (e.g., 14pt) define the space between the baselines of adjacent text lines. Relative values for {line-height} are calculated in relation to the element's {font-size}. Numbers such as 1, 1.5, and 2 signify the familiar single-spacing, space-and-a-half, and double-spacing. The percentage values 100%, 150%, and 200% have the same result.

The {line-height} property also allows for special effects. Combining negative values (for overlapping text) with color and other properties creates interesting text treatments and graphics composed only of type. Figure 4.8 uses different color text and a decorative font together with a {line-height} set to 50%.

*Figure 4.8 Textual graphics. The* line-height, font, *and* color *properties create an eye-catching graphic that displays more quickly than an equivalent image file.*

## text-indent

| | |
|---|---|
| **Syntax:** | {text-indent: value;} |
| **Acceptable values:** | length *or* percentage |
| **Example:** | {text-indent: 6px;} |

The {text-indent} property might more properly be the {first-line indent} property. It applies only to block-level elements (i.e., those that begin and end with a line break—such as <P>, <H1>, or <LI>—and indents only the first line of the element.

One of the more confusing aspects of the {text-indent} property is that when an element is broken by another element, the text-indent is lost at the break. So, for example, if a paragraph is broken with a <BR>, text after the <BR> is not indented. This can be a problem with lists: specifying an indent for <UL> or <OL> indents only the first <LI>. Subsequent <LI> revert to the original margin. For an indented text list, the text-indent must be applied to the list item <LI> element, not to the list type of <UL> or <OL>.

The {text-indent} values are fairly straightforward: length values (such as points, picas, inches) indent the first line of the block-level element the specified distance from the margin applied to the rest of the element. Percentage values indent the first line the percentage of the element's line-width. The {text-indent} property also accepts negative length values, creating hanging indents (also known as "undented" paragraphs).

# Color & background properties

In many ways, the {color} property belongs in its own category; however, the CSS recommendations place it with the background properties. The {color} property is inherited; the {background} properties are not.

## color

| | |
|---|---|
| **Syntax:** | { color: value; } |
| **Acceptable values:** | *see section on* Color values |
| **Example:** | { color: #CC0000; } |

The {color} property applies to most elements, from single-characters to entire pages, and even non-textual elements such as horizontal rules. Used with <SPAN> tags, it sets colors for any element or combination of elements. This property can be specified in RGB, hexadecimal, or simple key values (such as *red*). For details, see the earlier section on *Color values*.

## background-color

| | |
|---|---|
| **Syntax:** | { background-color: value; } |
| **Acceptable values:** | any color value *or* transparent |
| **Example:** | { background-color:  red; } |

The {background-color} property determines the base hue underlying an HTML page or specific elements on the page. Beginning with version 4.0 of Internet Explorer, the {background-color} is designed to reach to the margins of the specified element's *parent* element (in earlier versions, it appeared only under the text of the element itself). However, there are some interesting exceptions:

- Applied to an <LI> list item , or an <OL> or <UL> list , the color does *not* extend under the number or bullets for the individual items.

- Applied using a <SPAN> tag, the color underlays just the text, leaving gaps between the lines of text.

The path to the image file is specified relative to the CSS file, not relative to the final HTML file.

## background-image

| | |
|---|---|
| **Syntax:** | `{background-image: url(value)}` |
| **Acceptable values:** | filename (can be URL with complete path relative to CSS file) or `none` |
| **Example:** | `{background-image: url(../pix.jpg)}` |

Box properties work unpredictably, if at all, on block-level elements forced with `<SPAN>` or `<DIV>` tags.

The `{background-image}` property points to an image file (`*.gif` or `*.jpg`) that will be used as a background for the HTML pages. By default, the image tiles on the page, so the specified image must either be large enough to fill the screen or it must be borderless (unless you're trying to create a checkerboard effect!). When specifying a `{background-image}`, be sure you do not leave ANY spaces between "url" and the opening parenthesis.

A style sheet can specify both a `{background-color}` and a `{background-image}` property for the same element. By default, the image overlays the color, but the color shows through any transparent elements in the image.

## background (shorthand property for backgrounds)

| | |
|---|---|
| **Syntax:** | `{ background: value &/or value; }` |
| **Acceptable values:** | URL path for graphic file *and/or* any color value *or* `transparent` |
| **Example:** | `{ background: url(../IMAGES/paper.JPG);red;}` |

The `{background}` property sets the `{background-color}` and the `{background-image}` in a single rule. Like the `{font}` shorthand property, the order of the elements matters. The URL for the background-image graphic file (if any) should precede the color specification (if any). If any color other than transparent precedes the background-image specification, the color overlays the image, completely hiding it.

# Box properties (margin, padding, borders)

Just as users of early word processors put extra returns between paragraphs to add spacing, Web design pioneers resorted to <BR> tags to add space between paragraphs and nonbreaking spaces ( ) to create inline spacing. The brave ones even used tables to control the layout of text and images on the page. But now the CSS box properties {padding} and {margin} bring sophistication to the spacing between elements in HTML. In addition, CSS supports several border properties that control the style, color, and width of any borders applied to HTML elements.

The box properties generally apply to block-level elements (i.e., those that begin and end with a line break, such as <P>, <H1>, <OL>, or <LI>) The properties can also be applied to replaced elements (such as images), although the results are less reliable. Web browsers see these elements residing in a series of nested boxes, as shown in figure 4.9.Note also that:

- None of the box properties are inherited.

- Percentage values specify a percentage of the *parent* element's box.

- Beginning in IE 4, all box spacing values are absolute values (IE 3 added the specified value to the default value.)

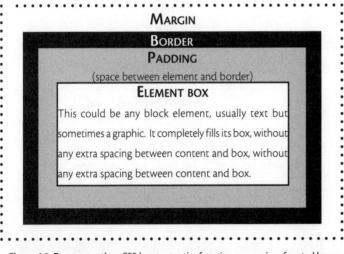

*Figure 4.9  Box properties.  CSS box properties function as a series of nested boxes, providing HTML Help authors with flexible—but complex—layout options.*

## Variants & shorthand versions

Each box property has four variants (marked with -top, -bottom, -right, and -left) as well as a shorthand version. To specify properties on a single side, or to set very different properties for each side, use one of the variants. The shorthand versions work best when all four borders are the same. However, the shorthand versions can take from one to four values to control individual borders separately:

1.  Specifying one value in a shorthand property makes all variants equal to the specified value.

2.  Specifying two values sets the horizontal (top and bottom) variants equal to the first value and the vertical side (left and right) variants equal to the second value.

3.  Specifying three values sets the top variant to the first value, the sides (left and right) variants to third value.

4.  Specifying four values sets the variants equal to the given values, proceeding in clockwise order from noon; that is, the first, second, third, and fourth values govern the top, right, bottom, and left variants, respectively.

### padding-top [-right, -left, -bottom]
### padding [shorthand property for padding on 2-4 sides]

| Syntax: | `{padding-top: value;}`<br>`{padding: value` and/or `value`<br>and/or `value` and/or `value;}` |
|---|---|
| **Acceptable values:** | `length` or `percentage` |
| **Example:** | `{padding-top: 6px;}`<br>`{padding: 120%; }` |

The `{padding}` properties exist to specify the distance between the content of the element (text or image) and its border (if any). It's best to use these properties only in conjunction with borders, to avoid confusion. If there's no border, the padding value is added to the margin value (if any), leaving potentially over-large areas of empty space between elements. Similarly, you can't use {padding} to control the horizontal space between elements (such as graphics) *unless* they're in adjacent table cells (where there is at least an implied border, even when no visible border exists).

Padding values default to 0, leaving no space at all between an element and its border. The {padding} properties do not allow negative values .

## border-top-style [-right-, -left-, -bottom-]
## border-style [shorthand property for border-style on 2-4 sides]

| | |
|---|---|
| **Syntax:** | {border-top-style: value;} {border-style: value *and/or* value *and/or* value *and/or* value;} |
| **Acceptable values:** | none *or* solid *or* double *or* groove *or* ridge *or* inset *or* outset |
| **Example:** | {border-top-style: ridge;} {border-style: double; } |

Since {border-style} properties default to none, you must specify a visible style before a border appears in a browser. The style can be set as a {border-style} property or as part of a {border} shorthand property.

The {border-style} property accepts six different values in addition to the default style of none . The graphic shows the available border styles in both light and dark colors. (The HTML page shown in figure 4.10 uses a table to control horizontal space between bordered elements. This spacing cannot be controlled with margins or padding alone.)

Current Web browsers always use black as the contrasting color for the groove, ridge, inset, and outset {border-style} properties (figure 4.10).

Because of this limitation, these styles display properly only with a light color specified as the {border-color} .

Borders properties are highly interdependent: no border appears until the {border-style} is set, and certain {border-style} values appear quite differently with different values for {border-color}.

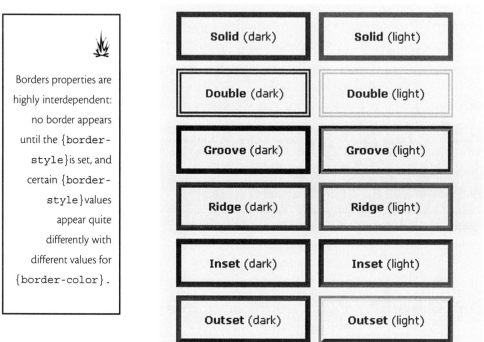

*Figure 4.10 Border styles.* *Border styles can be set in terms of both color and line style, but some line styles work better with light colors.*

## border-top-color [-right-, -left-, -bottom-]
## border-color [shorthand property for border-color on 2-4 sides]

| Syntax: | {border-top-color: value;} {border-color: value *and/or* value *and/or* value *and/or* value;} |
|---|---|
| **Acceptable values:** | see section on *Color values* |
| **Example:** | {border-top-color: red;} {border-color: #CC0000; } |

Not surprisingly, the {border-color} properties determine the color of the borders. These properties can take any of the color names, RGB, or hexadecimal values described in *Color values.* Don't forget that you must specify a {border-style} before any border will appear, and to use light colors for best results with groove, ridge, inset, or outset border styles.

## border-top-width [-right-, -left-, -bottom-]
## border-width [shorthand property for border-width on 2-4 sides]

| Syntax: | {border-top-width: value;} {border-width: value*and/or* value *and/or* value *and/or* value;} |
|---|---|
| **Acceptable values:** | thin *or* thick *or* medium *or* absolute length measurements (in, pc, cm, px, etc.) |
| **Example:** | {border-top-width: thin;} {border-width: medium; } |

The {border-width} properties are also very simple properties that determine the width of the border. In addition to the self-explanatory values of thin, thick, and medium, this property also accepts numerical length values specified in any of the standard absolute measurements: in, pc, cm, mm, pt, and px. (For more details, see the section on *Absolute: length values.*) This property does not accept percentage values.

## border-top [-right, -left, -bottom]
## border [shorthand property for all border properties on all 4 sides]

| | |
|---|---|
| **Syntax:** | `{border-top: value` *and/or* `value` *and/or* `value;}` `{border: value` *and/or* `value` *and/or* `value;}` |
| **Acceptable values:** | all acceptable values for `border-style`, `border-width`, and `border-color`.<br>• `border-style` is required<br>• unlike other shorthand properties `{border}` sets all four borders to be identical |
| **Example:** | `{border-top:thin blue solid }` `{border:6pt #CC0000 ridge }` |

Horizontal margin settings won't control space between block-level or replaced elements (images) unless they're in adjacent table cells.

The `{border}` variant properties allow you to set all aspects of any one side's border in a single property. Omitted attributes revert to their default values, so remember to set the border style attribute unless you want it to default to *none*. The color and style attributes are optional.

The shorthand `{border}` property is somewhat different from other shorthand properties. This shorthand property accepts only a single value for each attribute (style, width, color), so it requires all four borders of the element to be the same.

# margin-top (-right, -left, -bottom)
# margin (shorthand property for margins on 2-4 sides)

| Syntax: | {margin-top: value;} |
| | {margin: value *and/or* value *and/* |
| | *or* value *and/or* value;} |
| **Acceptable values:** | length *or* percentage *or* auto |
| **Example:** | {margin-top: 6px;} |
| | {margin: -75%; } |

The {margin} properties govern the space between an element's border and its external boundary. Since each element has its own external boundary, margins that meet are added together. So, for example, if an element with a {margin-bottom} of 10 points comes right before an element with a {margin-top} of 15 points, the total margin between the two elements is 25 points. Remember that these margin settings define the space outside the elements' borders and are in addition to any padding.

Margins also support negative values, which are added together as well. So if an element with a {margin-bottom} of 10 points comes right before an element with a {margin-top} of -10 points, the total margin between the two elements is 10 + (-10), or 0 points. Negative margins can also be used for interesting overlap effects.

Confused? Consider the following explanatory HTML code and the graphic (figure 4.11) showing its results:

```
<P STYLE="margin: 10pt; padding: 10 pt; border-
style: groove; border-color: red;">

This first paragraph has a 10 point margin all the
way around, plus a border and 10 points of padding
on all sides. It floats nicely within its
boundaries. </P>
```

```
<P STYLE="margin: 10pt; border-style: groove;
border-color: blue;">
```

This second paragraph has a 10 point margin all the way around. It has a border, but no padding on any side. See how tightly the border wraps the text? </P>

```
<P STYLE="margin: -10pt 0pt 10pt 0pt; padding: 10
pt; border-style: groove; border-color: aqua;">
```

This third paragraph has a <I>negative</I> top margin of 5 points. It has a border with 10 points of padding on all sides. It fits well within its border, but the negative top margin cancels out the previous paragraph's bottom margin.</P>

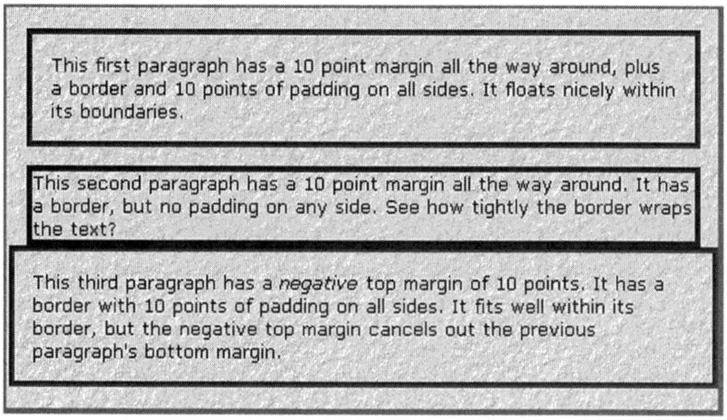

**Figure 4.11 Margin properties.** *Margin properties—which support both positive and negative values—provide both flexibility and confusion. .*

Notice also that the third paragraph extends beyond the left and right margins of the other two paragraphs. The first two paragraphs are set with 10 pt horizontal margins, while the third paragraph has no horizontal margins. (The gray box enclosing the graphic approximates the overall boundaries for the three paragraphs.)

# Classification (listing) properties

The CSS category of "classification" properties controls the numbering system or image used for notation and the positioning style (indented or undented) for list items. All classification properties are inherited.

Classification properties apply to list-item elements; that is, to `<LI>`, `<OL>`, and `<UL>`. In the existing major Web browsers, other elements (such as headings or paragraphs) simply ignore the classification properties. (The CSS recommendation includes a `display` property that would allow elements such as headings to be designated as `list-items`; however, this use of the display property is not yet widely implemented.)

Note that a style sheet rule designating the classification properties for `<LI>` will make all list items display in exactly the same way—there will not even be any difference between unordered and ordered lists (`<UL>` and `<OL>`). For this reason, it's best to assign classification properties to `<UL>`, `<OL>`, or a class selector rather than to `<LI>`. You can also create contextual selectors to set up different styles for list items in ordered and unordered lists, or even unordered lists within ordered lists.

Do not define classification styles for the basic `<LI>` element unless you want all items in all lists (both ordered and unordered) to be formatted identically.

## list-style-type

| Syntax: | {list-style-type: value;} |
|---|---|
| **Acceptable values:** | disk *or* circle *or* square *or* decimal *or* lower-roman *or* upper-roman *or* lower-alpha *or* upper-alpha |
| **Example:** | {list-style-type: square;} |

The {list-style-type} property supports eight separate styles:

- a disk appears as a filled-in circle: ●

- a circle appears as an open circle: ○

- a square appears as a filled-in box: ■

- a `decimal` list uses standard American/European-style numbers: 1,2,3

- `lower-roman` and `upper-roman` use lower-case and upper-case Roman numerals: iii and III, respectively

- `lower-alpha` and `upper-alpha` use lower-case and upper-case American/European-style letters: a, b, c and A, B, C, respectively

## list-style-image

| | |
|---|---|
| **Syntax:** | `{list-style-image:` `url(value);}` |
| **Acceptable values:** | `url` *or* `none` |
| **Example:** | `{list-style-image:` `url(pix.gif);}` |

If the eight list-style types don't meet a particular need, use the `{list-style-image}` property to designate any `.jpg` or `.gif` image as the list's bullet marker. The syntax for the `{list-style-image}` property works the same as the syntax for the `{background-image}` property: no space between "`url`" and the path; designate the path relative to the CSS file, not to the final HTML file.

## list-style-position

| | |
|---|---|
| **Syntax:** | `{list-style-position: value;}` |
| **Acceptable values:** | `inside` *or* `outside` |
| **Example:** | `{list-style-position:` `inside;}` |

`{list-style-position}` only works if users have installed IE 5.

Although Microsoft has publicly announced (on its Web page) that IE 4 supports the `{list-style-position}` property, "real-life" testing shows that it works only when the user has installed IE 5. IE 4 displays list items in the default outside position only.

When it works, the {list-style-position} property is like the margin settings in word processor lists. A value of inside puts the bullet inside the paragraph margins, so that the left edge of the bullet aligns with the left margin of the second and subsequent lines of text. The outside value gives the standard "undented" or "hanging indent" paragraph listing where the bullet hangs in the margin and all text is indented evenly.

> ▪ This is a list item with an *inside* **list-style-position.** The bullet lines up within the margins of the paragraph, so that second and subsequent text lines are even with the bullet.

> ▪ This is a list item with an *outside* **list-style-position.** Note that the text lines are all even at the left margin, with the bullet hanging *outside* the rest of the list.

## list-style [shorthand property for all list-style properties]

| | |
|---|---|
| **Syntax:** | {list-style: value *and/or* value *and/or* value;} |
| **Acceptable values:** | all acceptable values for list-style-image, list-style-position, *or* list-style-type |
| **Example:** | {list-style: square url(image.gif) inside;} |

This shorthand property sets all three list-style properties at once. The order in which the properties are specified does not matter. However, if you specify both a list-style-type and a list-style-image, the image overrides the type. The bullet specified as the type will then appear only when the specified image is unavailable (for example, if the path is incorrect or you inadvertently delete the image file before compiling the HTML Help file).

# Printing properties

## page-break-before [-after, -inside]

| | |
|---|---|
| **Syntax:** | {page-break-before: value;} |
| **Acceptable values:** | auto *or* always *or* left *or* right *or* avoid |

The crossover from online to printed Help has always been a problem for Help authors. The different demands of screen and paper formatting cause difficulties when users print an online Help system. While the page-break commands don't solve all the problems, at least they provide some control. Perhaps the most useful application for Help authors is the ability to avoid titles orphaned from their supporting text by *always* forcing a page break before or making the printer *avoid* page breaks after all headings.

The {page-break} properties default to auto, which means no control at all. Always forces a break before/after the element; avoid means there's never a break before/after the element). Avoid and auto are the only values supported by {page-break-inside}, allowing you to control breaks within tables, graphics, and other items that should be printed as a unit.

Even more interesting are the left and right values, designed to force 1-2 breaks as needed to start the element on a left- or right-facing page. Unfortunately, these values do not work reliably at the present time, but at least they offer hope for future functionality.

{page-break} properties work reliably only if users have installed IE 5.

# How CSS works with HTML Help— & how it doesn't

Since HTML Help is based on Microsoft's Internet Explorer display engine, it uses cascading style sheets according to the same rules applicable to IE. Basically, this means IE 4, which supports all the properties described in this chapter except page-break and list-style position. It does not support a number of other CSS properties, including first-letter pseudo, first-line pseudo, important, white space, and word spacing. If your users have IE 5, you can access page-break and list-style-position.

Using CSS within HTML Help requires only a few additional pieces of information to make it all work together smoothly.

## Adding the style sheet to the project

Theoretically, any files (such as images or CSS) referenced in an included HTML page will automatically be included at compile time. In practice, this ability is erratic at best. Therefore, it is necessary to manually add the CSS files to your HTML Help project.

To explicitly add a CSS file to the HTML Help project:

1. With the project (.hhp) file open in the HTML Help Workshop, go to the PROJECT tab and click the ADD/REMOVE TOPIC FILES button.

2. In the TOPIC FILES dialog, click ADD.

3. In the OPEN dialog, browse to the folder containing the CSS file. Type *.css in the FILE NAME text box to make the CSS file appear in the list. Choose the CSS file and click OPEN to add it to the project file list.

4. Click OK to return to the HTML Help Workshop.

> You can add the CSS manually by opening the .hhp file in Notepad and typing the full path and filename in the [FILES] section.

# Areas of enhancement: fonts

At present, compiled HTML Help works only on the Windows platform. On the positive side, this means that you can fairly accurately predict the fonts that will display in the HTML Help browser window.

The only truly universal fonts (at least, in the Windows universe of HTML Help) are Arial, Courier New, and Times New Roman (including their bold and italic versions), plus Symbol and Wingdings. Arial Narrow is also generally a safe bet.

In addition, Internet Explorer attempts to bring along its favorite fonts (Verdana, Tahoma, and Webdings), so users are likely to have access to these fonts as well. If you have reason to believe your users installed Internet Explorer independently of your HTML Help system, you'll want to at least experiment with Verdana, Tahoma, and Wingdings; designed specifically for the Web, they display quickly and cleanly onscreen.

The following lists detail the fonts installed by default on different versions of Microsoft Windows. If your product requires a certain Windows version, you may be able to expand the range of available fonts:

- **Windows 95 fonts:** Arial (bold/italic), Courier New (bold/italic), Marlett, Symbol, Times New Roman (bold/italic), Wingdings

- **Windows 98 fonts:** Arial (bold/italic), Arial Black, Comic Sans (bold), Courier New (bold/italic), Impact, Lucida Console, Marlett, Symbol, Tahoma (bold), Times New Roman (bold/italic), Verdana (bold/italic), Webdings, Wingdings

- **Windows NT 4 fonts:** Arial (bold/italic), Courier New (bold/italic), Lucida Console, Lucida Sans Unicode, Symbol, Times New Roman (bold/italic), Wingdings

In addition, Microsoft's embedded font technology allows you to include any font in your HTML Help system. Explore their Web Embedding Fonts Tool (WEFT) and its accompanying Wizard, which are freely available on the Microsoft Web site: `www.microsoft.com./typography`.

# Arenas of conflict: spacing, inheritance, & split files

The areas of conflict are relatively minor (beyond the limitations inherent in Internet Explorer itself.) They fall into three categories:

- **Inheritance:** Inheritance sometimes functions erratically within HTML Help. Always test and retest any specifications that depend on inheritance. When in doubt, it's best to overspecify (for example, setting the font for table data as well as for the table as a whole).

- **Split files:** Embedded and linked style sheets are lost if you also use the Workshop's SPLIT FILE command. This command is designed for authors who want to write all the topics in their entire system in a single, long file. The command inserts an ActiveX control that tells the HTML Help compiler to separate the single file into multiple topics. Unfortunately the command operates by just adding a sort of "break" and defining the new filename and title without capturing any other information in the HTML document's <HEAD> section. (The easiest way to think of it is to visualize the command simply closing and reopening the <BODY> and <HTML> tags, without repeating any of the information from the <HEAD> section after reopening the tags to start the second file.) In particular, the SPLIT FILE command does not pick up any <STYLE> or <LINK> information so, if you use this feature, linked and embedded cascading style sheet appear only in the first topic. Because of the way the Workshop stores this split (in an ActiveX object), you cannot even add the style sheet or its link manually to the new topic files. The answer? Don't use SPLIT FILE. HTML is easier to manage on a one topic/one file model—and CSS is too good to give up for the privilege of writing a megabyte-long file.

- **Measurement systems:** The most reliable measurement systems are picas and pixels, especially if you plan to use any DHTML. The least reliable measurements are inches. Percentages are also tricky except for elements and properties that depend on other elements and properties (for example, specifying the H2 point size as 75% of its parent H1 element, or setting line spacing as 120% of point size).

# 5

# Making Waves: DHTML

## [Dynamic HTML]

If HTML describes the structure of informational content and CSS describes its style, then DHTML captures the dynamics of both style and content. DHTML is best known for making graphics fly across the Web page. But DHTML not only adds the "dazzle" to the razzle-dazzle of the World Wide Web, it also makes the Web more useful with its ability to provide interactive content tailored to users' needs.

Before DHTML, most Web pages were static; that is, the same text stayed in the same place from the time the Web author created it through all the accesses by all the users who looked at that page with lots of different desires. Some clever designers used CGI scripts and forms to create a limited type of interactivity, but basically you could only change the content by following a link or by explicitly requesting information from the server. These approaches were slow and limited in scope. Also, the most sophisticated graphic layering involved text over a color or tiled background—or maybe different graphics if you used tables creatively. And the content was engraved in pixels, if not actually carved in stone.

With version 4.0 of the major browsers, dynamic HTML came to the Web. Graphic designers embraced the new technology early and enthusiastically, leading to all manner of visual effects and dynamics of style. But, as Web authors became proficient in DHTML, the dynamics of content came into play. User-specified needs can be collected and processed on the client's Web page, speeding up access and allowing ever more focused content. E-commerce sites may experience better sales with a customized product selection. Knowledge bases can become more effective in pointing users to answers . And in online Help systems, where the user is often not even connected to a server, dynamic HTML lets the author provide on-the-fly customizations for readers at different levels and in different situations.

Although many of these options are available through diverse technologies, DHTML scripting and style sheets generally offer a better solution than other approaches to interactivity. Because the DHTML technologies are native to the Web, they are smaller and faster than approaches such as Shockwave™, Flash®, and video (`.avi` and `.mov` files), nor do they require any downloads or plug-ins. DHTML also beats out CGI: as a client-side technology, DHTML is faster and less complex to implement. And it is far simpler to write DHTML than CGI!

This chapter discusses dynamic HTML primarily in terms of JavaScript, with a few bits of CSS. A full course in scripting and JavaScript is beyond the scope of this book; however, one of the best ways to learn is to get a general grasp of the basics and then experiment with simple implementations. The following sections provide an overview of JavaScript's history and general usage before presenting a number of scripts for use in online Help systems. To that end, this chapter does not go into detail on creating flying demos, but focuses on tasks more specifically related to HTML Help.

The Web is full of additional sources of DHTML code and tutorials. Any of the Web search engines can turn up dozens of locations. Some of my favorite reference sites are:

```
http://hotwired.lycos.com/webmonkey/
http://home.cnet.com/webbuilding
http://msdn.microsoft.com/workshop/author
http://www.dhtmlzone.com
http://www.webreference.com
```

The scripts in this chapter are also available for cut-and-paste copying at the companion Web site, `www.jmek.net/ html_help`.

# What it is & what it does

Although often used as a synonym for JavaScript, DHTML is actually a combination of cascading style sheet and scripting technologies, built on top of basic HTML, which brings movement and interactivity to Web pages. (Some definitions also include embedded objects and applets.) Cascading style sheets supply the ability to control the position and visibility of elements on the page. Scripting provides additional control over motion, layering, and visibility. Both react to user-input such as mouseovers, mouseclicks, and form-gathered information.

The cascading style sheet portion of DHTML draws primarily from CSS-P, the W3C standard for positioning variables, and CSS-2, which provides additional media-related items. If your users have Internet Explorer 4, you can safely call on the extremely helpful `visibility` and `display` characteristics of CSS; common positioning elements such as `top`, `left`, `vertical align`, and `z-index` (for three-dimensional layering); and a number of clever visual filters and transitions. Additional CSS elements are available in Internet Explorer 5, but this chapter will be confined to items requiring no more than IE 4.

The scripting component of DHTML may be written in JavaScript, JScript, or VBScript. This chapter works entirely with JavaScript. JavaScript is the de facto standard, supported by most of the common browsers, although VBScript is also widely used. The current JavaScript version 1.3 derives from ECMAScript, specifically from the ECMA-262 standards defined by the European Computer Manufacturers Association (ECMA). ECMA defines the standards for ECMAScript and, by extension, for JavaScript, just as the World Wide Web Consortium (W3C) defines the standards for HTML and CSS. (JScript is JavaScript with certain Internet Explorer-specific additions.)

JavaScript was originally created as LiveScript by Netscape in partnership with Sun Microsystems™ and has nothing to do with Java in any technical sense. The name came when an unknown but creative marketer decided

> ECMA-262 (the basis for JavaScript 1.3, released August 1998) and ECMA-290 (June 1999) are available for download at `www.ecma.ch/stand/standard.htm`.

to rename it "JavaScript" to take advantage of the popularity enjoyed by Java at that time. However, where Java is a compiled language designed to write complete applications, JavaScript is a noncompiled or interpreted scripting language designed for smaller bits of functionality; also, JavaScript is also much simpler to learn.

# Building a DHTML script

In basic HTML, when you put an image on the page, that image always appears in that position on the page (with some allowances for the user resizing the browser window). But using DHTML allows you to have the image change depending on the user's actions or other information. For example, you might want to make the image (`button.gif`) look as if it has actually been depressed when a user moves the mouse over the image. Often called an "image rollover," this technique can be used to provide visual feedback when a user clicks on a button in order to jump to another page or just to provide additional information or a short bit of animation. This technique can be accomplished by using DHTML *objects*, *properties*, and *events* to build *functions* that enact the desired changes.

The italicized terms are demonstrated in this example and explained in more detail later in the chapter.

To understand this technique, start by adding the image to the page with this basic HTML code:

```
<IMG SRC="button.gif">
```

This code adds an image *object* to the page, together with its source *property*. In order to make the image object easier to use in scripting, we'll add another *property* that gives the image a name, like this:

```
<IMG NAME="button1" SRC="button1.gif">
```

Next, imagine you have a second version of the button image that is shadowed so it looks like it's been pressed in (`button1Down.gif`). The untouched button should display `button1.gif`; when the user's mouse moves over the button, it it should change to `button1Down.gif`; and when the user moves away from the image, it should revert to `button1.gif`. You can use the rather clearly named DHTML *event handlers* onMouseOver and onMouseOut to trigger these actions:

```
<IMG NAME="button1" SRC="button1.gif"
onMouseOver="document.button1.src='button1Down.gif'"
onMouseOut="document.button1.src='button1.gif'">
```

The two new lines change the image object's source *property* whenever one of the specified *events* occurs (onMouseOver when the user's mouse moves over the image; onMouseOut when the user's mouse moves out of the image's area). The phrase document.button1.src uses *dot notation* to reference the specific image *object* as part of the entire document. (Dot notation is described later in this chapter).

Typing this code for numerous buttons on the page could get tedious and lead to errors. So we'll create a *function,* a set of actions which is given a name and put in the <HEAD> of the HTML document. From there, you can reuse the set of actions whenever you like. First, let's move the code to a function in the <HEAD> (we'll make it reusable in a moment):

```
<SCRIPT LANGUAGE="JavaScript" TYPE="text/
javascript">

function buttonDown()
{
  document.button1.src="button1Down.gif"
}

function buttonUp()
{
document.button1.src="button1.gif"
}

</SCRIPT>
```

Button1 is a naming convention for demonstration purposes only. Since numbered names quickly become confusing, you should develop your own conventions for meaningful names.

The <SCRIPT> and </SCRIPT> lines are always used to enclose the scripting section of an HTML document, much as the <STYLE> and </STYLE> lines are used for an embedded style sheet. The function buttonDown() line says that you're defining a *function* named buttonDown. Function names are always followed by a pair of parentheses (we'll see why in a moment) and their actual scripting lines are always set off by curly braces. In this case, the scripting line `document.button1.src="button1Down.gif"` echoes the `onMouseOver` line used to change the image source in the previous example.

These scripts demonstrate why you need to know what code works with which browser. These scripts work in IE4 and 5 (and thus in HTML Help), but not in Navigator, which does not support `onMouseOver` on images or `this`.

Once the function is defined in the `<HEAD>` section, you can "call" it from the body:

```
<IMG NAME="button1" SRC="button1.gif"
 onMouseover="buttonDown()"
 onMouseOut="buttonUp()">
```

But what, you ask, is the point? It's not any less typing; you've just moved the bulk of the text from the body to the head. The point comes when we make the function reusable so that the bulk of the code appears once in the `<HEAD>` and the repetitive `<BODY>` code is minimized and simplified. We do this by adding a *variable*, that is, a name that can change (vary) its value depending on the circumstances (like *x* in high school algebra). If we put the variable name in those empty parentheses after the function name and then substitute the appropriate value for the variable in the rest of the script, we can make each "call" from the body use a different variable and thus a different set of images. So our reusable functions with the variable `buttonName` look like this:

```
<SCRIPT LANGUAGE="JavaScript" TYPE="text/
javascript">

function buttonDown(buttonName)
{
document.images[buttonName].src=buttonName
+ "Down.gif";
}

function buttonUp(buttonName)
{
document.images[buttonName].src=buttonName +
".gif";
}

</SCRIPT>
```

In the body we'll call the function like this, using the parentheses after the function name to pass the appropriate value for the variable back to the function in the head :

```
<IMG NAME="button1" SRC="button1.gif">
  onMouseOver="buttonDown('button1')"
  onMouseOut="buttonUp('button1')">
```

This code allows you to simply cut and paste wherever needed; the only change you'll need to make is to change the "1" in the button name to 2, 3, 4,…, 268. And we can reduce the amount of editing even more by changing the value we pass in parentheses from the actual button name ('button1') to the dot notation this.name which automatically picks up the NAME= value of this item (whatever the current item may be).

```
<IMG NAME="button1" SRC="button1.gif"
  onMouseOver="buttonDown(this.name)"
  onMouseOut="buttonUp(this.name)">
```

Store this code as a reusable snippet using a text block in the HTML Help Workshop, assets capabilities in other HTML editors, or even in a plain old Notepad file. Any time you need to use the code, cut and paste it, changing only the image's name and source as you do when simply adding a new image. Just be sure that you name all of your buttons consistently, with the basic raised button image as X.gif (where X is the name given the IMG tag) and the version that looks pressed in as XDown.gif.

This approach brings us full circle, back to the point where the only custom coding involved is adding the image name and source. But whereas the original lines created a static image, you have now created a bit of dynamic HTML that responds interactively to your users.

> Note 'button1' (as a value passed backed to the function) requires quotes but this.name does not. That's because button1 is quoted literally to the function in the <HEAD>, while

# How to do it

The examples in this chapter use inline and embedded DHTML, simply because it is easier to see wtihin the context of a few lines. In a complete HTML Help system, external linked files are more efficient.

In many ways, DHTML scripting works much like cascading style sheets: both are created as simple ASCII text that can be written inline, embedded in the <HEAD> section, or in an external file. As with cascading style sheets, the most efficient use of DHTML is to use an external linked file for the function scripts with inline calls to trigger the functions. The linking and embedding approaches require the following steps:

1. In the <HEAD> section of each HTML file, add lines linking to a script file or setting off an embedded section for the scripts. (These lines can be added before or after creating the scripts.)

2. Define the desired scripts in an external script file (an ASCII text file with a .js extension) or in the embedded section of the document <HEAD>.

3. At the appropriate points within the <BODY> of the page, add the necessary script or event handlers to trigger the functions.

4. If you are linking to an external script file, explicitly add the .js file to the [FILES] section of your HTML Help project (.hhp).

The first and last steps are relatively simple and are described immediately below. The two intermediate steps involve the bulk of the work and are described in detail in the rest of this chapter.

## Linking to an external script file

If you are using an external script file, the first step described above simply involves adding lines to the individual HTML files in the form

```
<SCRIPT SRC="path\file.js">
<SCRIPT SRC="MS-ITS:main.chm::/common/file.js">
```

where the path in the first line is given relative to the HTML file and the path in the second line is relative to the main HTML Help file (main.chm). Note that the external path uses backslashes (the standard for Windows systems) but the internal path uses forward slashes (the standard for HTML systems).

In general, the first line is sufficient; however, some authors report that the browser has difficulties finding the file, especially in circumstances where the HTML Help file has been downloaded from a remote source and saved to the TEMP directory. To guard against these problems, add the second line as well. The browser uses whichever line works and ignores the other. The only time a problem occurs is if you have different script files in both locations, but this is mainly just a matter of keeping versions synchronized.

# Embedding a script file

If you are using an embedded script file, you simply need to add it to the HTML file, between the <HEAD> and </HEAD> tags. The complete recommended form is to begin the scripted section with the following lines, which set it off from the rest of the <HEAD> section and hide the scripts from older browsers that cannot process JavaScript:

```
<SCRIPT LANGUAGE="JavaScript" TYPE="text/
javascript">
  <!--start hiding script from older browsers
```

The script section should then close with these lines:

```
  // -->
</SCRIPT>
```

However, you can shorten the form, especially in compiled HTML Help which requires IE 3.02 and generally uses at least 4.0. You can use only first and last lines, with all script functions embedded between the two:

```
<SCRIPT LANGUAGE="JavaScript">
</SCRIPT>
```

# Adding the external script file to the project

As with cascading style sheets, external script files referenced in any page of an HTML Help file should theoretically be included in the finished project by the HTML Help compiler. Again, this is not a reliable theory, so it is necessary to manually add the `.js` file to your HTML Help project.

To explicitly add an external script file to the HTML Help project:

ADD/REMOVE TOPIC
FILES button

1. With the project (`.hhp`) file open in the HTML Help Workshop, go to the Project tab and click the **Add/remove topic files** button.

2. In the **Topic Files** dialog, click **Add.**

3. In the **Open** dialog, browse to the folder containing the script file. Type `*.js` in the **File name** text box to make the script file appear in the list. Choose the `.css` file and click **Open** to add it to the project file list.

4. Click **OK** to return to the HTML Help Workshop.

> You can manually add the script file to the project in Notepad. Open the `.hhp` and type the script file's full path and filename in the `[FILES]` section.

# Where to author

When it comes to actually creating scripts and inserting event handlers, dedicated scripting tools are few and far between. Most of the current crop of HTML editors include pre-canned DHTML scripts which you can use as is or edit; but they seldom offer much help for creating your own JavaScript. SoftQuad's HoTMetaL Pro, for example, includes an attribute inspector that automates the process of assigning IDs to elements and provides a list of available events for the currently selected element. Macromedia's Dreamweaver supplies some 300 custom functions and will record your scripts as you create them. The most robust tool is probably Microsoft's Visual InterDev, a full-fledged programming environment that is often more confusing than helpful to non-developers. But none of these actually offer much assistance in writing new code, perhaps because

JavaScript is a scripting *language*, offering all the richness, complexity, and flexibility of any language. After all, you don't expect word processors to actually choose the words that will convey the desired meaning, although many try to help with spelling and grammar checking facilities.

For the moment, then, the best scripting environment may be trial-and-error using Internet Explorer and the Windows Notepad. Beginning with version 5 of Internet Explorer, right-clicking in the window (anywhere except on a graphic or link) and selecting View Source from the shortcut menu brings up the code for the page in a new Notepad window. Make your edits and save the file in Notepad; then return to the IE window and press **F5** to refresh the HTML page and test your most recent edits.

Once the scripting works to your satisfaction, be sure to save a copy of the working file in a safe place! Scripts are amazingly delicate: a misplaced space or inappropriate capitalization can break the whole thing. For that reason, it's a good idea to cut and paste working scripts rather than retyping them from scratch. You can store the working scripts in a special Notepad file from which you cut and paste, or choose one of the HTML editors with support for libraries of assets. Even the HTML Help Workshop' s editor allows you to store some text blocks (which can be script), but you are limited to a total of nine blocks.

# Basic script syntax tips

Given the richness and flexibility of the JavaScript language, then, it is almost impossible to teach someone to "speak" (script) fluently in a few pages. The best way to learn is by examining sample scripts (such as the ones at the end of this chapter), taking them apart and putting them back together so that they serve slightly different purposes. Look at the scripts for DHTML supplied in the HTML Help Workshop; visit the Web sites referenced at the beginning of this chapter; right-click and select VIEW SOURCE whenever you find a Web page with an effect you admire. At first the scripts will appear impenetrable, but they will become clearer in time. To start, though, here are a few tips that you should know. If they aren't entirely clear now, just wait. As you work on your scripting, you will find that reminding yourself of these bits of information may often fix a stubborn script.

1. **JavaScript is case sensitive.** Typing `Document.write` instead of `document.write` can cause an entire script to fail. (Different versions of Internet Explorer vary in how well they interpret inappropriate capitalization.)

2. **Always use straight quotes, not curly quotes.** Also, if you nest sets of quotes, you must alternate between single quotes and double quotes.

3. **Spaces are crucial.** If a script should work but doesn't, try adjusting the spaces between script elements.

4. **Scripts can be in stored in the head or in the body of the page, but are most often stored in the head or in an external file.** Scripts stored in the head are processed before the rest of the page, so they're available immediately.

5. **Scripts are usually called from the body.** Once the script has been defined in the head, you still need to have code in the body next to the item that triggers the effect. Exceptions include scripts that are triggered when the page first loads, such as a splash screen or an opening effect.

6. **Scripts have a required syntax, just like any verbal or mathematical language.** Different script elements work in different ways, just like the parts of speech in spoken languages. Put very simply, scripts are made up of *objects* (things) which have specific *properties* (descriptive attributes) and *methods* (actions they are capable of performing). Not all properties and methods can apply to all objects, so be sure you're applying them appropriately. Also, you have to name or define an object or variable before you can use it. (These terms are discussed further in the rest of the chapter.)

7. **Scripts have a required punctuation, just like any verbal or mathematical language.** *Functions* are always nested inside curly braces {}; *functions* and *methods* are always followed by a pair of parentheses (). Items that should be quoted literally appear inside quotation marks; items that are names (of objects or variables) do not generally use quotation marks.

8. **Individual statements within a scripted function can be separated by semicolons, line breaks, or both.** For best results, end each script statement with both a semicolon and a line break.

9. **SPAN and DIV tags are useful for scripting non-defined objects.** If you want to apply a DHTML effect (with script or with CSS styles) to a section that is not an object, you can use these tags to set off and define the desired area. Setting items off with `<SPAN>   </SPAN>` tags applies the effect to the items without adding line breaks. Setting the items off with `<DIV>  </DIV>` tags defines the items as composing a block-level element, which causes the browser to insert line breaks before and after the spanned element.

`<DIV>` is defined by the W3C as a "generic language/style container" and is used in IE in much the same way that `<LAYER>` is used in Netscape Navigator. Automatic DHTML generators may use `<LAYER>`, but IE doesn't support it, so you may have to hand-edit the code.

# Basic JavaScript terminology

Most books on JavaScripting assume a level of previous scripting knowledge beyond that of the average HTML Help author. In general, the books immediately begin talking about how to use objects, properties, methods, and functions, without defining the terms or explaining how they fit together. This section presents the background an HTML Help author who is also an aspiring JavaScript author needs to learn this new language.

In the broadest terms, JavaScript uses *objects*, *properties*, and *methods*. It combines these items with *variables* and *operators*, using a special syntax, to write scripts that define *functions*. Functions are basically groups of actions that are given a name so that they can be run ("called") from multiple pages or multiple locations in a page. The following pages define these terms more fully, together with detailed information about specific instances (that is, information about particular objects, properties, methods, etc.)

## Objects

In the simplest terms, *objects* are things on an HTML page that you (the author) can see and manipulate; for example, in the image rollover presented earlier, the script manipulated an image object. Images may be the most commonly manipulated DHTML objects, but text, style sheets, and other objects can also be scripted. In technical programming terms, we say that the objects are "exposed" when they are available for script manipulations.

More technically, *objects* are named collections of data. These include custom objects (created by assigning a NAME to an HTML element), built-in (or global) objects, and browser objects. Browser objects are those "exposed" (made open) to scripting in the Document Object Model (DOM), a hierarchical list of objects wherein each object "owns" the objects below it. The list of "exposed" objects is determined by the people who write the browsers. The DOM standard is specified by the W3C, with varying implementations by Microsoft for IE and by Netscape for Navigator.

Under Internet Explorer 5, the main part of the Microsoft DOM travels from the browser window to the document and its constitutent objects (figure 5.1). (The full DOM has another branch with non-document objects; the additional objects are best left to advanced scripters.)

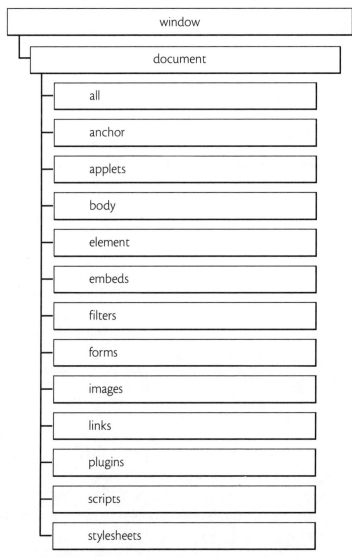

**Figure 5.1 The Microsoft DOM.** *In the main branch, the* window *object contains the* document *object which contains all the other objects shown . The idea of objects "belonging" to one another allows you to name and manipulate each object.*

Most of the objects in the DOM have specific correlations to common HTML tags. (In fact, the W3C recommendations state that the DOM should have an object for every HTML element and a property for every HTML attribute.) For example, *anchor objects* appear between <A> and </A> tags , *form objects* between <FORM> and </FORM> tags, and *image objects* appear within a single <IMG> tag's opening and closing brackets.

Except for the `body` and `all` objects, each of the objects below the `document` object can appear multiple times within a single HTML document. That's because each of the objects shown in the DOM is actually a collection of objects; for example, the `image` object collection includes all the images in a given HTML document. Technically speaking, each of these collections is called an *array*. The browser keeps track of the objects in each array by numbering them in the order that they occur. It's important to note that this numbering doesn't start at 1 but at 0, so that the first time the <IMG> tag occurs in a documents, its image is `images[0]` , the second occurrence is `images[1]` , etc.

In addition, JavaScript supports certain built-in or global objects  These include the `Date`, `Math`, and `Array` objects that let you work with dates and times, mathematical functions, and custom-defined groups of objects, respectively.  (The `Date` object is discussed later in this chapter.)

When using array numbers to refer to individual occurrences of an object type within a document, remember that the numbering begins with 0, not 1.

# Properties

Each object has certain properties that describe its particular characteristics. As explained previously, DHTML objects often have matching HTML elements; similarly, DHTML properties often have parallel HTML attributes. (There are also some commonalities between objects/elements and CSS selectors and between properties/attributes and CSS properties.)  The HTML/DHTML parallels are easiest to see with images, since a typical HTML tag for an image element uses the same names in both systems.

Thus, the properties for an image may include its `NAME`, `SOURCE (SRC)`, `BORDER`, `HEIGHT`, and `WIDTH`. Each object has its own special collection of applicable properties; in addition, there are some properties (such as

NAME and ID) that apply almost universally. In fact, the most commonly used DHTML properties are probably NAME and its sibling property ID. These properties make it even easier to access individual objects and their other properties through dot notation (figure 5.2).

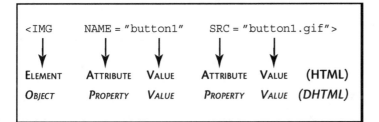

**Figure 5.2 HTML and DHTML naming conventions.** *W3C recommendations specify that every HTML element should relate to a DOM object and every HTML attribute should relate to a DOM object property, although the correlation is imperfectly implemented in the major browsers.*

# Dot notation

The DOM objects, together with their numbering within collections and their properties, provide the basis for the *dot notation* used to reference items in JavaScript. *Dot notation* just involves "walking the tree," specifying each object from the window on down as you move towards the desired reference. So, in order to manipulate the object marked by the first occurrence of the <IMG> tag in an HTML page, you could write:

```
window.document.images[0]
```

However, since there is always only a single window and it is the parent of all other objects, you can leave off the window item and just write

```
document.images[0]
```

You can't omit the document reference, however, because the DOM has another branch out of the window object (remember, it's not shown in the previous graphic of the Document Object Model).

This system allows you to refer to any of the elements on the tree by number, but it has two drawbacks:

1. The numbering is dynamic, so when a new object is added ahead of other objects in the same collection, each object's reference number changes.

2. What about other items not explicitly listed on the DOM tree, such as headings and paragraphs?

These problems are solved by using the ability to add a name to any object.

## Naming objects

W3C standards apply NAME to only a few tags and require ID to be unique within each document. The browsers do not implement the standards strictly.

The NAME and ID properties are probably the most useful properties in DHTML scripting, allowing you to call almost any HTML element that needs to be scripted. In general, you should assign a NAME or ID to any element you may want to script. For example,

```
<H1 ID="processDescription">The DOM</H1>
```

could be referenced in a script as

```
document.processDescription
```

Names and IDs must begin with a letter or an underscore and may not contain any spaces or punctuation other than the underscore. The identifier always appears after the property (NAME or ID) and an equals sign (=) and is enclosed within quotation marks. Since NAME is the more widely supported and backwards compatible property, start with NAME="whateverYouLike" and then, if you encounter difficulties, switch to ID="whateverYouLike" and see if that works.

Named objects can be referenced explicitly using dot notation, without the problems of references using the array number. Thus, the level 1 heading in the previous example would be referenced in dot notation as:

```
document.processDescription
```

In a `form` object, you can also reference its component parts, for example:

```
document.myForm.button1
```

would access the button named `button1` contained within the form named `myForm`.

## Referencing properties

Dot notation can also reference the properties within a particular object by simply adding another dot and the name of the desired property. For example, in the image rollover example that began this chapter, the first version of the function script references the source property of the images using the notation

```
document.button1.src
```

where `button1` is the name given to that particular image. This notation actually brings back the information `button1.gif`, since that is the `source` property for the `image`. Later in the example, a variable is used to make the script more modular, and the reference changes to:

```
document.images[buttonName].src
```

where `[buttonName]` is the variable that references the `NAME` property of the specific button image.

## Using "this" as a reference

In dot notation, the word `this` provides a wonderful way to simplify your scripts. Any object can refer to itself as `this`, so passing along an object name or property as `this` allows you to write the code calling the function once and then use it literally anywhere. For example, in the image rollover example, the final version of the script used the line

```
onMouseOver="buttonDown(this.name)"
```

One system recommended by many programmers is to make all names and IDs easily recognizable as such by giving them names and IDs that begin with an underscore (e.g., `_button1`).

to send its name back to the function in the header. The information that was actually sent to the script was `"button1"` since that is the "name" property of "`this`" image object. But do be careful: if `this` were used in the function, it would refer to the function, not to the image. The term `this` very specifically refers to the object within which it is used.

## Variables

Variables used in functions are also called *parameters* or *arguments* and are written inside parentheses immediately after the function name.

JavaScript variables are much like the old *x* and *y* variables from high school math: they allow you to assign names to an value and then to use specific steps to discover that value. In algebra, the variable's value was typically unknown at the beginning of the project; in JavaScript, you can set the value as soon as you define the variable. In addition, the value may vary from object to object even as *x* and *y* changed in different equations. The image rollover script at the beginning of the chapter used `buttonName` as a variable. Once we "discovered" its value for an image (in the example, `button1`), we could pass it back to the `buttonDown` and `buttonUp` functions (we called passing the variable to the function "plugging it in to the equation" in high school math) and solve those functions (equations).

To look at another common example, you can use a variable to work with the current date and/or time. Within a function, it might say:

```
var today=new Date()
```

This line says we're going to use a variable (`var`) named `today`. At the start of the operation, this variable equals a new occurrence of the built-in Date object. (`New` is a JavaScript reserved word that creates a new instance of something.) You can also assign a variable a "string" of characters (letters or numbers) that are substituted literally wherever that variable appears. To do this, put the desired string in quotes. For example,

```
var message="Hello world"
```

would then substitute the words *Hello world* wherever the variable message appeared.

Note that all variable names must begin with a letter or an underscore character and may not contain internal spaces. The names are also case sensitive, so today, TODAY, and Today would all be different variables.

# Events & event handlers

As you might guess from the name, *events* are things that happen on the Web page, particularly user actions; most often events refer to mouse movements (such as clicking or double-clicking on an object, moving over or away from an object), but they can also refer to form events (such as submitting a form), window events (such as opening or loading a new page), etc. *Event handlers* are code you can add to an object's HTML tags to process the event when it occurs. The most common events and event handlers have easily understandable names (table 5.1).

In the Microsoft DOM, the mouse event handlers apply to all visible objects except the window object.

TABLE 5.1 COMMON EVENTS AND EVENT HANDLERS

| EVENT | EVENT HANDLER |
|---|---|
| mouse click on object | onClick |
| mouse moves over object (no click required) | onMouseOver |
| mouse moves away from an object | onMouseOut |
| the browser loads a new HTML page | onLoad |
| the user leaves the HTML page | onUnLoad |
| the user changes part of a form | onChange |
| a scripting or other error occurs (good chance to write a better error message!) | onError |

To assign an event handler to a DHTML object, you simply include it as one of the HTML element's attributes in the form:

```
<ELEMENT NAME="foo"
eventHandler="function(variable)"
```

where

| | |
|---|---|
| *ELEMENT* | is H, IMG, or other valid HTML element tag; |
| *eventHandler* | is an appropriate handler, such as onClick; |
| *function* | is a function defined elsewhere; |
| *variable* | is the value passed from the event to the function. |

The "function(Variable)" section can also be replaced by a short script defining the actions to be taken when the event occurs. For example, in the image rollover example at the beginning of the chapter, we took the typical <IMG> tag with a named image:

```
<IMG NAME="button1" SRC="button1.gif">
```

We first added event handlers explicitly stating how to change the source when the mouse moved over the image and then away from it:

```
<IMG NAME="button1" SRC="button1.gif"
onMouseOver="document.button1.src='button1Down.gif'"
onMouseOut="document.button1.src='button1.gif'">
```

These event handlers say that when the mouse moves over or away from the image, the source (.src) of the object named button1 within the current document changes to a different gif file (button1Down.gif or button1.gif). We then made the code more modular by removing the explicit event handlers and substituting in pointers to generic functions and, finally, using the this pointer for enhanced reusability:

```
<IMG NAME="button1" SRC="button1.gif"
 onMouseOver="buttonDown(this.name)"
 onMouseOut="buttonUp(this.name)">
```

These revised event handlers call reusable functions. Each function call specifies what happens when the mouse moves over or away from the image; specifically, that the `buttonDown` or `buttonUp` function should be run, using the `name` property of the current object (`this`) as the parameter in the function.

# Functions

*Functions* are groups of scripts that are given names so that they may be run (or *called*) from various locations in an HTML page. Usually, the functions are defined in the `<HEAD>` of the HTML page, so that they are available as soon as the call is made on the page. Functions generally initiate an action or take a value, based on the *parameters* (or *arguments*) that are passed in from specific calls to the function.

The basic form of a function is:

```
function functionName(parameter, parameter,...)
{
scripts
}
```

where

| | |
|---|---|
| *functionName* | is the name used to call the function elsewhere; |
| *parameter* | is one or more named variables that will be passed in when the function is called; |
| *scripts* | are statements that define the function's variables and manipulate the data to return a value or initiate an action. |

The simplest functions specify that a certain action takes place whenever the function is called. But functions become more powerful (and more interesting) when they pass values from one script to another and when the component script statements evaluate the situation or passed value

Function names are case-sensitive, alphanumeric strings beginning with an underscore or letter. They may not contain spaces.

using *conditional logic*, that is, the ability to take different actions when faced with different conditions. The most common forms for conditional statements in DHTML functions are called `if...then` and `if...then...else` statements.

An `if...then` statement says that *if* condition A occurs, *then* perform action X. As a JavaScript statement used within a function, it takes the form:

```
if(condition)
  (
    scripted action(s) to perform
  }
```

An `if...then...else` statement goes one step further by deciding which of two (or more) actions to perform based on the status of a particular condition. This statement says that *if* condition A occurs, *then* perform action X; otherwise *(else)*, perform action Y. In JavaScript, this type of statement takes the form:

```
if(condition)
  {
    scripted actions to perform when condition is
  true
  }
else
  {
    scripted actions to perform when condition is
  false
  }
```

For example, a primitive passwording scheme could ask users to type in their names and then greet them (if they passed the test) or ask them to sign in.

```
<SCRIPT LANGUAGE="JavaScript">
{
var user=prompt("Hello, who are you?", "")
if(user=="Mike")
  {
```

```
    alert("Good morning, Mike"
    }
else
    {
    alert("Please sign in")
    }
}
</SCRIPT>
```

Writing functions lies at the core of DHTML. Once you learn to manipulate functions, your Web page can be as interactive as you like.

The *Window object* section explains the `alert` and `prompt` methods used in this script.

# Methods

*Methods* are *functions* that are predefined within JavaScript and are attached to specific *objects*. The most easily used method is the `write` method attached to the `document` object. As part of a function, a line such as

```
document.write("Hello world")
```

creates a new Web page that says "Hello world." The quotes around the "Hello World" parameter tell the browser that these letters should be written literally. The parameters for the `write` method can also pass on HTML code (remember, it's just ASCII text) so that a line such as

```
document.write("Hello <B>world</B>")
```

would create a new Web page saying "Hello world" with the "world" in boldface type. Passing in literal strings like this has limited usefulness; the real power comes when you pass in variables defined by the user's choices to build an entire Web page customized for individual needs. A simple e-commerce site could use variations on the `write` method to show customers only items in their sizes and favorite colors. HTML Help systems might use this method to create procedures customized to take account of the user's particular system setup. The built-in `Date` and `Math` objects each have a number of methods that allow you to perform a wide variety of date and mathematical transformations.

# Crucial DHTML elements for HTML Help

The previous sections provided an overview of how DHTML works, followed by general information on the terminology commonly used in JavaScript. This section provides reference information on common objects, properties, and event handlers to give you the tools to create your own DHTML.

NAME and ID are not explicitly listed, since most objects support these properties in practical terms, even when the standards don't recommend it.

## Common objects & their properties

The full Microsoft Document Object Model (a portion of which was shown previously in the *Objects* section ) includes approximately three dozen different objects. As you begin working with DHTML, you are unlikely to use them all. The objects described below are some of the most useful and easily understood for the beginning DHTML author.

### window

| | |
|---|---|
| **Properties & values** | location="URL of window" |
| | status="text for status bar" |
| | opener="window that opened this one" |
| | parent="window with defining frameset" |
| | self="this window or frame" |
| | top="topmost parent window" |
| **Methods (parameters)** | open("url", "name","options below") |
| | close() |
| | alert("text of message box") |
| | confirm("text requiring OK/Cancel response") |

| | |
|---|---|
| | `prompt("text prompting user to enter input")` |
| **Events** | `onLoad - action performed when window loads into browser`<br>`onUnload - action when window closes` |

The `window` object is the top level of the Document Object Model and, as such, contains all the other objects in the DOM. From a user's perspective, however, the `window` is just the whole browser window presented by the HTML Help Viewer (or Microsoft Internet Explorer). If you open secondary windows (top context-sensitive help, message boxes, etc.), each secondary window has its open `window` object.

You'll use the `window` object most often to open or close new windows for specific purposes. To open a new window, use the following format:

```
window.open("here.htm", "thisPlace", "height=100,
width=100, menubar=yes, resizable=yes,
scrollbars=yes, status=yes, toolbar=yes")
```

where

| | |
|---|---|
| *here.htm* | is the URL of the page displayed in the window; |
| *thisPlace* | is the name used to call the window in scripts; |
| *height, width* | are window's overall dimensions in pixels; |
| *menubar, scrollbars, toolbars* | are navigation elements which are displayed if *yes* (default); |
| *resizable* | is whether the the user can change the window's size (default=yes); |
| *status* | message area at the bottom of the window displayed if yes (the default). |

The `window.open` requires a URL to display and it's a good idea to include a name; the rest of the parameters are optional.

You can also open particular kinds of windows using the `alert`, `confirm`, and `prompt` methods. The `alert` is the simplest, presenting a message with only an OK option.

```
alert("Hello world!")
```

results in figure 5.3:

*Figure 5.3. Alert window.* *The* alert *method produces a window with a message. The user can only close the window.*

The `confirm` method lets the user choose **OK** or CANCEL so that

```
confirm("Shall we proceed?")
```

results in figure 5.4:

*Figure 5.4 Confirm window.* *The* confirm *method produces a window that asks a question. The user can choose to confirm or deny the question, which determines the subsequent actions taken by the script.*

The `prompt` method gathers user input and suggests default input, so that

```
prompt("Who are you?","your name goes here")
```

results in figure 5.5:

Explorer User Prompt     ☒

JavaScript Prompt:

Who are you?     OK     Cancel

your name goes here

*Figure 5.5. **Prompt window.** The prompt method produces a window that allows the user to provide input that is used in the subsequent script actions.*

# document

| | |
|---|---|
| **Properties & values** | url="location of current page" title="text for title bar" referrer="URL of document that opened this one; i.e., previous document" |
| **Methods (parameters)** | open("url","name","options below") close() write("text string" or dot notation) writeln("text string" or dot notation) |

The open() and close() methods work much the same for a document as they do for a window. The trick is knowing how their triggering mechanism affects their operation:

- If the open() or close() method is triggered by an event that is part of the <BODY> tag, the method affects the current *document*.

- Otherwise, if the open() or close() method is triggered by a function attached to an event that is not part of the <BODY> tag, the method affects the current *window*.

Probably the most commonly used method for the document object is the write method, which allows you to dynamically create a Web page, as described in the earlier section on *Methods*. The writeln method writes a single line, so using the writeln method repeatedly to create the page breaks up the individual elements and simplifies your coding.

Note that these methods can become much more complicated than suggested by the examples, which simply pass on plain text and HTML strings. As you become more proficient in writing DHTML functions, you can use dot notation to combine object references with user responses to dynamically "write" extremely customized pages.

## image <IMG>

| Properties & values | align="image position related to text" (default=left; also absbottom, absmiddle, baseline, bottom, middle, right, texttop, top) |
|---|---|
| | alt="alternative text" border="border width in pixels" |
| | height="vertical size in pixels or % of parent object's height" vspace="# pixels in top & bottom margins separating image from adjacent elements" width="horizontal size in pixels or % of parent object's height" hspace="# pixels in left & right margins separating image from adjacent elements" |
| | src="filename of image source" |
| **Methods (parameters)** | click() simulates mouse click to trigger onClick event handler |

Most of the image properties should be familiar from general HTML coding, and they work in much the same way. For examples of scripting images, see the image rollover example at the beginning of this chapter.

# anchor < A >

| | |
|---|---|
| **Properties & values** | `classname="name of class, for grouping named anchors together"` |
| | **`hash`**`="#specific area within HREF page"` |
| | **`href`**`="URLtoOpen.htm"` |
| | **`target`**`="name of window or frame in which HREF opens"` (see below for acceptable values) |
| **Methods (parameters)** | `click()`simulates mouse click to trigger onClick event handler |

An `anchor` object, like an anchor element in regular HTML, requires at least a `name` or `href` property. If the anchor has only an `href` property, it specifies the destination that should open when the anchor is activated. For example, `A href="there.htm"` means that activating the anchor opens the file `there.htm`.

An anchor's `name` property works in conjunction with the `hash` property. Once an anchor is assigned a name, it can become a destination for another anchor that uses the `hash` property. For example, if you specify one anchor as `A name="localJump"`, then another anchor in the same page can jump to it by using the syntax `A href="#localJump"`. Note that a hash mark (or number sign #) always precedes a hash value. The hash property is useful in HTML Help pages as a way to provide a quick internal table of contents for a long page. (You may have seen this in readme files that start with a list of items such as "System Requirements" or "Known Issues" that jump to those particular subsections.) If necessary, you can create an anchor object that goes nowhere.

The `target` property also works like the target attribute in standard HTML, specifying the name of the window or frame in which to open the location specified in the anchor's `href` or `hash` property. The `target` property is optional; if it is not specified, `_self` is assumed and the new location opens in the same window or frame that displayed the original anchor object. The values for the target property include:

| | |
|---|---|
| _self | the active window that displayed the anchor object |
| _blank | a new blank, unnamed window |
| anyName | a new window named "anyName" |
| _parent | the immediate parent of the document displaying the anchor object (usually a page containing the defining frameset) |
| _top | the topmost window of the current document hierarchy |

## style

| | |
|---|---|
| **Properties & values** | most CSS properties |
| **Methods (parameters)** | `setAttribute("attributeName, attribute value")` |

By using the `style` object, you can modify the CSS attributes of any scriptable element, dynamically changing its appearance. For example, the statement

```
descriptorPara.style.color="red"
```

makes the text in the paragraph named `descriptorPara` turn red. In addition to the more common CSS attributes, the `style` object can be used to change the `visibility` of an object, making it appear or disappear dynamically. For details, see the later sections on *Visibility & display properties* and *Show/hide text.*

# all

| Properties & values | length="number of objects contained in the ALL collection" |
|---|---|
| Methods (parameters) | item("ID or NAME") retrieves a list of all items on the page with the specified name or ID |
| | tags("HTML tag") retrieves a list of all elements in the page that use the specified HTML tag |

Strictly speaking, all is a *collection* not an *object,* but it's listed in the Micrrosoft Document Object Model (DOM) and acts as a generic object. The all collection lets you access any HTML element on the page, even if it is not named (standard dot notation takes care of named elements). For example, using the tags method, you could retrieve a list of all <H1> elements on the page, and then use a script to perform a transformation on each element.

# Date

| Methods (parameters) | getSeconds() retrieves current second of the minute (0-59) getMinutes() retrieves current minute of the hour (0-59) getHours() retrieves hour of the day, 0 (midnight) through 23 (11pm) getDay() retrieves day of the week, 0 (Sunday) through 6 (Saturday) getDate() retrieves current day of the month (1-31) getMonth() retrieves month, 0 (January) through 11 (December) getFullYear() retrieves year in four-digit format (e.g., 2000) |
|---|---|

The Date object's set methods only affect the script and HTML page; they do not affect the user's system clock.

> setXXX() a set method parallel to
> each of the above get methods sets
> the time to a specific value for
> the purposes of the script's
> calculations

You can *concatenate* items by enclosing literal strings (including spaces and punctuation) in quotes and putting plus signs (+) between each element in the concatenated string.

The Date object is useful for time calculations. For example, in an HTML Help tutorial, you might want to time how long it takes a user to complete an exercise or offer additional information after a certain amount of time has passed.

Note that the Date object has no properties, so you can't create a time-oriented script using dot notation. Instead, use the appropriate get method to obtain the desired time element. For example, the following code displays a message that says "It is now" plus the current date. It does this by creating a new Date object named now, then creating specific variables for the month, date, and year. These variables are strung together (*concatenated* in programming language) and then displayed using the document.write method, with the end result of a line saying something like "It is now 1/1/2000".

```
<SCRIPT LANGUAGE="JavaScript">

var now = new Date()
var month= now.getMonth()
var date=now.getDate()
var year=now.getFullYear()

document.write("It is now " + month +"/" + date + "/
" + year)

</SCRIPT>
```

# Common events & event handlers

DHTML supports a wide variety of events and event handlers. The most commonly used events involve mouse movements and the opening and closing of documents.

## onClick

| | |
|---|---|
| **Syntax** | onClick="handler" |
| **Events handled** | user clicks the mouse on the object or form item<br>user presses ENTER in a form<br>script invokes **click** method |
| **Examples** | onClick="confirm('Download now?')"<br><P onClick="this.style.display=''"> |

The onClick event handler works with the simplest and most common mouse movement in HTML: clicking.

The onClick event handler (as well as its relatives, onMouseOver and onMouseOut) can be used in scripts or can be added to an object's HTML tag as a property. For example, a button can have an onClick event that pops up an alert window displaying a related message:

```
<FORM>
<INPUT type="button" value="More information?"
onClick="alert('You must first set the
configuration parameters for this report.'>"
</FORM>
```

Alternately, the onClick event handler can be used in scripts. For example, imagine the user clicked a button to exit before finishing the entire lesson. The code for the button would look like this:

```
<FORM>
<INPUT type="button" value="Exit to main menu"
onClick="exitLesson()">
</FORM>
```

The script in the <HEAD> would loook like this:

```
<SCRIPT LANGUAGE="JavaScript">

function exitLesson()
{
if (confirm("You haven't finished this lesson.
Are you sure you want to exit?"))
  {location="mainMenu.htm"}
}

</SCRIPT>
```

This function pops up a confirm window asking the user if they're sure about leaving the lesson. If the user clicks OK in the confirm window, that information is passed back to the script so that the condition is true and the window's location property changes to the new value (mainMenu.htm). If the user clicks Cancel, the confirm window passes information back to the script that the condition is false and the move to the new location is aborted.

## onMouseOver
## onMouseOut

| | |
|---|---|
| **Syntax** | `onMouseOver="handler"`<br>`onMouseOut="handler"` |
| **Events handled** | user moves mouse over or away from an object |
| **Examples** | `<A HREF="there.htm"`<br>`onMouseOver="this.style.color='red'"`<br>`onMouseOut="this.style.color=''">`<br>`click here</A>` |

The `onMouseOver` and `onMouseOut` event handlers work much the same as the `onClick` event, except that they are generally used as a pair. The example directly above could be used to highlight the *click here* text link by turning it red whenever the user mouses over it. For a fuller example of using this pair of event handlers, see the image rollover script built at the beginning of this chapter.

## onLoad

| | |
|---|---|
| **Syntax** | `onLoad="handler"` |
| **Events handled** | Web browser loads a page (`onLoad` relating to BODY or FRAMESET tags) or graphic (`onLoad` relating to IMG tag) |
| **Examples** | `<IMG NAME="Configuration"`<br>`SRC="dialog.gif"`<br>`onLoad="window.status='This image`<br>`shows the Configuration dialog.`<br>`Click on image elements for`<br>`specific details.'">` |

The `onLoad` event handler fires when the HTML Help Viewer loads a new page or finishes loading an image. You could use it to display a welcome message at the beginning of a tutorial letting users know how long the module takes; to provide additional information about an image; or for other scriptable tasks.

Simple actions can be added directly to the `<BODY>`, `<FRAMESET>`, or `<IMG>` tags, as shown in the previous box. The example (using onLoad with an IMG tag) could be used on an image map, to provide a message in the status bar identifying the image and notifying the user of how to obtain additional information. It could just as easily have created an alert window or launched an accompanying movie.

Alternately, you can embed the actions in a script that is called from the element's HTML tag. For example, if you wanted to use the scripting approach with the previous example, the image tag would become:

```
<IMG NAME="Configuration" SRC="dialog.gif"
  onLoad="moreInfo(this.name)" >
```

and you would add these lines to the page's HEAD section between `<SCRIPT>` and `</SCRIPT>` tags:

```
function moreInfo(dialogName)

{
window.status="This image shows the " + dialogName
+ " dialog. Click on image elements for specific
details.";
}
```

Prefer a popup to a status bar message? Substitute `alert` for `window.status`, and a pair of parentheses for the equal sign and closing semicolon.

This script is similar to the image rollover at the beginning of the chapter; both use the `this` pointer to automatically pass information from the calling element to a script in the header. The advantage of the scripting approach over the inline element DHTML is its reusability. If you had multiple image maps of the product your HTML Help system was documenting, you could automatically display a status bar message for each image. The only editing required is to supply the appropriate information for the NAME and SOURCE properties.

# onUnload

| | |
|---|---|
| **Syntax** | onUnload="handler" |
| **Events handled** | closing or refreshing browser window; opening different page in the browser; invoking document.write, open, or close methods; invoking window.open method submitting a form |
| **Examples** | `<BODY onUnload="alert('Are you sure you want to exit before finishing the tutorial?')">` |

The onUnload event handler works much the same as onLoad, except that it applies only to windows and framesets, not to images. This event handler will only be used or called from a <BODY> or <FRAMESET> tag. Because of these limitations, it has two primary uses: to issue a departing message or to close any secondary windows opened from the page or frame.

# CSS properties for DHTML

Most of the standard CSS properties can be scripted by using dot notation together with the `style` object (described previously). As you begin adjusting content and display with JavaScript, you will also want to use the the `zIndex` property to determine the vertical position of objects, and the `visibility` and `display` properties to show or hide specific content.

## zIndex

| | |
|---|---|
| **Syntax:** | in style sheets:  `{z-index: value;}`<br>in dot notation:<br>`object.style.zIndex=value` |
| **Acceptable values:** | positive or negative integers representing the object's position in the vertical stacking order of objects on the page |
| **Example:** | `{z-index: -1;}`<br>`dialogImage.style.zIndex=2` |

The `zIndex` property lets you create sophisticated graphic effects without using large graphic files. You can use it to layer new images on top of existing images, creating a slide show effect. In fact, one of the best uses of the `zIndex` (and other positioning properties) in HTML Help is to create timelines showing changes that occur during a process. Simple timelines can be coded manually; more elaborate scenarios involving large numbers of positioning changes are best created in specially designed applications such as Macromedia's Dreamweaver or Microsoft's Visual InterDev.

## visibility & display

| | |
|---|---|
| **Syntax:** | in style sheets:  {visibility: value;}<br>in dot notation:<br>object.style.visibility="value" |
| **Acceptable values:** | visible or hidden or inherit or<br>" ""(blank) |
| **Example:** | <DIV STYLE="visibility:hidden"> |

. . . . . . . . . . . . . . . . . . . . . . . . . . . . . .

| | |
|---|---|
| **Syntax:** | in style sheets: {display: value;}<br>in dot notation:<br>object.style.display="value" |
| **Acceptable values:** | block or inline or none or " "(blank)<br>or list-item or table-header-group<br>or table-footer-group |
| **Example:** | definition.style.display="none"; |

The visibility and display properties control whether or not an object appears on the page.  For graphic effects, these properties allow you to hide an image in a timeline until you need it to appear; for text , they allow you to add definitions and additional information only when the user requests it or when it fits the current situation.  You can apply these properties to any HTML element; in addition, you can custom-define affected sections by using <DIV> and <SPAN> tags to create set-off block and inline elements, respectively.  For an example using the display property to add information on request, see the *Show/hide text* recipe later.

The difference between the two properties become apparent when they are hidden.  An object with its visibility property set to hidden  still takes up space on the page; that is, it forces the adjacent text and other elements to wrap around the hidden object. The display property, on the other hand, does not create a "box" to reserve space for its object. When an object's display property is set to none, the object cannot be seen and does not occupy space.

For example, consider the example lines below, where a "hidden" object separates the first two lines while an object with its display set to none neither displays on the page nor forces the last two lines apart.

> Text before object where object.style.visibility="hidden"
>
>
> Text after object where object.style.visibility="hidden"
>
> *Text before object where object.style.display="none"*
>
> *Text after object where object.style.display="none"*

Although the official specifications don't mention it, in practical usage the two properties accept a blank value specification; for example the line `<P onMouseOver="this.style.display=''">`. The blank value in this example sets the property back to whatever it was before the scripting began.

# DHTML recipes for HTML Help

This section includes a variety of "recipes" you can copy to create DHTML effects in your own HTML Help system. Some of the recipes were used as examples earlier in this chapter; others are new; all are collected together here to provide a single, easily accessed reference.

In each of the following recipes, the goal has been to use the least amount of manipulation needed to make each work in various situations. To that end, event handlers are used in place of functions where appropriate; in addition, all variable names are single words (so you can simply double-click to choose them) and are designed to be as meaningful as possible. Once you are comfortable with the scripts, you can change the variable names and make other adjustments to suit more situations.

These script "recipes" are available for cut-and-paste copying at the companion Web site,

`www.jmek.net/`
`html_help.`

## Quick & easy tool tip

Purpose: Although the HTML Help Workshop provides a way to include tool tips (pop-up messages that appear when the user's mouse pauses on the item), they've always appeared unnecessarily complicated, involving the insertion of an ActiveX control—and you still only get a plain text popup. The **TITLE** attribute (not covered elsewhere in this chapter) provides the same functionality much more easily.

Call within element:

```
<SPAN TITLE="toolTipText">affectedText</SPAN>
```

where

| | |
|---|---|
| *toolTipText* | is the text that appears in a small yellow text window when the user's mouse moves over the affected text; |
| *affectedText* | is the text that activates the tool tip popup. |

The tool tip appears in your HTML Help topic as shown below.

> This is the affected text.
>
> This is the toolTipText

# Change text color on mouseover

Purpose: This recipe makes the affected text change colors when the user's mouse moves over it and could be used as an alternate way to signal a link. It turns back to the default color (usually black) when the mouse moves away.

Call within element (using onClick event handler):

```
previousText

<SPAN
onClick="this.style.color='desiredHue'">
affectedText
</SPAN>

followingText
```

where

| | |
|---|---|
| *previousText* | is the text that appears on the Web page right before the affected text; |
| *desiredHue* | is the color the text turns, specified as a reserved color name or as an RGB value; (See *Color values* in Chapter 4, "Doing It in Style: CSS (Cascading Style Sheets.") |
| *affectedText* | is the text that changes color when the mouse moves over it; |
| *followingText* | is the text that appears on the Web page right after the affected text. |

# Show/hide text

Purpose: This recipe can be used to create inline definitions of terms that appear when the user mouses over the affected text and disappear when the mouse leaves the area. It moves a step beyond the earlier tool tip recipe, since you can add any amount of formatting or graphics.

Function: You could perform this task with a function, but it's less confusing to keep the term and its definition together on the HTML page.

Call within element (using onMouseOver event handler):

```
previousText

<SPAN
 onMouseOver="definitionID.style.display=''"
 onMouseOut="definitionID.style.display='none'">
 definedTerm
</SPAN>

<P ID="definitionID" STYLE="display:none">
    definition</P>

followingText
```

When the page first opens, it looks like this (the `definedTerm` has been made bold for easier visibility):

previousText **definedTerm** followingText

When the user mouses over the `definedTerm`, the definition appears. This recipe is flexible enough to include a small picture representing the onscreen icon identified by the `definedTerm`.

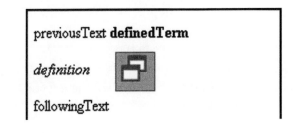

previousText **definedTerm**

*definition*

followingText

# Status bar explanation of an image map

Purpose: This recipe displays a message in the status bar (the gray bar at the bottom of the Web viewer) alerting the user that the graphic is an image map. Putting the message in the status bar allows you to use the entire contents pane to display a dialog box or a visualization of a process.

Function (in `<HEAD>` section):

```
<SCRIPT LANGUAGE="JavaScript">

function moreInfo(dialogName)
{
window.status="This image shows the " + dialogName
+ " dialog. Click on image elements for specific
details.";
}

</SCRIPT>
```

where

    *dialogName*    is a variable passed from the calling element to the function; in this case, it is the name of the dialog shown in the graphic.

Note how the status message combines static text with the variable. All static (literal) text is enclosed in quotation marks; variables are not. The literal text and variables are combined (concatenated) with plus signs.

Call to function (placed in the `<BODY>` section):

```
<IMG NAME="dialogName" SRC="picture.gif"
 onLoad="moreInfo(this.name)" >
```

Note that the SRC property can use any filename; it is not tied to the image's NAME property.

Possible modifications: This recipe can display other information in the status bar by substituting an onClick event handler for the onLoad handler used here (onLoad works with images and the document body; onClick works with virtually any HTML element).

# Open secondary window

Purpose: This recipe opens a prompt dialog asking the user for information, then uses that information to customize an alert message.

Function (in <HEAD> section):

```
<SCRIPT LANGUAGE="JavaScript">

function openWindow(url,windowName)
{
window.open("url", "windowName", "height=x,
width=y, menubar=yes, resizable=yes,
scrollbars=yes, status=yes, toolbar=yes")
}

</SCRIPT>
```

where

| | |
|---|---|
| *url* | is a variable passed from the calling element to the function.  This variable identifies the URL of the page displayed in the window; |
| *windowName* | is another variable passed from the calling element to the function.  This variable supplies the name used to refer to the window in scripts; |
| *x, y* | describe the overall size of the secondary window in terms of the number of pixels in the height and width (respectively); |
| *menubar, scrollbars, toolbars* | are navigation elements displayed if the value is *yes* (the default) or not displayed if the value is *no*; |
| *resizable* | is whether the user can change the window's size  (default=*yes*; may also =*no*); |
| *status* | is the message area at the bottom of the window; displayed if *yes* (the default), hidden if *no*. |

Call to function (placed in the `<BODY>` section, within the appropriate HTML element tag):

```
<P onClick="openWindow(url,windowName)"> Click
here to open a new window.</P>
```

Possible modifications: As it stands, this recipe allows you to specify the URL and window name for each link. If you will always use the same window name, you could remove the variable `windowName` from the first line of the function, so that you pass only the URL as a variable: `function openWindow(url)`. Then, within the body of the function, supply an actual name instead of using the `windowName` variable.

You can also open a new window directly from an event handler, without using a function at all. For example, to use a button to open a new window and show an animated demonstration of a process, you could include the following code:

```
<FORM><input type="button" value="Show Me How"
onClick="window.open('url', 'windowName',
'height=x, width=y, menubar=yes, resizable=yes,
scrollbars=yes, status=yes, toolbar=yes')"></FORM>
```

The components of the element handler have the same meaning as in the original function, except that `url` and `windowName` should be the actual URL and window name, rather than variable names.

# Image rollover

Purpose: This recipe changes the image that is displayed whenever the user's mouse moves over the image.

Preparation: The files for the two states of the image should be named `x.gif` and `xDown.gif`, where `x` can be anything you like.

Functions (placed in `<HEAD>` section):

```
<SCRIPT LANGUAGE="JavaScript">

function buttonDown(buttonName)
{
document.images[buttonName].src=buttonName
+ "Down.gif";
}

function buttonUp(buttonName)
{
document.images[buttonName].src=buttonName +
".gif";
}
</SCRIPT>
```

where

| | |
|---|---|
| `buttonName` | is a variable used to access the name property of the graphic or other element modified by the functions. |

Call to function (placed in the `<BODY>` section, within the appropriate HTML element tag):

```
<IMG NAME="button1" SRC="button1.gif"
  onMouseOver="buttonDown(this.name)"
  onMouseOut="buttonUp(this.name)">
```

Possible modifications: This recipe can be applied to text as well as graphics, if the call to the functions are placed within the text element's tag (such as `<P>` or `<H1>`) or if the text is enclosed in `<SPAN>` tags.

# Alert message using input from a prompt

Purpose: This recipe opens a prompt dialog asking the user for information, then uses that information to customize an alert message.

Function (placed in <HEAD> section):

```
<SCRIPT LANGUAGE="JavaScript">

function test()
{
var foo=prompt("Question?", "defaultResponse")

if(foo=="desiredResponse")
  {alert("desiredMessage"}
else
  {alert("alternateMessage")}

</SCRIPT>
```

where

| | |
|---|---|
| *foo* | is the variable used to pass information in scripts; |
| *Question* | is the question the prompt box poses to the user; |
| *defaultResponse* | is the answer used if the user does not respond to the *Question;* |
| *desiredResponse* | is the correct or preferred answer to the question; |
| *desiredMessage* | is the computer response to the correct or preferred answer (i.e., the desiredResponse); |
| *alternateMessage* | is the computer response to any answer other than the one specified as correct or preferred. |

Call to function (placed in the <BODY> section, within the appropriate HTML element tag):

```
<P onClick="test()">Click here to test your
knowledge.</P>
```

Possible modifications: In the chapter, this example was used in a primitive passwording scheme that greeted an approved user by name. It could also be used in a quiz situation to give reinforcement for correct answers ("Good job!") or ask the user to "Try again."

# How DHTML works with HTML Help— & how it doesn't

In general, dynamic HTML works quite well within compiled HTML Help systems; it even provides a few extra bonuses that enhance your ability to use DHTML snippets in your online system. The chief enhancements are the lack of cross-browser concerns and a collection of samples tailored to HTML Help systems; the primary areas of concern have to do with referencing windows and file paths. Also, it is best if you remember to always compile external .js files into the project.

## Areas of enhancement

Since HTML Help is currently confined to Windows-based systems, its implementation of DHTML is much simpler than in broader Web-based situations that have to take into account multiple platforms (Macintosh, UNIX, and perhaps Linux) as well as multiple browsers and browser versions. This situation even provides a few special enhancements.

### Single browser/limited versions

The best part of using DHTML within compiled HTML Help is that you need not worry about cross-browser compatibility. Compiled HTML Help interprets JavaScript according to Internet Explorer. In addition, the interpretation is most often in accord with version 4.0; however, if you know your users will have IE 5.0 or higher installed, you can exploit some of the newer features. Cross-browser concerns arise only if you build an uncompiled version of Help (that is, HTML-based Help rather than strict HTML Help).

## Focused examples

The HTML Help Workshop itself provides an additional area of enhancement: its online Help contains a useful section with examples of DHTML (figure 5.6). You can use these in your project or read them to understand more about DHTML.

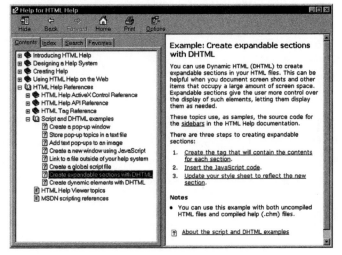

*Figure 5.6. Focused samples.* The online Help system of the HTML Help Workshop provides examples of DHTML for use in HTML Help Systems..

Additional information is available on Microsoft's Web site, in particular, at the MSDN Web Workshop (`http://msdn.microsoft.com/workshop/ author/default.asp`). Some MDSN content is by subscription only; however, a great deal of information is available to everyone.

# Arenas of conflict

Since HTML Help is designed for the Web, its areas of conflict with DHTML are relatively few and fairly easy to work around.

## Explicitly adding files to avoid lost paths

Linking to external `.js` or `.css` files is the most efficient way of using DHTML in your HTML Help; this approach allows you to make refinements in a single file, and have the changes available to all linked files. However, the HTML Help Viewer occasionally has difficulty following paths if these files remain external to your project. Fortunately, it's easy to avoid these problems by explicitly adding the external files into the compiled project. For instructions on how to do this, see the section on *Adding the external script file to the project* earlier in this chapter.

## Jumping to other topics

If linking to a file not included in the same compiled HTML Help system (within the same `.chm` file), you must use the special protocols. For a complete discussion of linking to topics in different .chm and to external `.htm` files, see the section on *Linkages* in Chapter 3, "Bringing It Together: HTML Templates & Topics."

## Linking to secondary windows

Some HTML Help authors have reported problems with topic pages containing more than one anchor element pointing to a secondary window (that is, something of the form `<A HREF="foo.htm" TARGET="popup">` or the equivalent call within a script). Although the causes have not yet been discovered, a workaround is available: instead of using the anchor form shown above, use an `onClick` event handler. This approach also requires you to format the link explicitly (either with local HTML formatting or with a class defined in your style sheet), since it will no longer use the anchor element's styling.

## Taking care with positioning elements

If you're writing DHTML that works with positioning elements, use pixels as your measurement system (picas usually work, but are not quite as reliable). Although DHTML supports positioning with other systems, these may prove unreliable if you can't predict your users' monitor setting. A monitor set to 800x600 may size and position elements differently than one set to 1024x768, so that your carefully layered demonstrations have the wrong layers peeking out beyond their edges.

## Splitting files

Once again, the HTML Help Workshop's **Split File** command (designed to split a single, long HTML file into multiple topics at compile time) will lose all links to external scripting files. Avoid this command.

# 6

# Creating Magic:
## The HTML Help Project file

The backbone of any HTML Help system is the project (*.hhp) file, the primary container for information about and pointers to all elements of the HTML Help project. The project file is where the magic occurs, bringing all the pieces together into one HTML Help system.

The project file itself is simply a text file; the information it contains is used by the HTML Help compiler to create the actual compiled HTML Help system (.chm file). The project file specifies the system parameters (such as window definitions, language and version compatibilities, and any other options) and keeps track of all the topic, contents, index, script, style sheet, and image files.

You can create this file in at least three ways:

- by adapting an existing project (.hhp) file;

- with Notepad or another text editor;

- with the HTML Help Workshop's New Project Wizard.

Once you establish a standard project style, the easiest way to create a new project is to open an existing project file; remove its specific pointers to files, table of contents, and index entries; then save the file under another name and add the new files, contents, etc. This approach insures that the setup you use once to create a successful HTML Help project will create a new project with the same parameters but different content. The drawback is that it works only after you have created the first successful project!

At the other end of the ease-of-use spectrum, you could type the entire project in Notepad or another text editor. The minimum requirements are a text file saved with the .hhp extension and containing the section headers [OPTIONS] and [FILES] on separate lines.

Once you add at least a few HTML files to the [FILES] section, the HTML Help Workshop and compiler will use this bare file to create an HTML Help project with the same name as the .hhp file, assuming certain basic project defaults concerning version and language compatibility. However, once past these basic settings, creating an .hhp file in Notepad is unnecessarily complicated. For an entirely new project, then, you will most often use the HTML Help Workshop, starting with its New Project Wizard.

# Setting up the project

## The trivial New Project Wizard

The NEW PROJECT WIZARD itself provides only the most basic functions for building a new HTML Help project, guiding you through the steps to specify the project filename, location, and any existing files (topics, table of contents, and index). It does *not* specify the default topic file, merge files, search options, or window types. These items are set up elsewhere in the HTML Help Workshop (primarily in the PROJECT OPTIONS dialog box).

All new projects files contain a few settings, whether you create them in the NEW PROJECT WIZARD or in Notepad. By default, these are:

- Compatibility with HTML Help Workshop version1.1 or later

- Compile progress not displayed

- Language settings, taken from the REGIONAL SETTINGS of the CONTROL PANEL on the machine where the HTML Help Workshop exists

The NEW PROJECT WIZARD offers additional functionality when converting an existing Windows Help project.

In addition, there is a default window type, although no mention of it appears in the project file itself. This window measures approximately 550x450 pixels, positions itself in the upper right corner of the screen, and displays the word HELP in its title bar. If you have not specified a contents or index file, the project has no navigation pane and no buttons. If you have specified a contents or index file, the project also displays a navigation pane as well as the default button set (HIDE, BACK, PRINT, and OPTIONS).

Before invoking the Wizard, take a few moments to consider the directory structure and a few naming conventions for your project.

# Directory structure

HTML Help uses relative file references and, in cases such as merged files, uses a unique syntax to specify these relative references. Because of this, it is best to locate your project (.hhp), table of contents (.hhc), and index (.hhk) files at the top level of your project's directory structure. If your project contains more than just a few topics, it's best to create subdirectories one level down to organize your topic files, graphics, and common elements (such as cascading style sheets and script files). The structure depicted here provides a well-organized approach for standardizing references to style sheets, graphics, and other cross-file references. Maintaining consistent relative paths helps insure that all links remain functional.

Whatever directory structure you choose, be sure that all files reside in the project file's folder or in one of its subfolders.

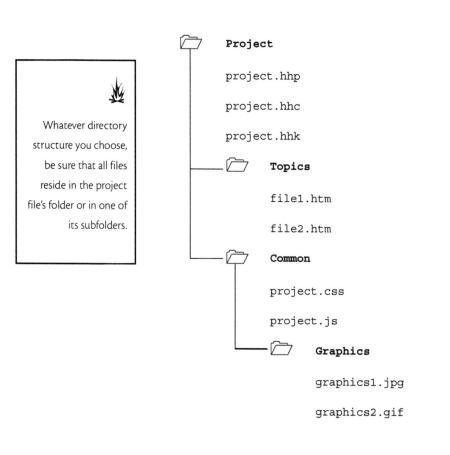

# File & directory conventions

In theory, HTML Help supports all filenames and paths accepted under Windows 95/98 and NT. This includes long filenames (more than 8.3; that is, eight characters followed by a period and then a three-character extensions) and spaces within filenames. In practice, however, the HTML Help Workshop and compiler are not completely reliable when working with complex filenames, so things are a bit more restricted.

In particular, avoid spaces in filenames and directory paths referenced from within the HTML Help project. Various HTML Help authors have reported projects that just "didn't work" until they removed the spaces in the file and directory names. (This occurs most frequently on inter-file references; for example, when the `main.chm` in a merged project references a subordinate `.chm` with a space in its name.) Instead of spaces, substitute internal capitalization (such as `myChoices\screenChoose.htm`). Underscores *usually* work (`my_choices\screen_choose.htm`), but they have been known to cause occasional problems, so it's best to avoid them as well.

It's also best to use relatively short filenames with meaningful beginnings. The length of file and directory names has no direct effect on HTML Help projects. However, most of the dialog boxes within the HTML Help Workshop are not resizable, so filenames are sometimes cut off, making it difficult to view all of a long filename or to see the identifier at the end of a filename. For example, if you're trying to specify your default file in the Workshop's PROJECT OPTIONS, it may be difficult to see in the dialog whether you're choosing `MyFirstHTMLHelpProject\MyTopicFiles\WhatIWouldUse.htm` or `MyFirstHTMLHelpProject\MyTopicFiles\WhatIWouldUse2.htm`.

Finally, use consistent and meaningful filenames for the table of contents, index, and project file. By default, the HTML Help Workshop names the table of contents file `Table of Contents.hhc` and the index file `Index.hhk`. Besides the problem of the spaces in the contents filename, these names offer no assistance when merging multiple projects. If the contents files for all of the merged projects have the same name, how will you know which one contains the desired topic file? Ideally, choose a single short name (such as `Colors`, `Printing`, or `Shapes` when writing help modules for a graphics program) and apply it to the project, contents, and index files (i.e., `Printing.hhp`, `Printing.hhc`, and `Printing.hhk`).

Also note that the HTML Help Workshop follows the current standard Web model of one topic per .htm file. Particularly if you're coming from a Windows help environment, you may be used to working with a single long file (the `rtf` in Windows help). The HTML Help Workshop does include a SPLIT FILE command (on the EDIT menu) that lets you use a single long file for many topics, but it has a number of limitations, the least of which is the fact that it only works in compiled files. Technically, the SPLIT FILE command adds an `<OBJECT>` tag at the current cursor location, notifying the compiler that it should treat what follows as a separate HTML file and, optionally, give it a new title. Unfortunately, the command does not add any of the other information you might have included in the file's `<HEAD>` section, such as links to external style sheets and script files. Also, the newly split file does not appear in any file lists. So, if you want to add it to the table of contents or index or jump to it from another file, you must manually type in the path to the split file, together with the file name you specified in the SPLIT FILE command. For example, if you split `LongFile.htm` located in your `Topics` directory and you named the split `SplitFile.htm`, you would link it to an index entry by typing in `Topics\SplitFile.htm`.

All in all, unless you have a very large backlog of topics in long files, it's easier to use a new file for each topic. At the least, consider manually splitting the content into individual files with unique names and all appropriate information.

# Using the New Project Wizard

Once you've made the preliminary decisions for your project, use the NEW PROJECT WIZARD to get started.

1. Go to the HTML Help Workshop's FILE menu and choose NEW > PROJECT, then click **OK** to invoke the Wizard.

2. Specify the filename and directory location of the new project.

3. Specify whether you have table of contents (`.hhc`), index (`.hhk`), or topic (`.htm`) files you wish to include in the project. If you choose any of these options, the Wizard offers additional options.

   - If you have selected the table of contents or index options, you must specify the name and location of the desired files. These may be previously existing files or you can set up empty files of the appropriate type. For existing files, use the BROWSE box to locate the desired files. To create the appropriate new files, type in a filename and use the BROWSE button to choose the desired directory.

   - If you have selected the topic (HTML files) option, you must use the NEW PROJECT—HTML FILES dialog to ADD these files to the project's list. The selected topic files must be previously existing HTML files.

4. Click the FINISH button to let the HTML Help Workshop create a new project file, using your specifications plus the basic compatibility, language, and compile progress display defaults.

# Refining the project

## Adding topic & navigation files

After setting up the basic HTML Help project with the Wizard, immediately add all available files. Don't worry if you don't have all the files you need or if the files you have aren't completely finalized. You can always add more files later and pick up any changed files by recompiling the project. But adding files to the project's file list now provides easy access when you choose files in other parts of the HTML Help Workshop.

Available files include not only HTML topic files, but graphics, scripts, and cascading style sheets. Theoretically, the HTML Help compiler adds all files referenced by the topic files; that is, it should "automatically" include the graphics, style sheets, and scripts used in your HTML topic files. In practice, the procedure is less than reliable. For example, if an external style sheet sets fonts and background images for your topic files, neither the style sheet nor the background image is automatically added to the project file. The result is a "plain vanilla" HTML Help file using the default fonts and a plain background.

So, in addition to adding all the .htm topic files, it's best to explicitly add all .jpg, .gif, .css, .js, and other files to the help project. You can add the files in the HTML Help Workshop or edit the project file directly in Notepad. If you add the files in Notepad, you can use wildcards (such as *.gif) to specify all files in a given directory. If you're working in the HTML Help Workshop, you'll have to type *.* in the FILE NAME box of the Workshop's BROWSE dialog to force the display of files with extensions other than *.htm.

> Once you add a file to the project's file list, any changes made to the file are picked up when you recompile the project. Changed files need not be added back into the project as long as they maintain the same name and location.

## To add files to an HTML Help project [in the Workshop]:

1. Open the project file (*.hhp) in the HTML Help Workshop.

2. Click the ADD/REMOVE TOPIC FILES button (second from top on the left). Then click the ADD button in the TOPIC FILES dialog.

ADD/REMOVE
TOPIC FILES
button

3. In the OPEN dialog, navigate to the directory containing the desired files. Type *.* in the FILE NAME text box to force the Workshop to display all available files, no matter what their extension or file type.

4. Select the files to add. You can use CTRL-click to select multiple files or you can use SHIFT-click to specify the first and last items in a block of files that you wish to include in the project. When you have selected all desired files in that directory, click OPEN to add the files to the project.

5. Repeat the previous two steps for each directory containing files that you wish to add to the project. Then click OK to close the dialogs.

## To add files to an HTML Help project [in Notepad]:

1. Open the project file (*.hhp) in Notepad or another text editor.

2. On the line following the [FILES] section heading, type the names of the files you wish to add to the project.

   - Specify filename with a path relative to the project (*.hhp) file. For example, using the directory structure recommended earlier, you would specify your style sheet as Common\project.css.

   - Use wildcards to add all files of a specific type within a specific directory. For example, to include all .jpg files in the Common\Graphics directory, type Common\Graphics\*.jpg.

   - List each file or file group in a separate line. Using the above examples, your file list would start out as:

     ```
     [FILES]
     Common\project.css
     Common\Graphics\*.jpg
     ```

3. Save the file, then open it in the HTML Help Workshop and recompile.

# Setting project options

Some of the most essential parts of the HTML project file are labeled project "options" in the HTML Help Workshop and are available only through the PROJECT OPTIONS and WINDOWS TYPES dialogs. Far from being optional, these surreptitious essentials are required to make your HTML Help project function as expected. In particular, be sure to set up the following options:

- Title bar text

- Opening topic (default file)

- Contents and index files (if you didn't specify them in the NEW PROJECT WIZARD)

- Search options

- Default window type, with tripane format (navigation pane, topic pane, and button bar)

## Those surreptitious essentials

Most of these crucial settings appear in the OPTIONS dialog, accessible by clicking the top button of the Workshop's vertical toolbar or by double-clicking the word [OPTIONS] in the display window of the HTML Help Workshop's PROJECT tab.

The PROJECT>OPTIONS dialog opens to the GENERAL tab (figure 6.1), which specifies several overall project options. Use the TITLE field to enter the text that appears in the title bar at the top of the Help Viewer. Remember that this text appears as the default for the Help file, although it is overridden by any text specified for the title bar in a specific window type. Make sure the title text specified under PROJECT > OPTIONS > GENERAL is broad enough to apply to all topics, but specific enough to be useful. For software, the title is usually the name of the application being documented.

The DEFAULT FILE identifies the topic that appears when the compiled HTML Help project opens. The HTML Help Workshop automatically sets this field to the first topic file you add to the project, whether you use the

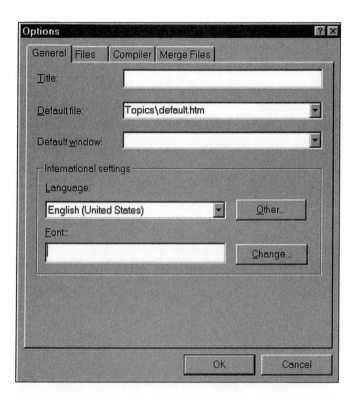

The FONT field controls the font used in the contents, index, search, and favorites tabs on the Help Viewer's navigation pane.

*Figure 6.1 Surreptitious essentials. The Workshop's* Options *dialogs contain a number of crucial settings that are not immediately obvious. On the* General *tab, you will set up the file and window that the compiled file defaults to, plus specify the default language—which affects search and indexing features as well as menu display.*

NEW PROJECT WIZARD, the Workshop's TOPIC FILES dialog, or type the file list into Notepad. Even if you later remove that file from the file list, the HTML Help Workshop retains it as the default (opening) file and automatically includes it during the compilation process. You can only change the default file from the Workshop's PROJECT OPTIONS dialog or by using Notepad to edit the line specifying that `Default topic=Directory\ FileName.htm`. You can type in the name of the desired default file, including its path relative to the project (`.hhp`) file, or you can use the drop-down list. This list draws its information from the `[FILES]` section of your project files—one of the reasons that it's best to add files to the project as soon as possible.

Besides specifying the project's default file, you must identify the files to use for the table of contents and index. Go to the Options dialog's Files tab (figure 6.2) to choose these files or to verify that you chose them correctly in the New Project Wizard. You can type the filenames directly into the Contents file and Index file fields or you can use the Browse button to locate the files. If you type the filenames manually, be sure to include the path relative to the project file. Of course, if you've used the suggested directory structure, these files will be in the same directory and need no path at all. (That is, you'll just type the filename; for example, `Printing.hhc`.)

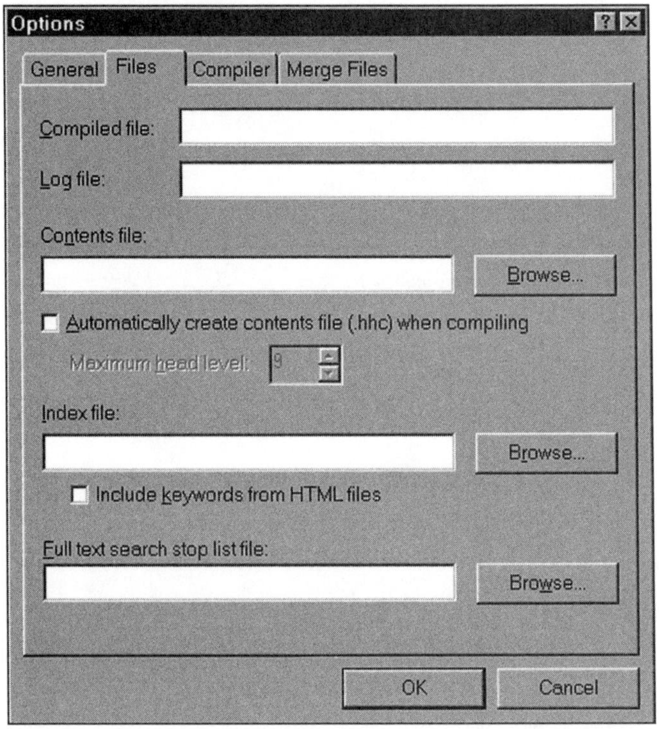

***Figure 6.2 File options.*** *The* Files *tab of the* Options *dialog defines the compiled project file's name and sets the files used for the table of contents and indexing. It also lets you create a full-text search stop list, which speeds up searches by excluding too-common words such as* as *and* or *or.*

The FULL TEXT SEARCH STOP LIST field at the bottom of this tab leads to one of HTML Help's more recent options: full-text search (FTS) that actually works. In earlier versions, FTS worked only if the default language was set to U.S. English and if the HTML Help components were on a hard drive (no CDs or other removable media). Beginning with version 1.22, these problems seem to have been fixed; the search facility even supports a stop list of too-common words (for example, *the, a, and*). The stop list words are not indexed, providing quicker searching of large HTML Help files. Of course, you still have to deal with searching's surreptitious essential: turning it on. The COMPILE FULL-TEXT SEARCH INFORMATION option is found on the COMPILER tab of the PROJECT OPTIONS dialogs. Simply mark its check box to make sure this option is enabled, and the HTML Help compiler will automatically create the search information.

The final surreptitious essential, the default window type, appears throughout the project file. To create a properly functioning HTML Help view, you should specify the same DEFAULT WINDOW type in three places:

- PROJECT tab: On the OPTIONS dialog's GENERAL tab
- CONTENTS tab: On the PROPERTIES dialog's GENERAL tab
- INDEX tab: On the PROPERTIES dialog's GENERAL tab

However, before you can set the default window, you must define the appropriate window in the WINDOW TYPES dialog, as described in the following section.

# Dealing with window types

Window types (or window definitions) specify the size, position, navigation options, buttons, and other attributes of the window that displays Help topics to the user. Although Help authors with a knowledge of Web design can create their own viewer design with a custom HTML frameset, the *de facto* standard for the HTML Help Viewer is a tripane window with a toolbar across the top, a navigation pane on the left, and a topic pane on the right (figure 6.3).

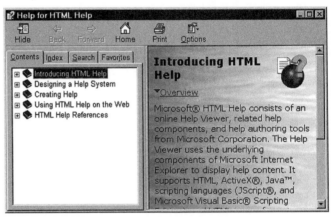

*Figure 6.3 The standard tripane window. The HTML Help Viewer's standard display model is a tripane window composed of a button bar (across the top), a navigation pane (on the left) and a topic pane (on the right).*

The HTML Help Workshop uses the terms *window definition* and *window type* interchangeably: the toolbar button is named ADD/MODIFY WINDOW DEFINITIONS; the dialog is named WINDOW TYPES.

Window types allow you to customize this tripane window from within the HTML Help Workshop; you can even do away with the navigation pane and button bar, if you like, or control which navigation tabs (contents, index, search, favorites) and buttons appear onscreen. These customizations are made by defining a window type and specifying it as the DEFAULT WINDOW on the PROJECT, CONTENTS, and INDEX tabs. (If you don't manually specify a DEFAULT WINDOW type, the first window type you define automatically becomes the default.)

Be sure to use the same window type as the default on all three Workshop tabs (PROJECT, CONTENTS, INDEX). Not setting these defaults, or setting the default to different window types, can result in very odd behavior in your compiled HTML Help project.

You can also use window types to define secondary windows for image maps, special topics, etc. The Workshop allows you to define up to 255 secondary window types, of which the user can display up to 9 at a time.

According to the HTML Help Workshop's online help, you can set these secondary windows as the home window for your table of contents and index (by using the PROPERTIES dialog for the contents and index); as the target window in which topics open when they are accessed from the contents or index (on the ADVANCED tab of individual contents and index entries); or as the window used when a topic opens from an anchor (<A>) tag. Unfortunately, HTML Help's implementation of secondary windows seems to break in every other release, so these methods only work occasionally. The only reliable way for the Help author to access secondary windows is to use them as the targets of anchor tags, and this requires using the HTML Help ActiveX Control Wizard to insert a RELATED TOPICS object. (For details on this procedure, see the section on related topics in Chapter 9, "Accelerating Links: Cross-Referencing Options.") Application developers can also use the secondary windows by calling them programmatically via the HTML Help API. (For details, check the Workshop's online Help system's section on the *HTML Help API Reference.*)

In 1.x versions of HTML Help, the most practical use of window types for Help authors is to customize the default window for your system.

## Creating window types

Once you design your default and secondary window types, the WINDOW TYPES dialog lets you create them in the HTML Help Workshop. Click the ADD/MODIFY WINDOW DEFINITION button (third from the top on the vertical toolbar). A small dialog appears, where you type the name of the window type you wish to create. You will use this name throughout the project so it should be short and descriptive (main often works well for the primary window type). If you are going to use this window type in multiple files

ADD/MODIFY
WINDOW DEFINITION
button

(for example, secondary popup windows in a merged project), it's a good idea to preface the name with $global_ (so the window name would be something like $global_pop).

Once you name the window type, click **OK** to close this dialog and open the main WINDOW TYPES dialog. The WINDOW TYPES dialog opens to the GENERAL tab, showing the name of the WINDOW TYPE and the TITLE BAR TEXT that appears at the top of the defined window and in the Windows taskbar when the HTML Help system is minimized. The only other features on this tab are the ADD and REMOVE buttons that allow you to create additional window types.

The place to start massaging the window type definition is the NAVIGATION PANE tab. By default, window types use the tripane format with a navigation pane, topic pane, and button bar. Make sure the proper WINDOW TYPE is selected from the drop-down list at the top of the tab, and then select or clear the option to use the tripane format. With this tripane option selected (for the standard HTML Help format), the rest of the dialog options appear, providing the following choices:

- The NAVIGATION PANE WIDTH specifies the width of the left pane in pixels. (This width is part of the total window width set on the POSITIONS tab.)

- The PROPERTIES section specifies whether (a) the navigation pane should be open when the HTML Help project opens; (b) the navigation pane should automatically hide whenever the user clicks in the topics pane or away from the compiled help project (AUTOMATICALLY SHOW/HIDE NAVIGATION PANE); and (c) the compiled HTML Help file should automatically focus on and highlight the entry in the navigation pane that corresponds to the item currently displayed in the topic pane (AUTO SYNC).

- The TABS section determines whether the navigation pane includes SEARCH and FAVORITES tabs and which tab displays when users first open the HTML Help project (DEFAULT TAB). This section includes the ability to enable ADVANCED options on the compiled project's SEARCH tab.

Always make sure the correct window type is named in the WINDOW TYPES list at the top of each tab before editing the various window definition elements.

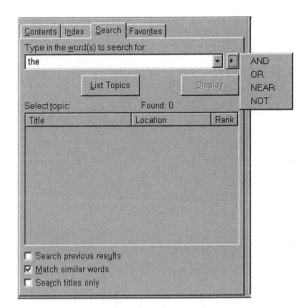

*Figure 6.4 Advanced search options. HTML Help's full-text search can supply a number of advanced options, including Boolean search terms (AND, OR, NEAR, NOT, on the fly-out menu at the top) and the ability to search only within titles or previous results, as well as the ability to match similar words (for example, plurals).*

Advanced search adds three options to the SEARCH tab of the compiled help project: SEARCH PREVIOUS RESULTS, MATCH SIMILAR WORDS, and SEARCH TITLES ONLY. It also allows complex searches using wildcards, nested expressions, and Boolean operators (AND, OR, NOT, NEAR) selected from a flyout menu (figure 6.4).

The POSITION tab offers some relatively simple choices about the window type's size and position. You can set these options numerically or visually:

- To set the HTML Help system's window size and position numerically, type in the desired value (in pixels) for the LEFT and TOP corners of the total window, then type in the desired WIDTH and HEIGHT for the total window. Note that the size of the window specified as the WIDTH is the width of the entire tripane window, including the width of the navigation pane (set on the NAVIGATION PANE tab).

The user-defined window position is stored in the `hh.dat` file in the user's `Windows` directory. When testing window type definitions, delete hh.dat each time you reopen the Help system for testing.

- To set the HTML Help system's window size and position visually, click the AUTOSIZER button. Resize and reposition the sample window to your liking, then click OK.

The POSITIONS tab also determines whether the system should SAVE USER DEFINED WINDOW POSITIONS AFTER FIRST USE. By default, the HTML Help system always opens in the size and position specified by the Help author. Choosing this options means that the HTML Help system will always open in the same place that the user last closed it. Note that this option overrides the DEFAULT TAB option set on the NAVIGATION PANE tab.

The BUTTONS tab (figure 6.5) specifies the contents of the button bar for the WINDOW TYPE shown on the drop-down list at the top of the tab. Select each desired button by putting a check mark in its box. For additional information about a particular button, click the ? at the top of the WINDOW

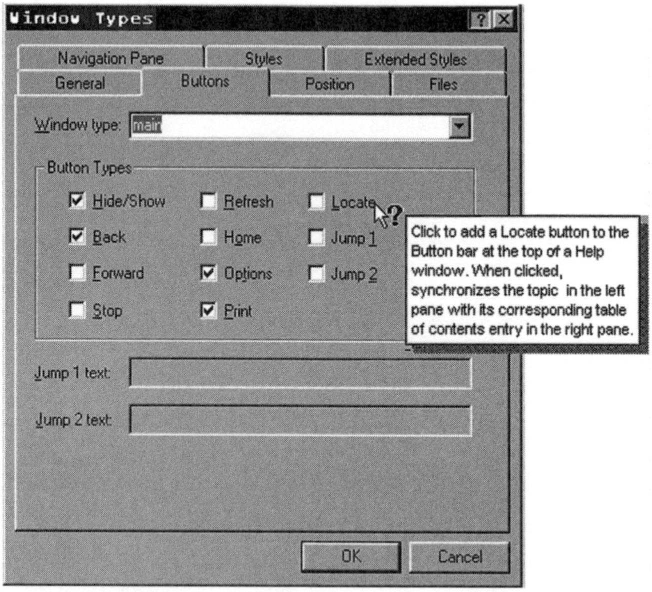

*Figure 6.5 Adding buttons to a window type.* The Buttons *tab of the* Window Types *dialog lets you define the buttons that appear on a custom window's button bar (top pane). For specific details about any button, click the question mark in the dialog's top right corner, then click on the button name.*

Types dialog, then click on the button name. A pop-up text box appears with additional information about that button.

The Jump 1 and Jump 2 buttons add a button with custom text that links to a specific help file topic or URL. Selecting one of these options enables the areas at the bottom of the dialog, where you specify the text that appears on the button in the compiled Help file. The targets for the jump buttons are set on the Files tab of the Window Types dialog.

The Files tab governs which files populate various parts of Window type shown on the drop-down list at the top of the tab. For each field, use the drop-down list to specify the file that will appear for that window type as the table of contents (TOC), Index, Default, and Home pages. The drop-down lists display all the files that you have added to the project as Topic Files or on the Project Options > Files tab. If you type in a different filename here, be sure to include the file's path relative to the project file.

The Styles and Extended Styles tabs can set advanced options for your window type. For additional information about a particular style or extended style, click the ? at the top of the Window Types dialog, then click on the style name. A pop-up text box appears with additional information about that style. Unfortunately, most of these window styles do not work reliably or offer functionality that can only be accessed programmatically through the HTML Help API. The most useful option is the Tool window (on Extended styles), which provides a floating window with just a text area, title bar, and close button.

## Advanced info: Understanding the project file's window type specs

Many HTML Help authors will never look into the project file, much less attempt to decipher the lines that define specific window types. However, being able to read the project file's window type definitions can be helpful in troubleshooting difficult projects and can allow you to set options not available in the Workshop.

The WINDOW TYPE definition is a single line with no line breaks!

For each window type set up in the HTML Help Workshop, the project file (*.hhp) contains a line that defines all the characteristics of that window type. For example, if you simply specify a window type name without setting any other parameters, the HTML Help Workshop adds a [WINDOWS] section to the project file with a line saying:

```
WindowType=,,,,,,,,,0x2120,,0x3006,,,,,,,0
```

where `WindowType` is the name you specified, `0x2120` describes the navigation pane settings (including the default settings of "off" for saving user-defined window positions after the first use, and "yes" for using the tripane window format), and `0x3006` displays the default button set (HIDE/SHOW, BACK, OPTIONS, PRINT). Each of the commas in the series sets off a place for specifying other parameters of the window type.

The full specification is:

```
WindowType="Title bar text","tocfile.hhc",
"indexfile.hhk","default.htm","home.htm","jump1
destination file", "jump1 button text","jump2
destination file","jump2 button text",
0xNavigation Pane,navigation pane width,
0xButtons,[l,t,w,h],0xstyles,0xextended
styles,,navigation pane closed,default tab,blank,0
```

The entire line is typed without line breaks. Table 6.1 describes the meaning of individual parameters and where they are defined in the Workshop. Most of the parameters are expressed as hexadecimal "bit flags" that tell the compiler how to build the window type. For an explanation of these hexadecimal values and an example of how they work in specifying the buttons that appear in a window type, see the *Fun with Hex* section.

**TABLE 6.1 WINDOW DEFINITION PARAMETERS**

| PARAMETER | EXPLANATION & WHERE DEFINED IN THE WORKSHOP |
|---|---|
| WindowType | Name specified when you create the window type; also appears as the WINDOW TYPE throughout the WINDOW TYPES dialog tabs |
| Title bar text | Name that appears in the window's title bar (defined in the WINDOW TYPES dialog on the GENERAL tab in the TITLE BAR TEXT field) |
| tocfile.hhc | File displayed on the CONTENTS tab in the navigation pane of this window type (defined in WINDOW TYPES>FILES>TOC) |
| indexfile.hhk | File displayed on the INDEX tab in the navigation pane of this window type (defined in WINDOW TYPES>FILES>INDEX) |
| default.htm | Topic displayed when user first opens the file (defined in WINDOW TYPES>FILES> DEFAULT) |
| home.htm | Topic file displayed when the user clicks the HOME button in the compiled HTML Help file (defined in WINDOW TYPES>FILES>HOME) |
| jump1 destination file | Topic file or URL displayed when the user clicks JUMP 1 button in the HTML Help file (defined in WINDOW TYPES > FILES > JUMP 1) |
| jump1 button text | Text displayed on JUMP 1 button on the compiled HTML Help file's button bar (defined in WINDOW TYPES>BUTTONS>JUMP 1 TEXT once you select the JUMP 1 check box) |
| jump2 destination file | Topic file or URL displayed when the user clicks JUMP 2 in the HTML Help file (defined in WINDOW TYPES>FILES>JUMP 2) |
| jump2 button text | Text displayed on the JUMP 2 button on the compiled HTML Help file's button bar (defined in WINDOW TYPES>BUTTONS>JUMP 2 TEXT once you select the JUMP 2 check box) |

| PARAMETER | EXPLANATION & WHERE DEFINED IN THE WORKSHOP |
|---|---|
| 0xNavigation pane | Hexadecimal "bit flag" specifying information about the navigation pane, including information about whether the HTML Help file:<br>• uses the standard tripane format<br>• always opens in the location defined by the Help author (default) or opens to position it was in the last time the user closed it<br>• automatically synchronizes contents highlight with currently displayed topic file<br>• displays SEARCH and FAVORITES tabs<br>(defined in WINDOW TYPES > NAVIGATION PANE and WINDOW TYPES> POSITION>SAVE USER DEFINED WINDOW POSITION AFTER FIRST USE) |
| navigation pane width | Default width of navigation (left) pane in pixels (defined in WINDOW TYPES>NAVIGATION PANE >NAVIGATION PANE WIDTH) |
| 0xButtons | Hexadecimal "bit flag" specifying buttons to display in the button bar (See *Fun with Hex* section for information about "bit flags" and how to determine hexadecimal value.) (defined in WINDOW TYPES>BUTTONS>BUTTON TYPES) |
| [l,t,w,h] | Default position for this window type, where:<br>• l is the number of pixels from the left edge of the computer screen that the left edge of the HTML Help window begins<br>• t is the number of pixels from the top of the computer screen that the top of the HTML Help window begins<br>• w is the width (in pixels) of the window<br>• h is the height (in pixels) of the window<br>(defined in WINDOW TYPES>POSITION> WINDOW SIZE AND POSITION) |

Setting the 0xNavigation pane bit flag to save the user-defined position overrides other window type choices, such as opening the window maximized (full screen) or setting the default tab.

| Parameter | Explanation & Where Defined in the Workshop |
|---|---|
| 0xStyles | Hexadecimal "bit flag" specifying "Style" elements included in the the HTML Help window, including:<br>• frames and border styles<br>• horizontal and vertical scroll bars<br>• child and pop-up windows<br>(defined in Window Types >Styles) |
| 0xExtended Styles | Hexadecimal "bit flag" specifying "Extended Style" elements included in the HTML Help window, including:<br>• tool window (floating window with no buttons except a close button)<br>• edge styles<br>• language settings for right-aligned and right-to-left reading order languages<br>• relationship between parent and child windows<br>(defined in Window Types>Extended Styles) |
| Navigation Pane Closed | Default state for the navigation pane in a tripane window where:<br>• "1" signifies that the statement "Open with navigation pane closed" is true (that is, the HTML Help file opens *without* a navigation pane)<br>• "0" signifies that the statement "Open with navigation pane closed" is false (that is, the HTML Help file opens *with* a navigation pane)<br>(defined in Window Types>Navigation Pane >"Open with navigation pane closed") |

"Tool window" is virtually the only style or extended style that is both useful and reliable.

| PARAMETER | EXPLANATION & WHERE DEFINED IN THE WORKSHOP |
|---|---|
| Default Tab | Default opening tab for the navigation (left) pane of the tripane HTML Viewer, where a value of:<br>• blank means the CONTENTS tab is the default<br>• 1 means the INDEX tab is the default<br>• 2 means the SEARCH tab is the default<br>• 3 means the FAVORITES tab is the default<br>(defined in WINDOW TYPES>NAVIGATION PANE>TABS>DEFAULT TAB) |
| blank,0 | Two final elements which appear only to signal the termination of the window type definition. |

## Fun with hex

Each bit flag used in a window type definition tells the compiler what to do about a particular element in window type; that is, it "flags" individual "bits" of the window for display, sizing, etc. (The programmers among you may recognize the language in that definition is not entirely technically appropriate; however, it is descriptive and works as a mnemonic.) Each flag is written as a hexadecimal nunber prefixed by `0x`. (Hexadecimal is a base-16 number system where the digits 0–9 represent themselves and the letters a–f provide single-place representations for the numbers 10–15.) For example, the bit flag for the default button set (HIDE/SHOW, BACK, OPTIONS, PRINT) is `0x3006`.

The values for the bit flags are drawn from the `htmlhelp.h` header file, installed by default in your HTML Help Workshop directory or in an `include` subdirectory of the HTML Help Workshop directory. Just to keep things interesting, the header file specifies bit flags as binary numbers which you must then convert to hexadecimal for the project (`.hhp`) file.

To make it all a bit more concrete, let's take a look at the section of `htmlhelp.h` that defines buttons for the window type:

```
#define HHWIN_BUTTON_EXPAND (1 << 1) // Expand/
contract button
#define HHWIN_BUTTON_BACK (1 << 2) // Back button
#define HHWIN_BUTTON_FORWARD (1 << 3) // Forward
button
#define HHWIN_BUTTON_STOP (1 << 4) // Stop button
#define HHWIN_BUTTON_REFRESH (1 << 5) // Refresh
button
#define HHWIN_BUTTON_HOME (1 << 6) // Home button
#define HHWIN_BUTTON_BROWSE_FWD (1 << 7) // not
implemented
#define HHWIN_BUTTON_BROWSE_BCK (1 << 8) // not
implemented
#define HHWIN_BUTTON_NOTES (1 << 9) // not
implemented
```

```
#define HHWIN_BUTTON_CONTENTS (1 << 10) // not
implemented
#define HHWIN_BUTTON_SYNC (1 << 11) // Sync
button
#define HHWIN_BUTTON_OPTIONS (1 << 12) // Options
button
#define HHWIN_BUTTON_PRINT (1 << 13) // Print
button
#define HHWIN_BUTTON_INDEX (1 << 14) // not
implemented
#define HHWIN_BUTTON_SEARCH (1 << 15) // not
implemented
#define HHWIN_BUTTON_HISTORY (1 << 16) // not
implemented
#define HHWIN_BUTTON_FAVORITES (1 << 17) // not
implemented
#define HHWIN_BUTTON_JUMP1 (1 << 18)
#define HHWIN_BUTTON_JUMP2 (1 << 19)
#define HHWIN_BUTTON_ZOOM (1 << 20)
#define HHWIN_BUTTON_TOC_NEXT (1 << 21)
#define HHWIN_BUTTON_TOC_PREV (1 << 22)
```

The parenthetical numbers (for example, (1<<22) for HHWIN_BUTTON
_TOC_PREV) give the binary number that displays that button. In binary,
(1<<22) displays as a 1 followed by 22 zeroes; its decimal equivalent is 2
raised to the $22^{nd}$ power, or 4,194,304; and the hex equivalent is 400000.
Fortunately, you need not be a mathematician to perform this arithmetic:
the scientific view of the Windows Calculator (figure 6.6) will do it for you.

To display the scientific view, open the calculator (from the START menu,
choose PROGRAMS > ACCESSORIES > CALCULATOR, or RUN > calc.exe). Go
to its VIEW menu and choose SCIENTIFIC.

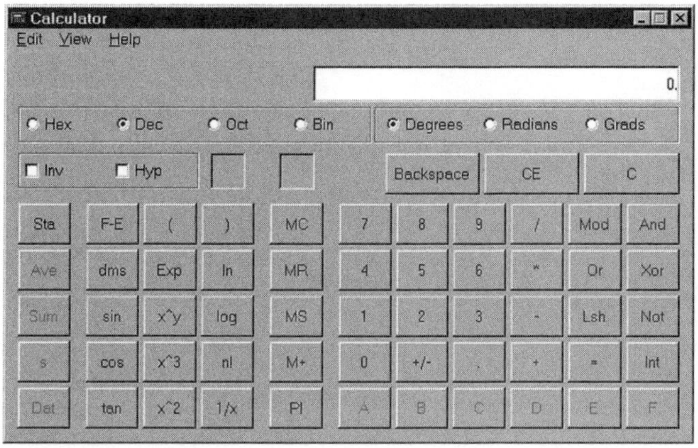

*Figure 6.6 Hexadecimal math with the Windows Scientific Calculator. The radio buttons labeled* Hex *and* Dec *change the Calculator's view between hexadecimal and decimal math. The key labeled* x^y *calculates a number raised to a power.*

To convert the header file's binary number to the project file's hexadecimal number:

1.  Set the calculator to decimal (DEC) format.

2.  Type in 2 followed by the x^y key and then the desired power (in the previous example, 22). Press ENTER to see the answer (4194304).

3.  Switch to HEX format to view the hexadecimal equivalent (400000) that you'll use in the project file.

Once you've determined the appropriate hex value for each item in a bit flag, you can also use the scientific calculator to total the values for all the desired buttons. Type that value (prefaced by 0x) in the appropriate place in the window definition, and you have a new element for your window type.

Using this approach to creating window type definitions allows you to use features not currently implemented in the HTML Help Workshop—nor obvious from the descriptions in the htmlhelp.h file. For example, the third last line of the buttons section in htmlhelp.h refers to a zoom button.

Not all buttons listed in the header file work, but a little experimentation can pay big dividends. For example, the ZOOM button lets users adjust the font size used for viewing the compiled HTML Help file—a nice accessibility feature.

When you add 0x100000 (the hexadecimal representation of 1 << 20) to your window definition's button flag, the resulting .chm file has a FONTS button. Pressing the FONTS button repeatedly cycles the user through enlarged and reduced views of the contents pane with larger and smaller fonts, but without affecting the "zoom" factor of the graphics.

Also, some of the buttons require additional settings to make them work. For example, the last two lines of the section of htmlhelp.h quoted previously refer to next and previous buttons that scroll users through the table of contents. You can't add these directly in the Workshop, but if you manually add their hex bit flag to the project file (that is, add 0x60000 to the current window definition value), the buttons magically appear in the compiled file. However, they don't do anything until you set the project options for a compiled TOC.

# Pulling it all together

Once the project is set up with all the files and options specified, it's time to pull it all together by compiling the HTML Help system that the user will see. If you've done all the setup work properly, this is a relatively simple step: just save, compile, and view the results. If necessary, troubleshoot problems and recompile.

## Save early, save often . . . and close the Workshop

As with any computer project, saving your work is important. But the HTML Help Workshop adds a new twist: not all save options affect all files, and not all save options work all of the time. Basically, the HTML Help Workshop offers the following ways to save your work:

- From the FILE menu: SAVE PROJECT is designed to save only the project (`*.hhp`) file. If you have any topic (`*.htm`) files open, this menu also contains commands to SAVE FILE, SAVE FILE AS, and SAVE ALL FILES. The first two commands are designed to act on the file currently visible in the right pane of the PROJECT tab, while SAVE ALL FILES is designed to save all currently open files.

- From the vertical toolbars on the PROJECT, CONTENTS, and INDEX tabs: Each tab includes a SAVE button. On the PROJECT tab, this is designed to affect the project, contents, and index (`*.hhp`, `*.hhc`, `*.hhk`) files. The buttons on the CONTENTS and INDEX tabs only affect the individual contents and index files. If a topic file is open for editing, an additional SAVE button on the horizontal toolbar applies to the topic files.

SAVE button

- Within the COMPILE options: The compile buttons on the horizontal toolbar and the PROJECT tab's vertical toolbars, as well as the FILE menu's COMPILE command, offer the ability to save all files before compiling.

COMPILE and SAVE & COMPILE buttons

Unfortunately, none of the options are 100% reliable. The best results come from the COMPILE options, but even these aren't failsafe. (To test this for yourself, try one of the save options while watching the file list in Windows Explorer. The timestamp does not always change.) If you think you've changed something in a file but it doesn't show up in the compiled project, force the files to be saved by closing the HTML Help Workshop. You'll be surprised at how often a dialog box pops up saying something hasn't been saved. Once the files actually are saved, reopen the Workshop and recompile the project.

## The moment of truth: compiling

Invoking the HTML Help compiler simply involves clicking on one of the two compiler buttons. Depending on how the options are set on the COMPILER tab of the PROJECT OPTIONS dialog, the right pane of the Workshop may display a log file containing various information about the compile as it proceeds.

If the NOTES option is selected, the right-pane of the HTML Help Workshop displays:

- the HTML Help Compiler version;

- a notice that compilation is in progress;

- the length of time it took to compile the file;

- a summary of the number of topic files, inter-topic links, Internet links, and graphics in the project; and

- the filename and path of the compiled project, including its size before and how much the size decreased due to compression.

If the PROGRESS option is selected, the right pane displays a list of each file as it is added to the project.

In either case, the log file also displays any relevant compiler messages about conditions that occur during the compile. These messages fall into the following categories:

- Note (numbered 1000–2999): informational messages about potential problems that do not prevent compilation or opening the compiled help file. The most common notes are for missing files or broken links.

- Warning (numbered 3000–4999): messages about problems that do not prevent compilation but will cause a defective compiled help file. Missing or invalid `.dlls` can cause warnings.

- Error (numbered 5000–6999): messages about problems that halt compilation. Probably the most common message occurs when you are recompiling a file. If you've already compiled the file, previewed it, and left it open, the HTML Help compiler can't work its magic on the open file.

- Internal Error (numbered 7000 and up): messages about problems caused by the HTML Help Workshop itself. These may signal Workshop bugs or may require reinstallation or updating of your Workshop. Sometimes you may also be able to circumvent these errors by compiling from the command line.

According to Microsoft, version 1.3 of the Workshop no longer sends warnings 3001 (links to non-existent files), or for 3003 and 3005 (both referencing invalid characters before the closing tag marker >). This makes for a cleaner log file, but less warning of broken links.

Under Windows 95/98, the log pane shows the messages until the log file reaches its limit of 64k; under Windows NT, the limit is 1 MB. Although the NT limit is seldom reached, large projects can easily exceed the Windows 95/98 limits. Fortunately, there is no limit to the size of the log file that can be saved (beyond the available hard drive space). To view large log files under 95/98, specify a Log file name on the Files tab of the Project Options.

To compile from the command line, hh.exe and hha.dll must be in the path statement.

## Compiling from the command line

Large projects and other limitations of the HTML Help Workshop may make it difficult to compile projects from within the GUI. More reliable results can sometimes be obtained by calling the command line compiler (hhc.exe).

To use the command line compiler, open a DOS prompt. From the Windows START menu, choose RUN. Either type hhc.exe and the project file name here, or type in command to open a DOS window and run the compiler from there.

# Previewing & troubleshooting the results

PREVIEW button

Once the compile finishes, use the PREVIEW button on the horizontal toolbar to view your results. (Note that the COMPILE button on the horizontal toolbar offers an option to AUTOMATICALLY DISPLAY COMPILED FILE WHEN DONE; however, this seldom works.)

When you finish previewing the file and want to make adjustments in the HTML Help Workshop, be sure to close the compiled file. One of the most common frustrations in compiling is getting the HHC 5003 error message "Compilation failed while compiling project.chm." Most of the time this simply means the compiler can't work with the .chm because you didn't close it after the last viewing.

By the way, if you do compile the same project multiple times during the troubleshooting stage, don't worry if the reported size differs. It is well known that the compiler does not necessarily order projects in the same way every time, resulting in slight differences between compiled file sizes, even when no changes have been made to the project.

You should also be sure to delete the hh.dat file after each previewing. This file, which stores user information such as the last navigation pane opened and changes to the FAVORITES tab, can corrupt the results of your troubleshooting. For example, if you change the default window size and position but opt to Save user-defined window position after first use, the compiled file will continue to appear in the same place until hh.dat is deleted. [Starting with version 1.3 of the Workshop, hh.dat is found in the Application Data\Microsoft\HTML Help subdirectory of your Windows system directory, usually named Windows or Winnnt. If your system is set up for multiple profiles, the HTML Help directory will be down two more levels, beneath Windows or Winnnt\Profiles\UserID. Workshop versions prior to 1.3 store hh.dat directly in the Windows system directory.]

If files are missing or links are broken in the project, be sure to double check that the files have been explicitly included in the project's file list, that their names do not contain spaces, and that they are specified with the correct path relative to the project file. For help with other problems, check the chapter referring to that area for relevant tips and tricks.

# Navigating the Waters:
## Table of Contents

The HTML Help table of contents (TOC) fills the Help Viewer's navigation (left) pane with a collapsible tree presenting a hierarchical view of the topics contained in the Help system. By clicking on various branches of the tree, the user can expand and contract topic levels before opening a specific page in the topic (right) pane of the Viewer. In a modular HTML Help system, the table of contents can include references to topics in other modules of the system. When these modules are present, the topics appear in the contents; when the other modules are not present on the user's system, the topics disappear from the contents, without any gap or other trace of their presence.

This apparently simple tree presents one of the most obvious usability advances over Windows Help—and one of the most challenging features to implement in HTML Help, especially in modular (merged) systems.

The usability advances come from HTML Help's tripane window format, which keeps the table of contents onscreen and synchronized with the currently displayed topic. In Windows Help, the system opened to display the navigation window, with three tabs for the table of contents, index, and find (search) capabilities. When the user selected an entry from the table of contents, Windows Help opened a new window to display the contents and immediately closed the navigation window. The user could return to the navigation window only by clicking a button at the top of the contents pane. As a result, the user constantly jumped between windows, with no clear idea of their current position in the "bigger picture."

In HTML Help, the navigation pane (including contents, index, and search tabs) remains onscreen unless the user explicitly chooses the HIDE button. Even when the navigation pane is hidden, a clearly marked SHOW button can bring it back. In addition, synchronization between the currently displayed topic and the table of contents is greatly improved; the author can even add a LOCATE button that allows the user to force a synchronization update. The synchronization capability keeps the user securely located within the HTML Help system. Synchronization can be a great help when similar topics exist in multiple locations; for example, the help system for a graphics application might have sections on "Color" referring to choosing colors, calibrating a monitor for accurate color display, working with color printers, or even changing user preferences for colors in the application's onscreen display. With a synchronized table of contents always onscreen, users know when they have wandered away from the desired topic.

The HTML Help TOC also supplies elements authors and users have come to expect in Windows Help. The contents displays as a hierarchical tree, with branches that expand or collapse just like the branches in the Windows Explorer Tree. HTML Help also supports merged modular systems. In these systems, the contents of each module shows up when the module is on the user's system, but silently disappears if the files are not available.

The challenges presented by the HTML Help table of contents arise from a variety of instabilities and unimplemented features in the Workshop's tools for working with the table of contents. The Contents pane has a number of video refresh bugs, and neither information types nor custom icon sets are implemented as of version 1.3 of the HTML Help Workshop. Fortunately, there are workarounds for the bugs; but the unimplemented features remain a promise for the future.

# Choosing the editing environment

The information displayed in the table of contents for an HTML Help system is contained in a single `.hhc` file (or, in the case of a modular help system, in multiple `.hhc` files). This specific information (i.e., book and page titles, together with their associated links and certain graphic settings) is read and displayed by the ActiveX control that the compiler embeds in the navigation pane of every compiled HTML Help system. While you can't directly manipulate the ActiveX control itself, you can edit the specific information of the `.hhc` file.

Like most HTML Help files, the .hhc is a plain text file using HTML components; in this case, the components appear as multiple layers of unordered lists `<UL>`, with objects and parameters specified for each list item `<LI>`. (For more information, see the section on *Manual TOC creation.*)

The `.hhc` file can be created and edited in three different ways:

- using the HTML Help Workshop's automatic generation feature;

- using the HTML Help Workshop's graphical interface (on the CONTENTS and PROJECT tabs);

- using Notepad to manually edit the file.

The automatic generation feature requires the least work, but also offers little control over the output and disables certain features (such as merged TOCs, links to bookmarks, and specifying icons). On the other hand, manual editing in Notepad offers full control, but can be extremely confusing with large TOCs. Between these two extremes lies the CONTENTS tab of the HTML Help Workshop. The Workshop provides a graphical interface with guided editing capabilities and is probably the most common environment for TOC creation. Fortunately, HTML Help allows you to move among the three options, making each adjustment in the most suitable environment. The only caveat is that automatically generated TOCs overwrite any changes made in the other environments, so you should not use the automatic facility after using one of the other approaches.

# The Workshop's graphical interface

The most commonly used way to create a table of contents for an HTML Help project is by using the Workshop's CONTENTS and PROJECT tabs. This approach offers access to most TOC features with the least difficult learning curve. As always, you'll need to be aware of a few "undocumented features" and, in the end, may find yourself making a few changes in a text editor. But the Workshop's graphical interface provides the quickest way to get up and running.

## Understanding how the Workshop tabs work

The Workshop's CONTENTS and PROJECT tabs provide a graphical interface for creating a table of contents.

From the CONTENTS tab, you can access dialog boxes to specify individual book and page entries, including their links, icons, and target frames/ windows; edit the order and heading level for each TOC entry; and set some of the TOC's default settings. As you work through the individual dialogs, the Workshop writes an .hhc file reflecting your selections. You can always open this file in a text editor and adjust your choices manually. Note that the CONTENTS file dialogs primarily govern the individual entries of the TOC (their text, links, window destinations, and icons); only the TABLE OF CONTENTS PROPERTIES dialog concerns overall display issues (default frame, window, and font).

The TOC file specification in the WINDOWS TYPES dialog overrides the setting in the OPTIONS dialog.

Most larger TOC design and display issues are addressed on the Workshop's PROJECT tab. On this tab, the OPTIONS dialog defines the contents file to be used in the project, whether it is created automatically, and whether the TOC is binary. The WINDOW TYPES dialog (also on the PROJECT tab) turns on the automatic synchronization between the TOC and the currently displayed topic; it also sets up the design of the Help Viewer's navigation pane and defines the contents file to be used. This last function points out one of the pitfalls of HTML Help TOCs: the various components are not necessarily coordinated. For example, both the OPTIONS and WINDOW TYPES dialogs allow you to specify a default .hhc file for the project, but the two dialogs write separate lines in the .hhp project file and neither the GUI nor the text file synchronizes the two specifications.

# Creating a TOC on the Contents tab

1. With the project open in the HTML Help Workshop, go to the PROJECT tab and click the CHANGE PROJECT OPTIONS button (top button on the left side). In the resulting OPTIONS dialog, click the FILES tab and fill in the CONTENTS FILE section by typing a file name or use the BROWSE button to locate the desired file.

CHANGE PROJECT OPTIONS button

2. Still on the HTML Help Workshop's PROJECT tab, click the ADD/MODIFY WINDOW DEFINITIONS button (third button down on the left side). In the resulting WINDOW TYPES dialog, click the FILES tab and set its **TOC** field to the same file that you specified in the PROJECT/OPTIONS dialog.

ADD/MODIFY WINDOW DEFINITIONS button

3. Click the CONTENTS tab. If the TOC file you specified in the above procedures does not match the name and location of an existing file on your hard drive, the Workshop pops up a dialog saying you have not yet associated a contents file with the project and offers to create a new file or open an existing one.

- If you do have an existing file and the dialog is in error, choose OPEN AN EXISTING CONTENTS FILE, and click **OK.** In the dialog that appears, choose the appropriate .hhc file and click SAVE.

- If you want to create a new file, choose OPEN A NEW CONTENTS FILE and click **OK.** In the dialog that appears, navigate to the desired folder, type the correct FILE NAME, and click SAVE.

4. When the CONTENTS window opens with your existing entries or a blank window, click the TABLE OF CONTENTS PROPERTIES button (top button on the left). On the GENERAL tab, specify the DEFAULT WINDOW, using the

TABLE OF CONTENTS PROPERTIES button

same window name as in the PROPERTIES/WINDOW TYPES dialog (defined in the section on *Basic TOC settings*). You may also choose to USE FOLDERS INSTEAD OF BOOKS as the default icons for TOC entries with subordinate entries. Click **OK** to close the dialog.

You will probably not use any of the other settings in this dialog; as of version 1.3 of the Workshop, these features work erratically or not at all. Some STYLES settings work; for example, START LINE FROM THE ROOT draws a dotted line from the root folder to its subfolders (useful for reinforcing hierarchy), while PLUS/MINUS SQUARES adds a small plus sign in front of headings with subordinate entries that are hidden and a minus sign when all subordinate entries are displayed. However, many style settings are flawed; for example, you can set the background color, but you'll still get a white background behind topic titles and the lines from the root, if selected. The biggest disappointment is the promise of INFORMATION TYPES, which have not yet been correctly implemented. (See the section on *Perils ahead.*)

INSERT A HEADING &
INSERT A PAGE buttons

5. To create new TOC entries, click the INSERT A HEADING or INSERT A PAGE button (respectively, the folder and page icons that appear as the second and third buttons from the top on the left).

- **Heading entries** default to book or page icons, which can be displayed in open or closed mode; may contain subordinate topics (headings or pages); and do not require an associated topic file.

- **Page entries** default to the page icon, which has only one state, requires an associated topic file, and should not contain subordinate topics (if you assign subordinate topics to a page entry, the HTML Help Workshop automatically assumes it is a heading and uses the default book/folder icon for the entry).

After the first TOC entry, all subsequent entries must be positioned in relation to the existing entries (the order can be adjusted later). To do this, click on the existing entry that will immediately precede the new entry, then click the INSERT A HEADING or INSERT A PAGE button. To add an entry at the beginning of the TOC, select the first entry in the TOC list, click an INSERT button, and respond YES to the dialog asking DO YOU WANT TO INSERT THIS ENTRY AT THE BEGINNING OF THE TABLE OF CONTENTS?

6.  In the resulting TABLE OF CONTENTS ENTRY dialog, type the text that will appear in the table of contents into the ENTRY TITLE text field. Then click the ADD button to specify the target file or URL for the entry.

In the PATH OR URL dialog, choose the desired file based on the FILE OR URL field at the bottom or by using the BROWSE button. The HTML TITLES list and the FILE OR URL field frequently lose their synchronization, and it is the FILE OR URL specification that the Workshop uses. For example, in figure 7.1 (taken from an actual project), the Common\ConsoleMsgReader.HTM file shown as the FILE OR URL actually correlates to the HTML TITLE Message Reader: Viewing Message Details (the title below the currently selected title). When you have selected the desired file, click OK.

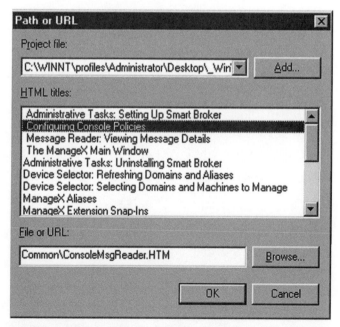

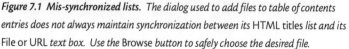

*Figure 7.1 Mis-synchronized lists. The dialog used to add files to table of contents entries does not always maintain synchronization between its HTML titles list and its File or URL text box. Use the Browse button to safely choose the desired file.*

7.  If you want a TOC entry to open to a particular location in a page, you must insert a bookmark into the page's HTML code at the desired location and then direct the TOC entry to that bookmark.

    ▪ To insert the bookmark, open the HTML page and insert appropriately named anchor tags. For example, to insert a bookmark named "bookmark" that opens to text saying "Open here," insert the code `<A NAME="bookmark">` before the "Open here" text and place the tag `</A>` after the "Open here" text.

    ▪ To direct the TOC entry to the bookmark, create the TOC entry as described above, then type "#bookmark" after the file name in the FILE OR URL text box. (In the example shown in the previous graphic, the text box would read `Common\ConsoleMsg Reader.HTM#bookmark.`)

**EDIT SELECTION**
button

8.  To change the TOC entry's icon, select the entry in the topic list, then click the EDIT SELECTION button (fourth from top on left) and select the ADVANCED tab. (Note that a bug in the Workshop disables this option when you first create the entry. You must create the entry, then return to it via the EDIT button.) Change the IMAGE INDEX number until the icon next to the field shows the desired icon. To designate the entry as a new entry, choose an icon with a red star in the corner. Do not use the MARK AS NEW ENTRY check box; this field overrides your image index selection and displays the icon of a page with a red star. Click **OK** to close the dialog.

**DELETE SELECTION**
button

9.  If you want to delete an entry from the TOC, select the entry in the list, then click the DELETE SELECTION icon. Be aware that the UNDO command on the Workshop's EDIT menu does not work for deleted TOC entries.

10. To adjust the order or hierarchy of the TOC entry list, select the entry you want to change, then click one of the arrow buttons on the left.

Up & Down
(list order) buttons

- The Up and Down arrows move the entry up or down in the order of the list; that is, if the entry were second in the list, clicking the Up button would make it the first entry in the list and clicking the Down button would make it the third item in the list. These buttons do not change the entry's level (hierarchical position).

Left & Right
(hierarchical) buttons

- The Right and Left arrows demote and promote the entry one level; that is, clicking the Right arrow indents the entry one level to the right and clicking the Left arrow removes one level of indentation from the entry.

Note that the exact results of these arrows may vary if you move entries that are at a different hierarchical level than the entries next to them. For example, if you have a heading entry followed by several page entries, using the down arrow may move the entry below all of its subordinate page entries. This portion of the Workshop is not predictable, so watch the results carefully in the list window.

11. When you finish adjusting your TOC, click the Save button. However, note that this button does not always work, so it's best to also close the entire Workshop and then reopen the project. This activates a message asking if you want to save the files—a save action that does work reliably.

# Automatic generation

The HTML Help Workshop provides an option to automatically generate the table of contents for your HTML Help system. While this makes the actual generation of the TOC quick and easy, it does require some advance planning and an understanding of how the HTML Help compiler creates automatic TOCs.

Also note that not all functions are available in an automatically generated TOC. For example, you cannot create an automatically generated TOC that references merged files (in a modular system), and you cannot force a TOC entry to open to a specific section of a file (that is, to a bookmark).

## Understanding how the automatic TOC works

The order of the topics in an automatically generated TOC follows the order of the file list in the project (.hhp) file.

When the HTML Help compiler generates the table of contents, it displays the contents of your HTML Help system in a hierarchical tree. The order of the topics mirrors the order in which they appear in the project file list (that is, the [FILES] section of the .hhp file).

The text displayed in the TOC is taken from the HTML heading codes (that is, <H1>, <H2>, <H3>, through <H9>) on each topic (*.htm) page. Each heading displays with a collapsible book icon if it has subordinate headings (that is, if lower level headings follow it on the topic page). If a heading has no subordinate headings, it uses a page icon.

Unfortunately, this runs counter to standard HTML usage with a single topic in each file. Normally, these .htm files begin with a level 1 heading <H1> and other heading levels follow as needed within the page. With an automatically generated table of contents, this standard approach produces a TOC with multiple entries for each .htm file. For example, consider an individual topic page on printing, using the fairly typical online Help format of an overall title, a descriptive paragraph, and then specific procedural instructions. The headings would include the following:

```
<H1>Color Printing</H1>
    <H2>To print a document in color</H2>
```

Normally, you would include this topic once in the TOC, under the heading Color Printing. However, an automatically generated TOC would look like this, where both the entries shown point to the same page:

 Color Printing

 To print a document in color

Most TOCs don't require multiple, adjacent entries pointing to the same page, with the potential for confusing the user. Therefore, in order to efficiently use the automatic TOC feature, you must design your Help system around the way it works. There are at least two workarounds, neither of which is a perfect solution:

1.  **Store all topics for a single section (book) within a single topic file.** In this approach, each `.htm` file contains an entire section of your Help system. For example, if you had 12 topics related to printing, all would be in a single file (for example, `printing.htm`) which opened with a level 1 heading (for example, `<H1>Printing</H1>`) followed by level 2 headings for each individual topic (for example, `<H2>Basic Printing</H2>`, `<H2>Color Printing</H2>`, and `<H2>Troubleshooting Printer Problems</H2>`). However, note that the automatic TOC entries will always open to the *top* of the topic file, which could still be confusing to users.

2.  **Pre-plan the TOC, assigning appropriate heading levels to individual topic files.** In this approach, each `.htm` file contains a single topic from your Help system, but not every topic begins with a level 1 heading. In essence, this requires an outline of your Help system that identifies at least the top two topic levels, which will appear as books and pages in your TOC. You must also be sure to add the files in the order you want them to appear in the TOC or edit the project's file list to reflect the desired order. Unfortunately, all this preparation rather negates the "automatic" part of the TOC generation.

# Creating an automatic TOC

Once the planning is complete, it's simple to actually create an automatically generated TOC, but it does require a few steps that are not immediately obvious.

CHANGE PROJECT OPTIONS
button

1. With the project open in the HTML Help Workshop, go to the PROJECT tab and click the CHANGE PROJECT OPTIONS button (top button on the left side). In the resulting OPTIONS dialog, click the FILES tab and fill in the CONTENTS FILE section by typing a file name or use the BROWSE button to locate the desired file.

ADD/MODIFY WINDOW
DEFINITIONS button

2. Still on the HTML Help Workshop's PROJECT tab, click the ADD/MODIFY WINDOW DEFINITIONS button (third button down on the left side). In the resulting WINDOW TYPES dialog, click the FILES tab and set its TOC field to the same file that you specified in the PROJECT/OPTIONS dialog.

CHANGE PROJECT OPTIONS
button

3. On the HTML Help Workshop's PROJECT tab, click the CHANGE PROJECT OPTIONS button (top button on the left side). In the resulting OPTIONS dialog, click the FILES tab and go to the CONTENTS FILE section.

- Click to select the AUTOMATICALLY CREATE CONTENTS FILE (.HHC) WHEN COMPILING.

- Change the MAXIMUM HEAD LEVEL to specify which of the available heading levels (i.e., <H1> through <H9>) will be used for TOC entries.

- Click **OK** to close the dialog.

# Editing automatic TOCs

You can use the HTML Help Workshop's CONTENTS tab or Windows Notepad to edit an automatically generated table of contents file. Opening the file allows you to change icons, add references to individual topics from multiple contents entries, and generally fine-tune the project's table of contents. For example, you may see odd blank spaces within contents entries. These blanks occur when the original HTML heading includes a line break <BR> between its start and end tags, forcing the heading to display on separate lines. Once the automatic TOC has processed these breaks, they appear as multiple spaces that can be removed in the Workshop or in Notepad.

Note, however, that automatically generated contents files are re-created every time your recompile the project (in fact, you'll see a warning message to this effect when you first click on the CONTENTS tab of an automatically generated TOC). On the one hand, this means that changes made to the project's file list or to individual topics within the project are automatically reflected in the table of contents. On the other hand, if you have done any manual editing of the automatic TOC, your manual edits will be lost when you recompile. To avoid losing manual edits, turn off the automatic contents feature before recompiling the project. (In the Workshop's PROJECT tab, click the CHANGE PROJECT OPTIONS button, select the FILES tab of the dialog, and clear the check box marked AUTOMATICALLY CREATE CONTENTS FILE (.HHC) WHEN COMPILING.)

A final caveat: automatically generated TOCs do not work well on projects with binary TOCs (PROJECT/OPTIONS/COMPILER: CREATE A BINARY TOC).

# Manual TOC creation

Don't forget that you must also set the TOC specifications in the project file. For details, see the sections on *Basic TOC settings* and *Graphic considerations*.

The specific information displayed in an HTML Help file's table of contents is stored in a text file labeled with an .hhc extension. Items in this file specify the text for the contents entries, the .htm files which the contents entries access, and additional parameters such as the choice of icon. While it is possible to create the .hhc file entirely by hand, you will more often use this approach to fine-tune a TOC that isn't working as desired. Be aware that this is a delicate operation that should not be attempted unless you are very comfortable with hand-coding HTML and have at least a general grasp of scripting principles.

If you open the .hhc file in Notepad or another text editor, you will see what looks like a variation on an HTML unordered list <UL>. This format is actually called a *sitemap* and is designed to *populate* the ActiveX control (hhctrl.exe) that reads and displays the contents of the file in the compiled HTML Help file. Sitemaps are becoming more common in various Microsoft components; in fact, Microsoft proposed the sitemap format as a W3C standard as long ago as 1996. (The proposal was rejected by the W3C, but the format still lives in a variety of Microsoft applications, including Internet Explorer and HTML Help.) In the sitemap format, each list item <LI> is defined by an object and its parameters. In coding terms, an <OBJECT> is a reusable component or instance of a class; in HTML, it is most often used to insert an ActiveX control into a Web page. Each object can have multiple parameters, or values given to variables. In the sitemap format, you'll see numerous instances of the tag

```
<param name="X" value="Y">
```

This tag specifies a particular parameter, that is, the value (Y) assigned in this particular case to the variable with the name of X.

The .hhc sitemap starts with fairly standard HTML header code (specifying the document type, marking it as HTML, opening the head, and adding a META tag specifying the program used to create the file) plus a commented tag marking this as a sitemap (the second last line in the following code):

```
<!DOCTYPE HTML PUBLIC "-//IETF//DTD HTML//EN">
<HTML>
<HEAD>
<meta name="GENERATOR" content="Microsoft&reg; HTML
Help Workshop 4.1">
<!- Sitemap 1.0 ->
</HEAD>
```

The `<BODY>` section starts with an `<OBJECT>` tag setting up properties for the TOC in the navigation pane. With only the default settings, these opening lines look like this:

```
<BODY>
<OBJECT type="text/site properties">
    <param name="Window Styles" value="0x800025">
</OBJECT>
```

The opening `<OBJECT>` tag includes the type specification of `"text/`
**`site properties`**`"` to indicate that it sets up properties for the entire TOC "site" (objects used for the various TOC entires are given a type of `"text/`**`sitemap`**`"`). The next line defines a parameter for the Window Styles variable. Its value is given in a hexadecimal format like that used in the window types defined for the overall project. (For more information on the window type hex format, see the section *Advanced info: Understanding the project file's window type specs*, in Chapter 6, "Creating Magic: The HTML Help Project File.")

After the site properties object, the file is composed of unordered lists of objects. A basic heading (or "book") entry in the TOC is specified by lines of the following type:

```
<OBJECT type="text/sitemap">
<param name="Name" value="Book 1">
</OBJECT>
```

where the name that appears as the TOC entry is "Book 1." A basic page entry in the TOC is specified by a similar set of lines, but it must also have a "Local" parameter specifying the HTML file that is displayed when the user selects the entry. Its general format is:

Manual TOC editing is not for the faint-of-heart. At the least, be sure to keep a backup copy of the existing `.hhc` before making any manual changes.

To decipher the window styles hex values, consult the `htmlhelp.h` header file (found in the HTML Help Workshop directory or its `include` subdirectory).

```
<OBJECT type="text/sitemap">
<param name="Name" value="Page 1a">
<param name="Local" value="1a.htm">
</OBJECT>
```

For an entry that opens to a specific bookmark (anchor tag) within an HTML file, add #bookmark after the filename, where bookmark is the name of the anchor tag (for example, you could use <A NAME="bookmark" open here</A>).

Both headings and pages can take various other parameters. In the following example, the Book 1 heading also has specific Frame and Window targets (FrameName and WindowName, respectively), a comment, and a custom icon (ImageNumber). Note that the icon's ImageNumber would not be specified for entries that use the default book and page icons:

```
<OBJECT type="text/sitemap">
<param name="Name" value="Book 1">
<param name="FrameName" value="frameX">
<param name="WindowName" value="windowY">
<param name="ImageNumber" value="6">
</OBJECT>
```

As you become more proficient with HTML Help and DHTML, you can experiment with adding JavaScript to the sitemap objects, using a line of the format

```
<param name="Local" value="javascript:X;">
```

where X is a valid script. Note that users must have version 4 or higher of Internet Explorer installed for these commands to work correctly.

The various heading and page objects are strung together in nested unordered lists. For example, consider the three-level TOC shown in figure 7.2. To create this TOC, create a sitemap which includes the following lines within the <BODY> tags (for clarity, no optional parameters are included):

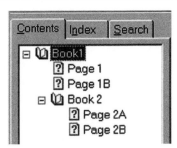

**Figure 7.2 Three-level TOC.** *The code for this multi-level table of contents shows a nested series of <LI> list items in <UL> undented lists.*

```
<UL>
  <LI> <OBJECT type="text/sitemap">
        <param name="Name" value="Book1">
        </OBJECT>
    <UL>
      <LI><OBJECT type="text/sitemap">
          <param name="Name" value="Page 1A">
          <param name="Local" value="1A.htm">
          </OBJECT>
      <LI><OBJECT type="text/sitemap">
          <param name="Name" value="Page 1B">
          <param name="Local" value="1B.HTM">
          </OBJECT>
      <LI><OBJECT type="text/sitemap">
          <param name="Name" value="Book 2">
          </OBJECT>
        <UL>
          <LI><OBJECT type="text/sitemap">
              <param name="Name" value="Page 2A">
              <param name="Local" value="2A.htm">
              </OBJECT>
          <LI><OBJECT type="text/sitemap">
            <param name="Name" value="Page 2B">
            <param name="Local" value="2B.htm">
            </OBJECT>
        </UL>
    </UL>
</UL>
```

Each level adds another nested `<UL>`. While most sitemap coding uses the HTML form of start tag, information, and end tag, individual `<LI>` do not require an end tag (although end tags sometimes help troubleshooting).

# Basic TOC settings

Whether you use an automatically generated TOC, build one in the Workshop's GUI, or manually craft it in Notepad, you must specify the TOC file and its relations to the window types. These settings are easily done in the GUI, but may also be entered manually into the .hhp file.

The settings described below *must* be specified in order for your table of contents to work. Additional control over the appearance of the TOC is described in the following section on *Graphic considerations*. (Because these are required settings, they are also listed in the previous sections on *Creating a TOC on the Contents tab* and *Creating an automatic TOC*.)

## Setting up the TOC in the Workshop

CHANGE PROJECT OPTIONS
button

1.  On the HTML Help Workshop's PROJECT tab, click the CHANGE PROJECT OPTIONS button (top button on the left side). In the resulting OPTIONS dialog, click the FILES tab and fill in the CONTENTS FILE section by typing a file name or use the BROWSE button to locate the desired file. Note that you do not have to specify an existing file; if no file of the specified name exists, the Workshop will offer to create a new .hhc file the next time you click on the CONTENTS tab.

ADD/MODIFY WINDOW
DEFINITIONS button

2.  Still on the HTML Help Workshop's PROJECT tab, click the ADD/MODIFY WINDOW DEFINITIONS button (third button down on the left side). In the resulting WINDOW TYPES dialog, click the FILES tab and set its **TOC** field to the same file that you specified in the PROJECT/OPTIONS dialog. (If the two specifications conflict, the setting in the WINDOW TYPES dialog takes precedence.)

# Setting up the TOC manually

1. Open the project (`*.hhp`) file in the Windows Notepad or another text editor.

2. In the [OPTIONS] section of the file, specify the project's default TOC file with a line of the form

   ```
   Contents file=PATH\foo.hhc
   ```

   where PATH is the full path to the contents file, relative to the location of the project file; and foo is the name of the desired contents file.

3. In the [WINDOWS] section of the file, locate the line starting with the name of the window type that your contents file uses for display; for example

   ```
   Main="Title","PATH\foo.hhc"...
   ```

   where Title is the title displayed in the window's title bar, PATH is the full path to the contents file, and foo.hhc is the name of the contents file. Make sure that PATH\foo.hhc specifies the same path and file used in the [OPTIONS] section.

# Graphic considerations

The HTML Help Workshop offers a few opportunities to customize the graphic and presentation aspects of your table of contents. You can also set the font for the TOC (and other elements appearing in the navigation pane) and add stylistic touches such as plus/minus squares to indicate headings with subordinate topics. Unfortunately, however, many of the options in the TABLE OF CONTENTS PROPERTIES dialog are broken in the current version of the Workshop (1.3). Most of the styles don't appear onscreen or work incorrectly. For example, while you can specify the background color, you'll soon find that the TOC entries are not transparent, leaving a white box around each entry. Finally, a problem with the HTML Help compiler's approach to paths prevents you from reliably accessing custom images for your icons.

Many of the presentation options available occur when creating a window type for the project. Window types allow you to control the navigation pane in which the TOC appears, setting its width, default tab, automatic synchronization between the currently displayed topic file and the TOC entry, and other stylistic options. (For details on creating window types, see Chapter 6, "Creating Magic: The HTML Help Project File.")

## Changing the TOC font

The font used in the TOC (and all other navigation pane items) is selected from the PROJECT tab's OPTIONS dialog. On the GENERAL tab, use the CHANGE button to select the desired font. Be careful, though: fonts not installed on your user's systems will not show up when they access the HTML Help file. So your choices are generally limited to universally available fonts. For a list of fonts installed on particular Windows platforms, see the section *How CSS works with HTML Help—& how it doesn't* in Chapter 4, "Doing It In Style: CSS (Cascading Style Sheets)."

# Available styles

The CONTENTS tab's TABLE OF CONTENTS PROPERTIES dialog includes a STYLES tab for setting some aspects of the TOC window's presentation. While most of the styles work unreliably, if at all, at least three options can be trusted (figure 7.3):

- Dialog Frame adds a title-bar like border at the top of the navigation pane. Clicking and holding on this border allows the user to move the TOC around within the navigation pane's borders.

- Plus/Minus squares adds lightly boxed plus and minus signs next to TOC entries with subordinate entries. The plus sign signals that the entry is "closed" and has subordinate topics that are currently hidden. The minus sign indicates that the entry is "open" with all of its subordinate topics displayed.

- Draw lines between items adds light pencil lines tracing the overall hierarchy of the TOC entries.

To use these styles, click the STYLE tab's ADD button, select the desired style, and click **OK.** Be sure to close and reopen the entire project file to force the Workshop to save your changes. Also note that these customizations to the contents window work only if you have created at least one new window type and specified it as the DEFAULT WINDOW (on the CONTENTS/PROPERTIES/GENERAL tab).

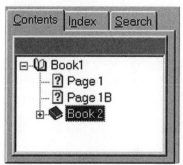

**Figure 7.3  Styles for the TOC navigation pane.** *This table of contents includes a* dialog frame *(the gray bar above Book 1),* plus/minus squares *next to the individual entries, and* drawn lines between items *in the left margin.*

# Binary or not?

The default HTML Help TOC format is known as a "sitemap," and uses a special ActiveX control to display a "map" of the HTML Help "site" described in the table of contents (*.hhc) file. In addition, HTML Help also supports a binary table of contents setting, which is useful in large online Help systems or those using a modular (merged) approach. It is important to note that a binary table of contents can be used only with compiled (compressed) HTML Help; it is not available with uncompiled HTML-based Help. On the other hand, it is required for merged TOCs in modular Help systems.

**CHANGE PROJECT OPTIONS**
button

Setting the type of TOC is, at most, a one-step process: if you want a sitemap version, you need do nothing at all. Choosing a binary table of contents is as simple as clicking the CHANGE PROJECT OPTIONS button (in the Workshop's Project tab), selecting the OPTIONS dialog's COMPILER tab, and choosing the option to CREATE A BINARY TOC. (This choice is only available if the COMPATIBILITY option is set to **1.1 OR LATER.**)

The primary advantages of a binary TOC are support for modular systems using a merged table of contents and faster display for large systems, since a binary TOC doesn't load subordinate branches of the contents tree until the user explicitly accesses them. For example, imagine an HTML Help system with ten top-level branches in the contents where each top-level branch also contains ten subordinate branches. When first opened, a binary TOC only populates (accesses and displays) the top level of the tree (that is, ten books). When the user clicks on a particular top-level book, HTML Help also displays its ten subordinate branches, but it does not access the other 90 books subordinate to the other branches. In contrast, a sitemap TOC populates the entire tree at once (in this case, all 110 books with their component topics).

The limitations of a binary TOC are primarily cosmetic: it does not support sitemap customizations, modified window styles, or any icons other than the book and page icons. Also, it does not work properly with automatically generated TOCs. When generating an automatic TOC for a project with a binary TOC, the compiler seems to pick up the lowest level heading in a topic file and repeat it for all the heading levels above it. For example, imagine that the topic file used as an example includes three levels of headings:

```
<H1>Color Printing</H1>
    <H2>To print a document in color</H2>
            <H3>Adjusting color options</H3>
```

An automatically generated TOC with the binary TOC option set would create the following contents entries, all pointing to the same page:

Adjusting color options

Adjusting color options

Adjusting color options

# Perils ahead

While HTML Help's table of contents features are powerful and offer many areas of improvement over previous systems, the actual implementation is probably the most unreliable part of the HTML Help Workshop. Some challenges can be worked around; others simply require patience while waiting for future releases.

## The unfixables

Probably the most long awaited and urgently desired of the unimplemented features are "information types." Information types would allow the HTML Help author to include a variety of subsets targeted at different users and different situations. For example, some topics could be marked for "novices" while others could be designated for "experts." Novice topics would describe only the required, basic information; the expert versions would include obscure tips and programming tricks. Users could then choose their knowledge level and see only those topics that suit their needs. This feature has its own tab in the CONTENTS/PROPERTIES dialog; it is documented in the Workshop's Help system. But it just doesn't work yet.

Also missing is the ability to create and access a custom set of icons for the table of contents. This worked in earlier versions of the Workshop, where you could create a 42-image strip of 16-color, 16x16 pixel icons, specify the filename in the CONTENTS/PROPERTIES tab, and compile the custom images into your project. Unfortunately, the last several versions of the HTML Help compiler have had a problem with following the paths to this image, and resolutely revert to the supplied images.

# TOC workarounds

Fortunately, most of the problems in the HTML Help's TOC can be worked around, with just a little patience and ingenuity.

- **Two-step icon specification:** If you add a new book or page on the GENERAL tab of the TABLE OF CONTENTS ENTRY dialog and then go directly to the ADVANCED tab, the IMAGE NUMBER field is disabled (figure 7.4). You must click **OK** to exit the dialog, then select the new entry in the contents list and click on the EDIT SELECTION icon (the pencil). Now when you go to the ADVANCED tab, you will be able to change the icon image with the spin controls or by typing in the desired image number. This problem has consistently appeared in all versions of the Workshop, from 1.0 through the most recent version (1.31).

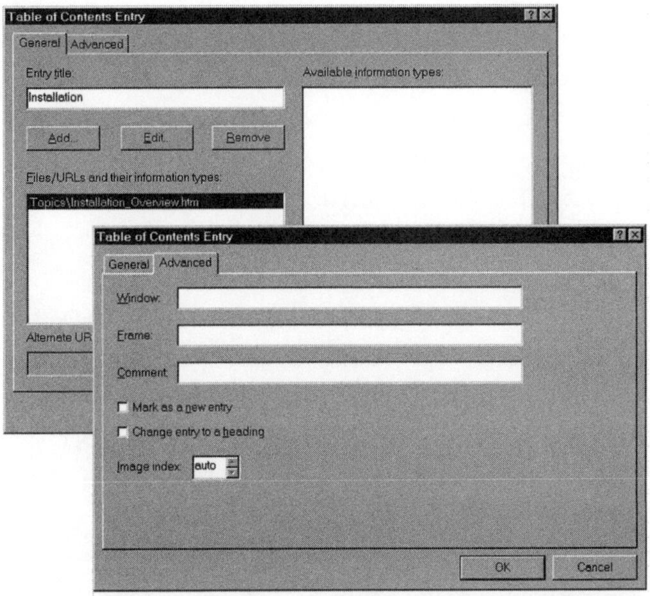

*Figure 7.4 **Disabled Image Index.** The Advanced tab of the Table of Contents Entry dialog does not allow you to change the Image Index when you first create the entry. You must click OK to exit the dialog, then use the Edit selection button to return and change the image index number to reference the desired TOC icon.*

- **Video refresh bug:** As your TOC list grows, it may eventually become longer than the available window space. When this happens, the tab occasionally freezes or goes blank when you finish adding a new item in the TABLE OF CONTENTS ENTRY dialog. To display the current state of the TOC, you must force a video refresh by clicking on the CONTENTS or INDEX tab and then returning to the CONTENTS tab.

- **Mis-synchronized file and topic names:** When you add a new TOC entry by clicking the ADD button in the TABLE OF CONTENTS ENTRY dialog, using the PATH OR URL dialog's list of HTML TITLES is likely to result in the Workshop using the wrong file. For some reason, the actual HTML file (listed as the FILE OR URL) often correlates to the title above or below the one selected. The workaround? Use the BROWSE button to access a standard Windows browse dialog and choose your files there.

- **Filenames with spaces or underlines:** If the name of the file referenced by a TOC entry contains a space or underline, the compiled file often cannot find the designated topic. This has been a problem in Workshop versions through 1.21; it's supposed to be fixed in version 1.3, but it's probably safer just to avoid breaking filenames with either spaces or underlines.

- **TOC changes are not saved:** Do not rely on either the SAVE button in the CONTENTS tab or the FILE menu's SAVE commands. To be sure your changes have been saved, close the Workshop and then reopen the project. At the least, have a Windows Explorer or File Manager window open when you attempt to save your `.hhc` file and make sure that the contents file's MODIFIED date changes.

- **Unreliable hierarchy editing:** The hierarchy of books and pages displayed in the Workshop's CONTENTS file list is not always accurately reflected in the compiled file. Many Help authors have reported setting up their books and pages very carefully, only to find everything at one level—or at levels other than the ones shown in the Workshop. There's no simple workaround for this. You must just keep trying different levels and recompiling to see what works. You can also open the .hhc file in Notepad and manually unravel the <UL> levels.

- **Custom image sets not supported:** The Contents Properties dialog offers the option to create a custom image set with specialized icons for your table of contents. Unfortunately, as of version 1.31, a problem with the HTML Help compiler's approach to paths prevents you from reliably accessing custom images for your icons.

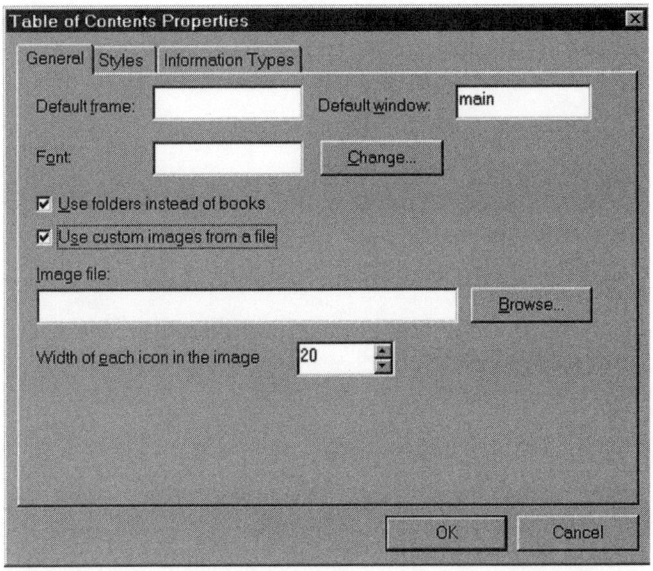

*Figure 7.5 Custom image set. The* Table of Contents Property *dialog suggests that you can specify a file of custom images, but it does not work as of version 1.31x.*

# 8

---

# Out of Many, One:
## Merging Modular Files

Modular systems provide an additional layer of control for HTML Help projects that have grown unwieldy in terms of size or the number of permutations, or that require frequent updates. When a project grows too large for one author to work with at one time, the modular approach allows the project to be split among multiple authors or scheduled for incremental development. Update modules can also be shipped to the customers (or distributed via the Internet), allowing you to add newly available information without requiring a new installation or disturbing the currently installed application and HTML Help system.

Modular HTML Help systems are also invaluable when the project involves different types of expertise or a variety of "plug-in" modules that users purchase separately from the main module. For example, the tree-planting project used for the overview (see Chapter 2: "So How Does It Work? Process & Product Overview") put the bulk of its content within a main file named `tree.chm`, but suggested creating individual files with plants specific to each planting zone (i.e., `zone01.chm`, `zone02.chm`, etc.). Tree.chm, installed with the original product, is complete in itself, but also contains provision (in the form of a project merge statement and INCLUDE statements in  the table of contents) for the integration of the planting zone files.  Not only does this approach allow multiple authors to work on the subordinate products, but the marketing department will like this idea of add-ons to generate additional revenue.  The same idea could be used in a financial product (with separate modules for home and business, or accounts receivable and accounts payable), graphics products (with modules for separate filter packs), etc.

You can see modular HTML Help at work in many Microsoft products.  For example, `iexplore.chm` is the main file for Internet Explorer's HTML Help system; however, a separate `ratings.chm` file provides information about using IE's Internet content ratings feature.  To see for yourself, open the CONTENT AND INDEX for Internet Explorer's online Help and locate the book CONTROLLING ACCESS TO INAPPROPRIATE INTERNET CONTENT.  Right-click any *page* within the book (not the book itself) and select JUMP TO URL.  The CURRENT URL field will show that you are looking at a page within `ratings.chm`.  Checking the CURRENT URL for most of the rest of IE's Help will yield a URL within `iexplore.chm`.

At the present time, the ultimate use of merged HTML Help files may be the MSDN Library from the Microsoft Developer's Network.  Designed for program developers (but also very useful to HTML Help authors), MSDN includes information on development in a wide variety of languages, applications, and platforms, including Visual Studio®, MS Office, Windows CE, Visual Basic®, and HTML Help—it even includes entire online books and periodicals.  This enormous volume of material is distributed in *collections*, a proprietary extension of the merge concept.  Although Microsoft does not yet support this approach for external use, many HTML Help authors are looking into this new technology and anticipating its eventual release to the online Help community.

# What it is & what it does

In a standard HTML Help system, all of the individual topics are compiled into a single .chm file. The user opens this file and navigates through the various topics by selecting entries from the contents or index tabs. For example, in the sample tree-planting project discussed in the earlier overview chapter (Chapter 2, "So How Does It Work? Process & Product Overview"), the user's primary approach through the table of contents looks something like figure 8.1:

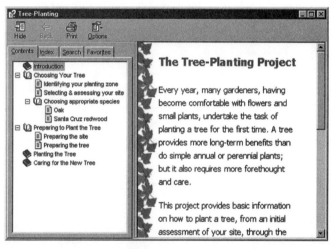

**Figure 8.1 A single-module HTML Help file.** *The basic module of the tree-planting project built in a previous chapter shows a limited selection of species (oak and Santa Cruz redwood).*

In a merged system, the user's experience should be no different: the user opens the HTML Help system by double-clicking a single .chm file or accessing the Help menu of an application. Individual topics are selected from the contents and index tabs, and full-text search supplies a list of topics containing the specified text.

You may remember that the sample tree-planting project suggested preparing for additional modules that would cover more tree species in specific geographic zones. In this approach, the limited choice of two species (oak and Santa Cruz redwood) would be expanded to include an array of species appropriate to the user's location. For example, if the user purchased the West Coast module, the primary approach to the HTML Help system might look something like figure 8.2:

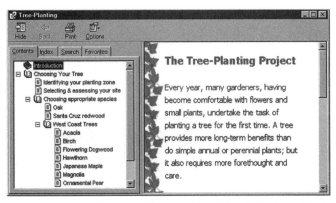

*Figure 8.2 An HTML Help system with a merged module. The basic module shown in the previous graphic described only two species. Adding a merged module named* West Coast Trees *provides the user with a larger variety of choices.*

## The HTML Help author's experience

The remainder of this chapter details the procedures the HTML Help author must follow to created a merged modular project.

As users purchase additional modules, their experience of using the system remains the same except for the expanded selection of appropriate species. The HTML Help author's experience expands more completely and now involves a number of additional steps. In a merged HTML Help system, the items available on the machine when a user opens the Help file determines what actually displays onscreen. Special coding by the HTML Help author makes the changing display possible.

In order to create a modular project, the HTML Help author must create a main project or module (in the example, `tree.chm`) that includes a number of settings that allow the HTML Help system to display additional subordinate projects or modules (in the example, these were named `zone01.chm`, `zone02.chm`, etc., and appear in the table of contents under headings such as WEST COAST TREES and EAST COAST TREES.) The HTML author's additional tasks include defining a window type as the global default setting project options to allow for a binary index, and adding `include` statements to the table of contents. For example, the new species displayed in the example of a merged project shown previously were added to the contents file of the main project by using the INSERT A FILE command available from the Workshop's CONTENTS pane. Another section in the main module's project file lists all possible subordinate modules, whether or not they yet exist, and determines the total universe of possible inclusions.

# Benefits

One of the benefits of a merged system of HTML Help files is the ability to transparently show or hide the table of contents entries for the individual merged modules. When the TOC for the main module opens, it displays the subordinate TOC entries for any subordinate modules present on the user's system. Properly done, the main module's TOC does not have any gaps or error messages for the TOC entries from subordinate modules not currently installed.

In addition to the combined TOC, the merged project displays index entries from the main module and all subordinate modules installed on the user's system. Similarly, a full-text search in the main module returns topics from all installed subordinate modules as well.

Another benefit of merged HTML Help systems is that no recompilation is required for expansion or customization. The compilation is performed when you create the main file with its "stubbed-in" links to current or future modules. Once these stubs are in place, the actual merging process occurs as the user opens the HTML Help file, so that only those files actually present on the user's system appear within the merged project. This approach also allows for expansion, since the actual subordinate files need not exist when the main file is created and compiled. Only the module names are required when the main file is coded, and these may be a predefined set of module names as generic as `module01.chm` and `module02.chm`, since the user never sees these filenames.

# Merging requirements

Merged projects require a single main project that specifies all the subordinate modules. The merged project may then include any of the subordinate modules specified in the main project file's [MERGE] section.

Coordination is the key issue in creating a successfully merged HTML Help system. Properly structured, the individual modules in a merged system should join as invisibly as the chapters in a book. Even as each chapter uses the same page size, paper, fonts, and numbering system, each subordinate project in a modular Help system should have the same window definitions, project options, styles, and cross-file referencing system. In addition, the table of contents and index should transparently span the entire book or HTML Help system.

In order to obtain this coordination wtihin a merged HTML Help system, you must set up a main project that governs the merged system. The main project should contain the following items:

- **A list of merge files in the project file:** The main project file (.hhp) must have a [MERGE FILES] section with a list of the files that will be merged into the project if present at run time. Without this list, the subordinate projects will not be merged. The file list may specify known subordinate modules or provide a list of generic names to allow for future expansion. The list can be created in the HTML Help Workshop from the PROJECT tab's OPTIONS dialog (on the MERGE FILES tab) or it can be written directly into the project file using Notepad. Within Notepad, a merge files list using generic project names might appear something like this:

```
[MERGE FILES]
project01.chm
project02.chm
project03.chm
```

If you use generic filenames, be sure to use these same names when specifying their linkages as INCLUDE statements in the main project's contents file and when creating the subordinate modules. You must also name the modular files with these names before distributing them to users for installation and merging into the main file.

- **Include statements in the table of contents:** The main project's contents file (.hhc) must have INCLUDE statements if you want the subordinate modules to appear on the contents tab of the merged project's navigation pane. Without these statements, the subordinate modules will be accessible only from the merged project's index and search tabs or via inter-project jumps from the main project. Within the main project's contents file, the INCLUDE statements appear the same as any other TOC entry, except that their NAME parameter line takes the form

```
<param name="Merge"
        value="project01.chm::\project01.hhc">
```

  assuming that the subordinate project's compiled file is named project01.chm and its contents file is named project01.hhc. The include statements can be created in the HTML Help Workshop by right-clicking in the list area of the CONTENTS tab and choosing the INSERT FILE option, or the statements may be typed directly into the contents file in Notepad.

In addition, both the main and the subordinate projects should have the following items consistently specified.

The next sections provide specific directions for creating the required elements within the main and subordinate projects.

- **Default window definitions:** The default window definition specifies the size and placement of the Help project's "pages," or viewing area within the HTML Help Viewer. Consistent visual specifications serve the user's need for ease-of-reading; consistent naming conventions and a consistent default window type serve the compiler's needs. Note that the default window type must be consistent for the project, contents, and index files of the main project and all subordinate modules.

- **Project options:** The project options serve the needs of the compiler, defining the ways that the individual modules are put together. These options tell the compiler which choices to make in terms of index and table of content format (merged projects require a binary index but a non-binary table of contents), as well as version compatibility options (merged projects require compatibility with version 1.1 or higher).

- Visual styles: Although the HTML Help compiler does not require consistent style sheets throughout a merged project, coordinated visual styles serve the needs of the user for easy readability. Note that these styles should be coordinated, but do not necessarily need to be completely consistent. To extend our book metaphor, sample or reference chapters may use fonts, colors, and page setups that differ from the main text of the book. Similarly, individual modules in a merged project may use somewhat different styles, but they should not clash. The easiest way to create consistent styles is through the use of cascading style sheets; if necessary, different modules may use variations of the primary style sheet or variant styles may be defined within a single main style sheet.

- Cross-file navigation: Modular projects do support hyperlinks between different modules in the project; however, you should exercise caution in using these jumps, so that you don't end up with broken links when a subordinate module is not installed on the user's system. In order to jump between compiled HTML Help modules, use the following syntax

```
<A HREF="ms-its:project01.chm::/page.htm>
```

where `project01.chm` is the name of the target module and `page.htm` is the name of the target page within that module. If the target module uses directories within its project structure, you should also include the full relative path. For example, if `page.htm` is located in a folder named `section1` within the compiled HTML Help file, the reference would be:

```
<A HREF="ms-its:project01.chm::/section1/page.htm>
```

Do not use a relative path to the `.chm` file itself, since the HTML Help compiler requires all merged modules to be installed within the same directory on the user's machine.

It's also worthwhile to think about consistency in topic titles as well as index and contents entries in the various merged modules. Users may not consciously notice if one module uses gerunds ("printing") while the other uses infinitives ("to print"), but the dissonance may eventually lead to confusion and reduced effectiveness for your HTML Help system.

If some of your users may still have versions of Internet Explorer prior to 4.0, replace `ms-its` with `mk:@MSITStore`.

# Meeting the requirements efficiently

The easiest and most efficient way to insure coordination and consistency among the main and subordinate projects is by creating templates for the project files (`*.hhp`, `*.hhc`, and `*.hhk`) used in each module. While some third-party tools may explicitly support templates for project files, you can also perform the task with Notepad or the HTML Help Workshop. Simply create your main module to meet the merging requirements. Then make a copy of the three project files (`*.hhp`, `*.hhc`, and `*.hhk`), renaming them something like "`template.hhp`," and save them in read-only format. Open these "templates" in Notepad or the Workshop, remove unnecessary topics from the file list (if you're using global style sheet and DHTML files, leave them in the file list), delete the list of merge files (unless you're using the same group of merge modules), and edit out the contents/index entries. Now whenever you start a new module in the merged project, just create new copies of the template files with the appropriate names and you're set to go!

# Procedures for merging

Most of the requirements for creating a merged HTML Help system can either be set up in the HTML Help Workshop or typed directly into the project files using Notepad or another text editor. However, the syntax for some of the requirements is quite complex, so it's generally best to use the Workshop's interface.

This section explains how to set up a merged modular HTML Help system within the Workshop. If you want to work in Notepad, experiment by setting up a test system in the Workshop then opening it in Notepad for examination.

## External procedures

Aside from verbal styles (the syntactical choices that create a consistent linguistic tone for your HTML Help system), there are really only two aspects of a merged system that you will not set up within the Workshop:

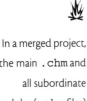

In a merged project, the main .chm and all subordinate modules (.chm files) must be installed in the same directory on the user's system.

- **Visual styles** (fonts, colors, spacing, backgrounds) are best set up primarily with cascading style sheets, although particular styles may be defined and applied within individual HTML topic files.

- **Directory structure** concerns both the organization of components within the individual modules and the way the modules are installed on the user's system.

For information on the best way to organize the components within individual HTML Help modules, refer to the section on *Directory structure* in Chapter 6, "Creating Magic: The HTML Help Project File." As for the installed directory structure, there's only one acceptable plan: HTML Help requires that the main and all subordinate modules in a merged system reside in the same directory on the user's system. Fortunately, this has the side effect of simplifying the list of merged files and any cross-file references incorporated in your HTML Help topics.

# Main module settings

As explained in the previous section, the main module's project file must have
a list of all merged files and its contents file should have INCLUDE statements
providing access to the contents files of subordinate modules.

1. Open the main project file in the HTML Help Workshop.

2. Specify the subordinate files that will be merged into the project.

   ▪ On the PROJECT tab, click the OPTIONS button. Click to move to the
     MERGE FILES tab, then click the ADD button.

CHANGE PROJECT OPTIONS
button

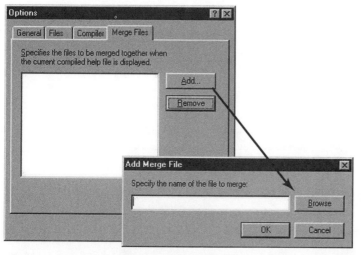

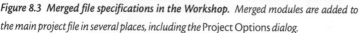

*Figure 8.3 **Merged file specifications in the Workshop.** Merged modules are added to
the main project file in several places, including the* Project Options *dialog.*

   ▪ In the ADD MERGE FILES dialog that appears (figure 8.3), type the name
     of the first subordinate file (for example, project01.chm) and
     click **OK**.   If the subordinate module exists on your system, you
     can use the BROWSE button to find the .chm file and fill in the dialog.
     Be sure that no path is added to the filename; the main and all
     subordinate modules in the merged project must be installed in the
     same directory on the user's system.

     Don't forget the subordinate files need not exist yet. Just type the
     future filename and click **OK** to add the files to the project.

- Repeat the procedure for each subordinate module. When all modules appear in the file list, click **OK** to close the dialog.

- From the FILE menu, choose SAVE PROJECT.

3. Add INCLUDE statements for each subordinate module to the main project's table of contents.

Note that you must select the entry, then right-click it: a two-step process. If you simply right-click an entry, the focus will not change from your previous selection, and you may add the subordinate TOC in the wrong location.

- On the CONTENTS tab, select the entry that should appear immediately before the merged contents file. Usually this will be the last entry of the main file or, if you have already added contents files from other subordinate modules, one of these other INCLUDE statements. With the desired entry selected, right-click and choose INSERT FILE from the shortcut menu (figure 8.4).

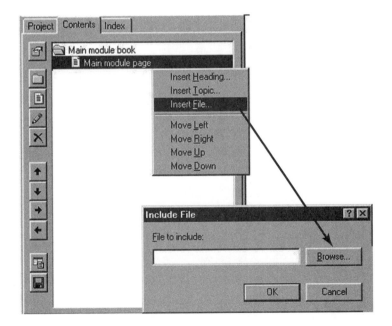

**Figure 8.4 Merging files into the TOC.** *In order to have the contents from the merged modules appear in the main project's TOC, you must add the files to the main project's contents file ( .hhc).*

- In the resulting INCLUDE FILE dialog, type a compiled HTML Help file name/contents name pair in the form

    ```
    project01.chm::/project01.hhc
    ```

    where `project01.chm` is the name of one of the subordinate file and `project01.hhc` is the name of the corresponding contents file. As with the `MERGE FILES` list, the file you add here need not exist yet. However, if the contents file does exist on your system, you can use the BROWSE button to locate the `.chm` file and fill in the blank. You will still have to type in the second part of the statement (`::/project01.hhc`). Again, be sure not to include a path to the file.

- When you click **OK** to close the dialog, the Workshop will display a dialog saying CANNOT FIND THE FILE PROJECT01.CHM::/PROJECT01.HHC. DO YOU WANT TO INCLUDE THIS FILE ANYWAY? Click YES to add the file to the main module's contents list.

- Repeat the procedure for each additional subordinate module.

- From the FILE menu, choose SAVE PROJECT. The added file appears as an `INCLUDE` statement in the main window (figure 8.5)

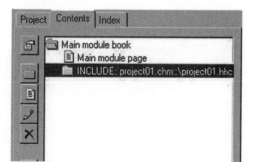

**Figure 8.5 Slashed syntax.** *The "official" syntax for the* INCLUDE *statement uses a forward slash, but the Workshop automatically converts it to a backslash—with no explanation for the switch.*

SAVE ALL FILES &
COMPILE button

VIEW button

4. Compile and test the main module to be sure the included contents files appear at the correct level in the merged table of contents.

- If the subordinate files do not exist on your system, create dummy .chm and .hhc files with the correct names. Store these files in the same directory with the main module's .hhp and .chm files.

- Go to the PROJECT tab and click the SAVE ALL FILES AND COMPILE button.

- When the compile is complete, click the VIEW button. Check the display of the included contents files.

- If the included contents files do not display at the correct level, return to the CONTENTS tab of the main module in the HTML Help Workshop. Select then right-click the misaligned entry and choose MOVE LEFT or MOVE RIGHT to adjust its position. Recompile the project and recheck the alignment of the TOC entries. Continue with adjustments until all entries appear at the correct level.

# Global settings

In addition to the settings for the main module described previously, the default window type definition and certain project options must be set to match in the main and all subordinate project files.

For each of the procedures below, open the main and all subordinate modules in the HTML Help Workshop and follow the steps as described. Be careful to match your options exactly in each file designed for the merged project.

1. Create a common default window type definition in the main and all subordinate modules. Even if you make no changes to the Workshop default settings for window types, merged projects must have at least one named window definition that can be used as the common default window type:

   • On the PROJECT tab, click the ADD/MODIFY WINDOW DEFINITIONS button. In the small dialog that appears, type the name of the window type you wish to create and then click OK.

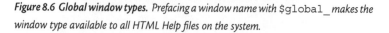

ADD/MODIFY WINDOW
DEFINITIONS button

**Figure 8.6 Global window types.** *Prefacing a window name with* $global_ *makes the window type available to all HTML Help files on the system.*

   For merged projects, it's best to prefix the window name with $global_, so the window name is something like $global_main (figure 8.6). Setting the window type as "global" helps avoid the problem of opening multiple instances of the HTML Help Viewer when the user clicks a topic in a different subordinate module. The $global_ prefix tells HTML Help that, once the initial window is open, it is available to any *.chm file.

For more details on how to create window types, see Chapter 6, "Creating Magic: The HTML Help Project File."

- On the GENERAL tab, type a generic name for the TITLE BAR TEXT. Usually, this is the name of the overall application or project.

- Click the FILES tab. Making sure that the WINDOW TYPE field shows the name of the window type you're defining, set the TOC and INDEX fields to show the main module's .hhc and .hhk files, respectively.

- Click the NAVIGATION PANE tab. Making sure that the WINDOW TYPE field shows the name of the window type you're defining, select the WINDOW WITH NAVIGATION PANE, TOPIC PANE, AND BUTTON bar option if you want to make sure that your merged table of contents is always available in the project. You may also want to select the AUTO SYNC option and set the DEFAULT TAB to CONTENTS.

- Change any other window definition settings as you wish, then click OK to close the dialog and save your window type definition.

2. Specify the new window type as the default for the project, contents, and index in the main and all subordinate modules (figure 8.7).

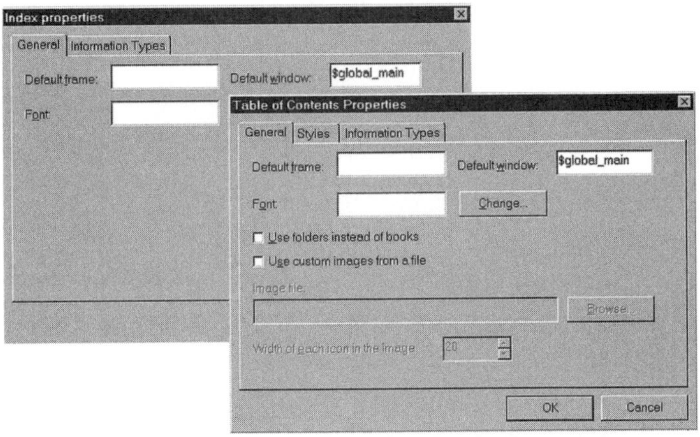

*Figure 8.7 Consistent window types. Specify the same window type for the contents and index of all modules, or the information may show up in unexpected locations—or not at all.*

- On the PROJECT tab, click the OPTIONS button. On the GENERAL tab of the resulting dialog, set the DEFAULT WINDOW to the window type you just created. If you are creating a system in a language other than U.S. English, set the LANGUAGE option.

OPTIONS button
(same for PROJECT, CONTENTS, & INDEX)

- On the CONTENTS and INDEX tabs, click the PROPERTIES button. (Note that the CONTENTS and INDEX tabs use the same icon for their PROPERTIES button as the PROJECT tab uses for the OPTIONS button.) On the GENERAL tab of the resulting dialogs, set the DEFAULT WINDOW to the window type you just created.

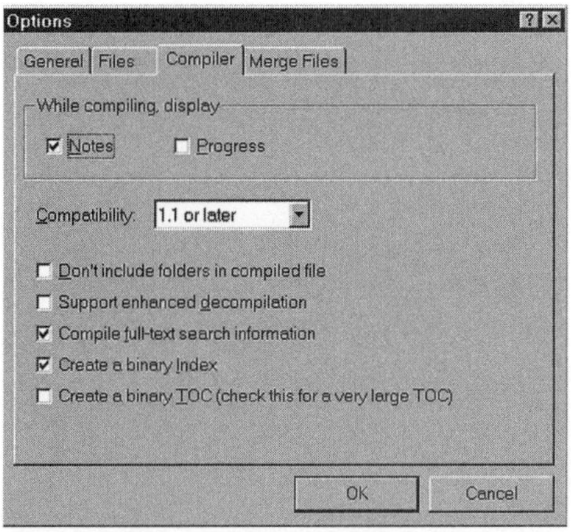

**Figure 8.8 Compiler options.** *Project options must be set to enable modular functionality in the main and all subordinate projects.*

3. Set project options consistently in the main and subordinate modules.
   - On the PROJECT tab, click the OPTIONS button, then select the COMPILER tab (figure 8.8).
   - Set the COMPATIBILITY option to **1.1** OR LATER.
   - Select the CREATE A BINARY INDEX option.
   - Make sure you have *not* chosen the CREATE A BINARY TOC option.
   - Click **OK** to close the dialog.

4. Compile and test the modules to be sure all settings are correct.

- If there are any subordinate files that do not yet exist on your system, create dummy .chm and .hhc files with the correct names. Store these files in the same directory with the main module's .hhp and .chm files.

SAVE ALL FILES &
COMPILE button

- For each subordinate module, go to the PROJECT tab and click the SAVE ALL FILES AND COMPILE button. Make sure the compiled file is saved in the same directory as the main module's compiled file.

VIEW button

- In the main module, go to the PROJECT tab and click the SAVE ALL FILES AND COMPILE button. When the compile is complete, click the VIEW button. Select various topics in the TOC to make sure that they display correctly and in a consistent window.

# Perils ahead

HTML Help's ability to merge modules into an apparently seamless system is very powerful—but it is also very delicate. The settings must be perfectly aligned in the main and all subordinate modules, and sometimes that "perfect alignment" can be achieved only through repeated trial and error. An obvious example is the question of hierarchies in the table of contents: sometimes the only way to make an included TOC appear at the right level is by repeated nudging with the CONTENTS tab's arrow keys!

The following paragraphs offer suggestions for troubleshooting and information about known bugs. With these tips and tricks—and a little patience—you can create a beautifully merged HTML Help system to meet your users' needs.

## General troubleshooting tips

Merged projects are subject to all of the difficulties of single-module projects, plus a whole new set of problems. For general issues, see the troubleshooting sections in the other individual chapters. The following tips refer to problems that occur specifically in merged projects.

- **Verifying file locations:** When experiencing difficulties with a merged system, make sure that all subordinate .chm files (or a dummy file of the same name) are actually present on the system and are stored in the same directory as the main .chm Also, make sure that the main module is installed!

- **Viewing merged projects over the Internet:** Merged projects do not work over Internet http connections. When users open a .chm file from the Web, they will see a dialog asking if they want to save the file to their disk. This dialog does *not* download any included files, so the subordinate modules will not be present in the same directory as the main modules, and will not appear in the merged project.

- **Simplifying filenames:** Another common problem involves .chm or .hhc filenames. Although HTML Help does not require eight-dot-three naming conventions, it works best if the filenames do not include any "breaks" in the form of spaces or underscores. (The length of the filenames doesn't seem to pose any problems.) If your .chm or .hhc files include these "breaks," rename the files to remove the offending break characters, then recompile all modules and try again.

- **Matching default window type settings:** If merged modules do not appear correctly, double-check that the default window type is specified consistently in the PROJECT/OPTIONS, CONTENTS/PROPERTIES, and INDEX/PROPERTIES dialogs for the main and all subordinate modules (figure 8.9). Also make sure that specifications for the default window type are set consistently in the PROJECT/WINDOW TYPES dialog for all modules.

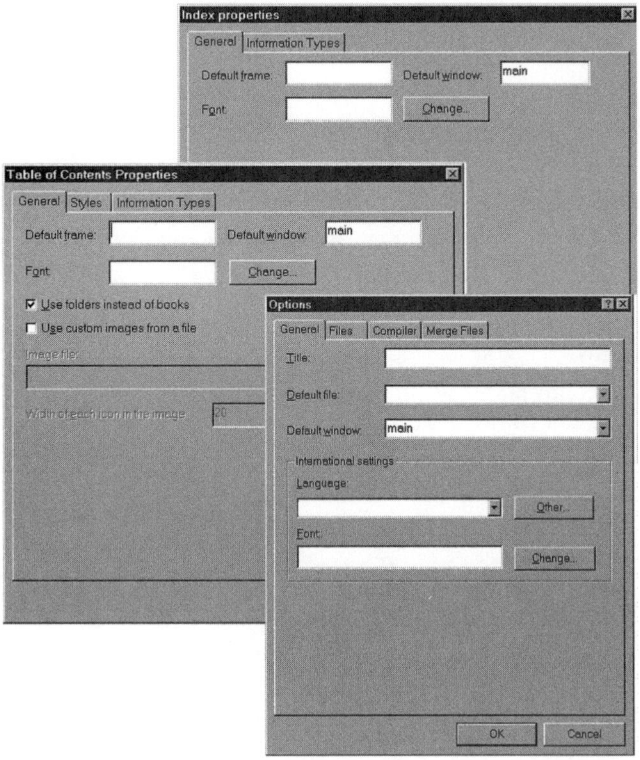

*Figure 8.9 Matching window type settings.* *All modules in a merged project must have the same default window type specified for the project, contents, and index.*

- **Setting a binary TOC:** If your merged modules don't appear, check that you have not turned on the binary TOC option in the main or any subordinate modules. (The binary TOC option is set from the PROJECT tab's OPTIONS dialog. Go to the COMPILER tab and make sure there is no check before the CREATE A BINARY TOC option.)

- **Merged projects for MMC applications:** If you're developing HTML Help for an application that works within the Microsoft Management Console (MMC), it's best not to use a merged system. MMC requires a binary TOC; merged HTML Help systems require a non-binary TOC.

- **Viewing merged projects over the Internet:** Merged projects do not work over Internet http connections. When users open a .chm file from the Web, they will see a dialog asking if they want to save the file to their disk. This dialog does *not* download any included files, so the subordinate modules will not be present in the same directory as the main modules, and will not appear in the merged project.

- **Disappearing indexes:** If the merged project does not display index entries from the subordinate modules, make sure that you have set the main and all subordinate modules to use the binary index option. (The binary index option is set from the PROJECT tab's OPTIONS dialog. Go to the COMPILER tab and make sure the CREATE A BINARY INDEX option has a check mark in its box.) Also, make sure that the main module includes at least one entry in its index (.hhk file), especially if you're working with version 1.3x of the Workshop.

# Troubleshooting the TOC

Merged table of contents files provide some of the greatest sources of frustration to the HTML Help author. Some of the problems you may encounter (and some possible solutions) include:

- **Syntax for INCLUDE statements:** The recommended syntax for including a subordinate module's table of contents is:

  ```
  foobar01.chm::/foobar01.hhc
  ```

  assuming that foobar is the name of both the compiled HTML Help (.chm) file and its table of contents (.hhc) file. However, the HTML Help Workshop converts the forward slash to a back slash in the Workshop display and in the actual .hhc file. In general, the syntax still works. If, however, your included TOCs suddenly disappear, you may wish to edit the .hhc file in Notepad and recompile the project without opening the Contents tab of the HTML Help Workshop.

- **Contents file hierarchy:** Included contents files often appear at a different level in the compiled HTML Help file than that displayed in the Workshop's CONTENTS pane. If an INCLUDE statement looks as if it's at the same level as the previous book or page from the main file, the previous item will become a book (if it isn't already) and the included TOC will be displayed within the book. Use the left-arrow button on the Workshop's CONTENTS tab to move the INCLUDE statement up a level (so it looks as though it's one level *higher*—that is, to the left—than the previous entry). Recompile and check the levels again.

- **TOC Autosync doesn't sync:** Sometimes the autosync feature for the TOC does not work properly for merged projects. This problem occurs most often in projects having duplicate filenames in the various merged modules; for example, many projects start with a file named introduction.htm The solution is to either rename the files with unique names or to set up a directory structure so that the full path differs. (For example, in the sample tree-planting project, you might set up the merged modules with zone01\introduction.htm, zone02\introduction.htm, etc.).

- **Disappearing INCLUDED contents:** Despite the correct syntax and repeated attempts to adjust its hierarchical level, sometimes an In-cluded contents file simply refuses to appear in the merged project. First check the general troubleshooting tips (listed previously) to make sure that you have created a binary TOC, stored the files correctly, and named the modules correctly.

  If the INCLUDED TOCs still do not appear, verify that the top-level entry in the main project's TOC is an actual entry (page or book). Merged TOCs often refuse to display without an actual book or page entry for the opening, top-level entry. If nothing else, use this entry for a welcome screen, a how-to-use-the-help topic, or splash screen.

  Upon rare occasions, INCLUDED TOCs have refused to appear if the immediately preceding entry in the main TOC is also an INCLUDED file. For example, if your main project only serves to gather the subordinate projects together, you may have a main TOC that is nothing but a list of INCLUDED files. In this situation, you may have to add a page or book introducing each subordinate module. Since you can't know for certain if the module will be present on the user's system, the topic must be carefully worded to explain what the potential module is without actually claiming that it is present (generally that means a topic that walks the thin line between online Help and marketing). This problem appeared more frequently under version 1.0 and 1.1 of the HTML Help compiler, but still shows up occasionally.

  Finally, you may need to edit the .hhc file in Notepad. The TOC's sitemap format does not requiring closing </LI> and </UL> tags; however, adding them sometimes helps when nothing else works. Be sure to add closing tags for the entries immediately preceding your INCLUDED files. In particular, if you're trying to force an INCLUDED entry to appear at the top level, make sure that any preceding <UL> "lists" are closed *before* the INCLUDE statement.

# 9

# Accelerating Links:
## Cross-Referencing Options

Cross-referencing is one area where HTML Help leaps ahead of standard HTML pages. Most Web users are familiar with the in-text links of the ubiquitous `<A HREF>` tag and the use of a top or left-hand frame to position the user within the overall "map" of the site. But because Web pages are so often designed to be standalone containers of content and sizzle, the ability to create cross-references is frequently neglected. HTML Help accepts all the standard HTML links, allowing the author to connect content in different parts of the same Web page, across multiple pages in the same project, across multiple HTML Help projects, and in pages located elsewhere on the World Wide Web. But HTML Help also takes these standard links and accelerates them into hyperlinkages through indexing, explicitly grouped cross-references, full-text search, and even shortcuts to other software applications.

HTML's indexing allows users to quickly find the information by typing in the words related to the desired topic. The HTML Help index works as a sort of accelerated version of the classic Yahoo™ or AltaVista® type of Web page "home": a listing of available information categories that you can drill down to find the desired content. But the HTML Help index is a specialized search engine designed for online Help and book-type content rather than an all-purpose tool for Web-crawling. Indexes can be single- or multi-level, and the author can add synonyms to the index list, so that users can find their information without already knowing the "correct" term. In addition, indexes can grow automatically, adding content from new modules in merged projects.

The grouped cross-references in HTML Help provide another means of access to information. These groupings can be based on the same keywords listed in the index, or they can have a separate set of classifications (ALinks), or the author can explicitly list the desired topics. Cross-references based on keywords and ALinks automatically merge the data from multiple projects.

Full-text search provides yet another means of access to the HTML Help project content. Perhaps the easiest of all the cross-referencing mechanisms to implement, full-text search lets the user locate any word, phrase, or combination of words appearing in the project. With the advanced search capabilities, the user can even create complex Boolean queries using AND, OR, NOT, and NEAR, nested as many as five levels deep. Yet the HTML Help author need only specify a handful of settings to enable the full range of search mechanisms.

Finally, HTML Help offers the ability to link to other applications using shortcuts. An HTML Help shortcut provides a one-click method to open another application, in a specific state, with a specific file, even at a specific dialog box. You can also help users set up their Windows machines through the CONTROL PANEL icons—and all it takes from the user is a single click of the mouse.

# Indexes

Indexes provide one of the most popular ways for HTML Help users to access the information they need. Many usability studies have shown that users turn to the index and search tabs more often than they use other navigational facilities, such as the table of contents.

## How it works

In a compiled HTML Help file, the user accesses the index from the navigation pane's INDEX tab (figure 9.1). As the user types the desired term in the box labeled TYPE IN THE KEYWORD TO FIND, the topic list moves to the section of the index matching the letters typed (an effect sometimes called a "word wheel"). Note that the index entries are words and phrases specified by the HTML Help author as *keywords;* they need not appear in the actual topic or represent a topic title. When the user spies an interesting-looking index entry, the associated topic can be opened by double-clicking the index entry or by clicking the index entry once and then clicking the DIS- PLAY button. If the index entry is associated with more than one topic, a

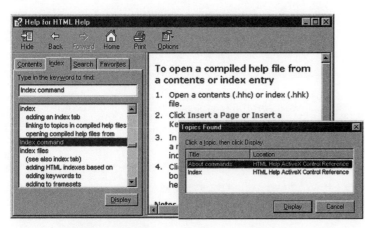

**Figure 9.1 Index tab.** *If the index term is associated with multiple topics, the HTML Help Viewer displays a* Topics Found *dialog listing all available topics.*

TOPICS FOUND dialog displays the titles and location of all associated topics. The user double-clicks the title or clicks the title once and clicks the DISPLAY button. The selected topic file appears in the topic (right) pane.

The mechanics underlying the index can use either of the two index formats supported by HTML Help—binary or sitemap—and, if you choose the binary format, the index keywords can be authored as KLinks in the individual topic files (.htm) or as entries in an index file (.hhk). The choices you make depend on where your HTML Help will be used and your own preferences for working with indexes.

## Binary vs. sitemap indexes

A binary index requires the compiled HTML Help format (so it cannot be used in an uncompiled file for a Web site) and the project's compatibility option set to version 1.1 or higher. When using the binary format, you can author index entries both in an index file (.hhk) created on the Workshop's INDEX tab and as keywords (KLinks) inserted directly into individual HTML topic files. When the binary index is compiled into the project, the compiler merges together both entry types and sorts them in alphabetical order. In merged modular projects, the compiled binary indexes (with both kinds of keywords) from all installed modules are merged and resorted at run time, so that all index entries from all modules appear in the same index in a single A to Z ordering. (More precisely, it's A to Z in American English and most European languages, but the exact definition of "alphabetical order" depends on the project's language setting.)

A binary index is smaller than a sitemap index (in fact, the compiler creates a binary index by compressing a sitemap index, if one is present) and is automatically sorted when the project is compiled (no author intervention or customization is possible). It offers maximum flexibility in merging index entries from disparate sources (the .hhk file, KLinks in topic files, and from multiple modules in a merged project).

A sitemap index, on the other hand, offers the flexibility of using either compiled or uncompiled systems. It also allows you to present index topics in any order you like (that is, it is not limited to alphabetical order). It is, however, more constrained in its sources, since it does not incorporate KLinks from topics or merge the indexes from multiple modular projecrts.

Basically, a sitemap index is an HTML file (with an .hhk extension) in much the same format as the default HTML Help table of contents sitemap format. Both use an ActiveX control to display a "map" of the HTML Help site. Like the table of contents, a sitemap index can be created manually in Notepad or another text editor, but the recommended editing environment for the index is the HTML Help Workshop.

The index file's sitemap format (like a sitemap table of contents) is a variation of an unordered list where the <BODY> looks something like this:

```
<BODY>
  <OBJECT type="text/site properties">
    <param name="WindowName"
value="DefaultWindowType">
  </OBJECT>
  <UL>
    <LI> <OBJECT type="text/sitemap">
      <param name="Name" value="Main index entry">
      <param name="Name" value="Main Topic Title">
      <param name="Local" value="MainTopicFile.htm">
    </OBJECT>
    <UL>
      <LI> <OBJECT type="text/sitemap">
        <param name="Name" value="SubIndex entry">
        <param name="Name" value="SubIndex Title">
        <param name="Local" value="SubTopic.htm">
        <param name="Name" value="SubIndex
Title2">
        <param name="Local" value="SubTopic2.htm">
      </OBJECT>
    </UL>
  </UL>
</BODY>
```

For additional information about the sitemap format, see *Manual TOC creation* in Chapter 7, "Navigating the Waters: Table of Contents."

The initial object tag appearing at the beginning of the <BODY> section identifies the file as a sitemap and specifies the name (`param name="WindowName"`) of the window type in the HTML Help project that will be used to display the index (here, `value="DefaultWindowType"`).

The rest of the file is an unordered list or, in the case of a multi-level index such as the one excerpted previously, a series of nested unordered lists. Note that most of the sitemap coding (such as the ordered list <OL> and object tags) uses the typical HTML form of start tag, information, end tag. However, individual list items <LI> do not require an end tag in a sitemap (although adding end tags sometimes helps when troubleshooting).

The parameters for each <LI>begin with two NAME parameters, one with a value specifying the text that appears in the index (for example, `value="Main index entry"`) and a second with a value (for example, `value="Main Topic Title"`) showing the HTML page's <TITLE>. This title will display in a TOPICS FOUND dialog if the index entry has multiple associated files. Each <LI> list item also has a LOCAL parameter with a value specifying the filename and path (relative to the project file) of the associated HTML topic file (for example, `value="MainTopicFile.htm"`).

The index excerpted previously—with two levels of index entries and two associated files for the subentry—would display something like figure 9.2 if a user double-clicked the subentry:

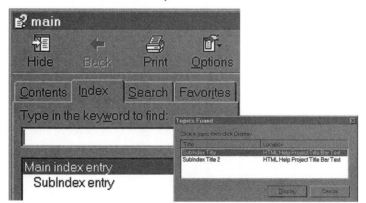

*9.2 Sample index file. The previous sitemap code produces this partial index. Note that the selected entry, which has multiple associated topics, activates a Topics Found dialog.*

## Location, location, location: Where to put keywords

Not only does HTML Help supports two types of index files, it also supports two styles of keyword creation. You can specify the keywords and their associated HTML files in an .hhk file (usually created from the Workshop's INDEX tab) *or* you can insert the keywords as KLinks in the individual HTML topic files. Specifying the keywords in the index file makes it easier to index consistently (so you don't forget if you used "print" or "printing" as your keyword) and it works for both compiled and uncompiled HTML Help files (so it's reusable if you're going to put the HTML Help file on a Web site). Putting the keywords as KLinks in individual HTML files provides better reusability if an HTML topic file is likely to be included in various projects. The KLink approach may also make it easier to index as you are writing your topics, rather than at the end of the project. A binary index supports both approaches and merges the results; a sitemap index only includes the information from the .hhk file.

If you are creating a binary index, you may use KLinks in topic files *and* keywords in index files. The compiler will combine all entries into a single index.

The first approach (specifying the keywords and their associated HTML files in an .hhk file) creates a sitemap index as described in the previous section. The second approach, adding a KLink to the individual topic files, inserts an <OBJECT> tag within the body of the HTML file, where the inserted tag takes the form:

```
<OBJECT
 TYPE="application/x-oleobject"
 CLASSID="clsid:1e2a7bd0-dab9-11d0-b93a-00c04fc99f9e">
 <PARAM NAME="Keyword" VALUE="foo">
</OBJECT>
```

The code for the <OBJECT> tag is identical in every KLink, except for VALUE text (here, "foo"). If you add multiple entries to a KLink <OBJECT> tag, the entries are separated by semicolons (for example VALUE="foo; foo2"). This text appears as an index entry on the INDEX tab of the final compiled file's navigation pane and, when the user selects the index entry, the topic file containing the <OBJECT> tag appears in the topic pane.

# Setting up an index

Creating the index in your HTML Help file requires you to specify the desired keywords (either by adding KLinks in the individual topic files or by creating an index file and adding keywords to it directly), and to specify the project settings.

## To create a binary index

1.  Open the project in the Workshop.

2.  Add the KLinks in the desired HTML topic files (.htm).

    -   Open the desired topic file in the HTML Workshop. If the file is not yet in the project, click the PROJECT tab's ADD/REMOVE TOPIC FILES button (second from the top) and use the ADD and BROWSE buttons to locate the file and add it to the project. Once the topic file is in the project, double-click the topic file in the PROJECT tab list of included [FILES].

    -   When the HTML file appears in the Workshop's right pane for editing, position the cursor within the topic's <BODY> and </BODY> tags. For easiest editing, it's usually best to position the cursor just prior to the closing body tag </BODY>.

    -   From the Workshop's EDIT menu, select COMPILER INFORMATION. On the KEYWORDS tab, click ADD.

    -   In the ADD KEYWORD dialog that appears, type the desired keywords, then click OK to close the dialog.

        -   To add multiple keywords at once, type each keyword followed by a semicolon.

        -   To add a secondary keyword, first enter the primary keyword on its own. Then reopen the ADD KEYWORD dialog and type the primary keyword, a comma, and the secondary keyword.

For example, if you wish to have a primary keyword of "printing" with secondary entries for "color" and "black-and-white" under it, you will need to use the ADD KEYWORD dialog three times, once each to add *printing, printing, color,* and *printing, black-and-white.*

- You may add, remove, or change the keywords in the <OBJECT> tag by using the ADD, REMOVE, and EDIT buttons. When you have finished all your changes, click OK TO return to the Workshop. To make sure all changes to the topic file have been saved, close the file by clicking the X in the *file's* top right corner and answering YES if you are asked whether you want to save your changes.

3. Repeat the previous step with every file for which you want to add keywords as KLinks. Note that, since the code for the KLink is always identical accept for the Value of the keyword, you can also index individual HTML topic files by cutting and pasting the following code. For each desired keyword, repeat the <PARAM NAME="Keyword" VALUE="foo"> line, replacing foo with a keyword. You must also make sure the files are included in the project.

```
<OBJECT
 TYPE="application/x-oleobject"
 CLASSID="clsid:1e2a7bd0-dab9-11d0-b93a-00c04fc99f9e">
 <PARAM NAME="Keyword" VALUE="foo">
</OBJECT>
```

4. Set up the HTML Help project's options to use the KLinks from the topic files and to create a binary index.

- On the Workshop's PROJECT tab, click the OPTIONS button.

- In the OPTIONS dialog, go to the FILES tab and click to select the textbox labeled INCLUDE KEYWORDS FROM HTML FILES.

- Go to the COMPILER tab and click to select the textbox labeled CREATE A BINARY INDEX.

- Click OK to close the dialog.

The INCLUDE KEYWORDS FROM HTML FILE options adds a line to the project file saying AutoIndex=Yes. But don't worry: unlike an auto TOC, an "auto index" (here, KLinks) does not overwrite manual edits to the index file.

5. If you want to combine the KLink index entries with entries from an index (.hhk) file, create the index file by following the instructions in the next section, *To create an index file (sitemap or binary index)*.

6. When you next compile your HTML Help project (remember, KLinks require a binary index and a compiled project), all KLink keywords from the topic files will appear in your index, alphabetized and merged with any entries inserted directly into the Index (.hhk) file.

## To create an index file (sitemap or binary index)

1. Open the desired project in the HTML Help Workshop.

2. Set up the project options.

CHANGE PROJECT OPTIONS

button

- Go to the PROJECT tab and click the CHANGE PROJECT OPTIONS button (top button on the left side).

- In the resulting OPTIONS dialog, click the FILES tab and fill in the INDEX FILE section by typing a file name or use the BROWSE button to locate the desired file.

- If you are creating a binary index and want to merge KLink keywords from the topic files with the entries in the index (*.hhk) file, click to select the textbox labeled INCLUDE KEYWORDS FROM HTML FILES.

- To have the compiler compile the .hhk file as a binary index (with or without KLinks), go to the COMPILER tab and click to select the textbox labeled CREATE A BINARY INDEX.

- When you have made all desired changes, click OK to close the dialog.

3.  Set up the project to use the index in the desired window.

    ▪   Still on the HTML Help Workshop's PROJECT tab, click the ADD/
        MODIFY WINDOW DEFINITIONS button (third button down on the left
        side).

    ADD/MODIFY WINDOW
    DEFINITIONS button

    ▪   In the resulting WINDOW TYPES dialog, click the FILES tab and set its
        INDEX field to the same file that you specified in the PROJECT/OPTIONS
        dialog.

    ▪   Go to the NAVIGATION PANE tab and make sure that you have
        selected the WINDOW WITH NAVIGATION PANE, TOPIC PANE, AND BUTTON
        BAR option. Set any other options as desired, then click OK to
        close the dialog.

4.  Create the index file and set its properties.

    ▪   Click the Workshop's INDEX tab. If the index file you specified in
        the above procedures does not exist, a dialog appears saying you
        have not yet associated an index with the project, and offers to
        create a new file or open an existing one.

        If you do have an existing file and the dialog is in error, choose
        OPEN AN EXISTING INDEX FILE, and click OK. In the dialog that appears,
        choose the appropriate .hhc file and click SAVE.

        If you want to create a new file, choose OPEN A NEW INDEX FILE and
        click OK. In the dialog that appears, navigate to the desired folder,
        type the correct FILE NAME, and click SAVE.

    ▪   When the INDEX window opens with your existing entries or a
        blank window, click the INDEX PROPERTIES button (top button on
        the left). On the GENERAL tab, specify the DEFAULT WINDOW, using
        the same window name you just used in step 3 above. You may
        also specify the FONT for the index, if desired. Click OK to close
        the dialog.

The options offered
on the INFORMATION
TYPES tab do not work
as of HTML Help
workshop, version
1.3x.

5. Create the desired index entries:

INSERT A KEYWORD
button

- Click in the window containing the existing keywords (if you have no keywords yet, this window will be blank). Click on the INSERT A KEYWORD icon (second from the top on the left). If necessary, position your keyword by responding to the dialog asking DO YOU WANT TO INSERT THIS ENTRY AT THE BEGINNING OF THE INDEX?

- In the resulting INDEX ENTRY dialog, type the text that will appear in the index into the KEYWORD text field.

- Click the ADD button to specify the target file or URL for the entry. In the PATH OR URL dialog, be sure to choose the desired file based on the FILE OR URL field at the bottom, or by using the BROWSE button. Note that, although you may type new text into the TITLE text box, the index will not pick up this text. Instead, it always displays the text specified between the `<TITLE>` and `</TITLE>` tags in the selected HTML file. When you have selected the desired file, click OK.

- If you want to associate multiple topic files with a single keyword, click the ADD button again and add another file. You may repeat this step as necessary. With multiple destinations, clicking the index entry in the compiled HTML Help file will display a TOPICS FOUND dialog listing all available topics.

- If you want to specify a particular file for display when the other associated files are not available, click the ADD/EDIT button next to the ALTERNATE URL field, and add the desired file. This option is often used to point to a generic HTML file with an error message such as "Sorry, topic could not be found. For more information, try www.ourWebSite.com".

- If you want to have this index entry jump to another keyword, use the ADD button to specify the target file or URL. Then click the ADVANCED tab and click to select the check box labeled TARGET IS ANOTHER KEYWORD.

- If you want to have the associated file for this index entry open in a special Window Type or frame, use the **ADD** button to specify the target file or URL. Then click the **ADVANCED** tab and type in the name of the desired **WINDOW** or **FRAME.**

- When you finish specifying all aspects of this keyword, click **OK.**

6. To edit an existing index entry, click on the entry, then click the **EDIT SELECTION** button (third from the top). Use the previous techniques to revise you index entry, then click **OK** to save it.

**EDIT SELECTION**
button

7. To delete an entry from the TOC, select the entry in the index entry list, then click the **DELETE SELECTION** button. Be aware that the **UNDO** command on the Workshop's **EDIT** menu does not work for deleted index entries.

**DELETE SELECTION**
button

8. To adjust the order or hierarchy of the index entry list, select the entry you want to change, then click one of the buttons on the left.

- The **UP** and **DOWN** arrows move the entry up or down in the list order; that is, if the entry is second in the list, clicking the **UP** button makes it the first entry in the list and clicking the **DOWN** button makes it the third item in the list. These buttons do not change the entry's level (hierarchical position).

**UP & DOWN (order)**
buttons

- The **RIGHT** and **LEFT** arrows demote and promote the entry one level; that is, clicking the **RIGHT** arrow indents the entry one level to the right and clicking the **LEFT** arrow removes one level of indentation from the entry.

**RIGHT & LEFT**
**(hierarchical)** buttons

- The **AZ** button automatically alphabetizes the existing index entries. Remember that the index will be resorted during compile if you are creating a binary index.

**AZ (alphabetize)**
button

9. When you finish adjusting your index, click the SAVE button. However, note that this button does not always work, so it's best to also close the entire Workshop and then reopen the project. This activates a message asking if you want to save the files—a save action that does work reliably.

10. When you compile your HTML Help project, the index file (including KLinks, if set up) will appear in the Navigation pane of the .chm file.

## Troubleshooting index settings

Since many of the steps involved in creating an index overlap and some of the project options (such as the default window) appear in multiple locations, it's easy to get confused. If you experience unexpected situations in your index file, check the following settings.

1. If you are missing KLinks in the index, check the following:

   - Is the project set to create a binary index? On the PROJECT tab, click the OPTIONS button. On the COMPILER tab, make sure that the textbox labeled CREATE A BINARY INDEX is checked.

   - Is the project set to add the KLink keywords? On the PROJECT tab, click the OPTIONS button. Go to the FILES tab and make sure the INCLUDE KEYWORDS FROM HTML FILES option is selected.

2. If the index is not appearing or opens a new window, check the following:

- On the PROJECT tab, click the OPTIONS button, then select the FILES tab. Make sure the correct INDEX FILE is named here.

- On the Workshop's PROJECT tab, click the ADD/MODIFY WINDOW DEFINITIONS button, then select the FILES tab. Make sure the INDEX field is set to the same file specified in the PROJECT/OPTIONS dialog.

- On the Workshop's INDEX tab, click the INDEX PROPERTIES button, then select the GENERAL tab. Make sure the DEFAULT WINDOW is set to the same window name used in the PROJECT tab's ADD/MODIFY WINDOW DEFINITIONS dialog.

3. If the index is composed entirely of KLinks included from the topic (*.htm) files, it does not officially require a pre-created index (*.hhk) file but creating one sometimes fixes problems with missing indexes. If your KLink index is not working correctly, create and specify an index file with the following steps:

- Open the project in the HTML Help Workshop and click on the INDEX tab. When an INDEX NOT SPECIFIED dialog appears, choose to CREATE A NEW INDEX FILE, click OK, specify a name and location for the file, and click SAVE. (If you do not see the INDEX NOT SPECIFIED dialog, proceed to the next step.)

- Click the INDEX PROPERTIES button, then select the GENERAL tab. Make sure the DEFAULT WINDOW is set to the window name specified in the PROJECT's ADD/MODIFY WINDOW DEFINITIONS dialog.

- On the PROJECT tab, click the ADD/MODIFY WINDOW DEFINITIONS button, then select the FILES tab. Choose the DEFAULT WINDOW specified in the INDEX PROPERTIES dialog and make sure the INDEX field is set to correct file.

- On the PROJECT tab, click the OPTIONS button, then select the FILES tab. Make sure the same INDEX FILE is named here.

4. If a binary index is alphabetizing incorrectly, check the following:

- On the PROJECT tab, click the OPTIONS button. On the GENERAL tab, check the LANGUAGE setting.

- You may also find that it is necessary to compile the final HTML Help project with your machine set to the same language (in the Windows Control Panel).

5. If the index displays in an unexpected font, check the following:

- On the PROJECT tab, click the OPTIONS button. On the GENERAL tab, check the FONT setting.

- On the INDEX tab, click the OPTIONS button. On the GENERAL tab, check the FONT setting.

- Make sure that both FONT settings use a font available on your users' systems. For a list of fonts installed on particular Windows platforms, see the section *How CSS works with HTML Help—& how it doesn't* in Chapter 4, "Doing It In Style: CSS (Cascading Style Sheets)".

6. If the index for a merged modular project displays "No topics found" for some users, check if they are running the HTML Help from a CD. HTML Help uses a temporary `.chw` file (similar to the Windows Help `.gid` file) to store the merged keywords. If it cannot write the `.chw` to the CD when the user initiates a search, the search may fail. To correct the situation, be sure to open the `.chm` files once before shipping, and to include the `.chw` file this creates when you create the CD master. (This problem was supposed to be fixed in version 1.21a of the HTML Help Workshop, so you may also want to check what version you're using.)

7. If the .chm crashes or freezes when the user accesses some topics from their index entries but works on other index entries in the same file, check the location of the <OBJECT> tags in the topic pages (*.htm) being accessed. The standard location for the <OBJECT> tag is in the <BODY> of the topic. However, some HTML Help authors have reported crashes in a system where some <OBJECT> tags were located in the <HEAD> and others were located in the <BODY>, and they were best able to fix the problem by moving all <OBJECT> tags to the <HEAD> section. If your HTML Help system displays this behavior, experiment with the location of your <OBJECT> tags.

8. If you are using KLinks in topic files and the second-level keywords do not appear correctly under the first-level keywords, make sure that you have specified the first-level keyword at least once in the project. You can specify the primary keyword once in any file of the project; it does not need to be specified in the same file as the secondary keyword.

# Cross-references

HTML Help lets you create cross-referencing links that group related topics and link them all one to the other. These linkages serve much the same function in HTML Help files that the *See also* notation serves in books and manuals: both provide a way for the author to point the user to other "related topics" on the same or similar subjects. But the HTML Help implementation offers some advantages over the static print notation, including the ability to automatically update the list of topics when new topics are added. In addition, the user need not "page through" the entire project as a reader must do with a book; rather, they click the cross-reference button or link, choose the desired topic from a TOPICS FOUND dialog or a pop-up menu, and click to jump to the selected topic.

## Available options

HTML Help supports three types of cross-references: Keyword Search (using KLinks), ALink Search, and Related Topics.

A Keyword Search with KLinks is probably the most efficient way to create cross-referencing links, since the KLinks can also appear as entries in the project's index. However, you can also use an ALink Search, which differs from a KLink search in two ways: ALinks are not included in the index; and the actual ALink name never appears to the user. This last differentiation can be useful if you are localizing your project into several languages, since these link names need not be translated. Both ALink and KLink cross-references are updated automatically as new topics with the cross-reference name are added to the project.

The final way to create cross-referencing links is with the Related Topics control. Unlike ALink and KLink searches, the Related Topics control does not update automatically; instead, it is based on a static list of topic (.htm) files entered by the HTML Help author. Thus, it is not much different from the standard HTML list of links that appears at the bottom of many

Web pages. The primary value of the Related Topics control is aesthetic, since it displays a neat button or image instead of a list of text links.

However, you may want to use a standard HTML list of links for related topics, for reasons that benefit both you as an author and your users. When an associate at Hewlett-Packard conducted usability tests that gave end users the choice of Related Topics displayed in a menu, Related Topics displayed in a Topics Found dialog, and an HTML list of links, users preferred the HTML list of links. Their preference relates to the original concept of this book, that much of the power of HTML Help springs from users' familiarity with and acceptance of HTML standards. In addition, the links list required fewer clicks to access the desired information.

## To create cross-referencing links

1. Add the cross-reference names to the topics you wish to display when the cross-reference link is activated. If you will be using related topics, skip to step 3.

   - Open one of the HTML topic files that will be a target destination for your cross-reference link.

   - Position your cursor anywhere in the file's <BODY>, then go to the EDIT menu and choose COMPILER INFORMATION. In the dialog that appears, click either the KEYWORD or the ALINK NAMES tab, depending on the format you will use.

   - Click ADD. In the dialog that appears, type in the name you will use for this set of cross-references. You may specify multiple names if you separate them by a semicolon. Click OK. You can then use the ADD, EDIT, and REMOVE buttons to add more names, change existing items, or remove an item. When all desired names have been created, click OK.

   - Close and save the file by clicking the X in the *file's* top right corner and answering YES if asked to save changes.

2. Repeat the previous step for every file you wish to use as a target destination.

3. Add an instance of the HTML Help ActiveX control object in the topic that will display the option to jump to the cross-referenced topics.

   - Open the file where you wish to have the cross-referencing option.

   - From the TAGS menu, choose HTML HELP CONTROL. In the dialog that appears, use the drop-down list labeled SPECIFY THE COMMAND to choose ALINK SEARCH, KEYWORD SEARCH, or RELATED TOPICS. If you are going to have other instances of the control in this file, or if you will use the search for scripting, enter an ID name in the bottom text box. Click NEXT.

   - In the HHCTRL DISPLAY TYPE dialog, choose whether the cross-referencing can be accessed from a button on the page or if it will be hidden (for scripting). Then choose whether it will DISPLAY ON A POP-UP MENU (if not selected, the associated topics display in a TOPICS FOUND dialog), and whether the Help Viewer will DISPLAY DIALOG OR MENU EVEN IF ONLY ONE TITLE. Click NEXT.

   - If you chose to display the cross-referenced topics as a button, you'll see the HHCTRL: BUTTON OPTIONS dialog. Select whether to display text, a bitmap, or an icon on the button, with the text box at the bottom changing to accommodate your selection. Make a choice and then specify the text, bitmap, or icon. Click NEXT.

   - **If you are creating a Keyword Search or an ALink Search,** you will see a dialog for specifying the KLink or ALink names. Click the ADD button and type in the name you used for the cross-referencing links in the HTML topic files. You can then use the ADD, EDIT, and REMOVE buttons to add more names, change existing items, or remove an item. You may optionally choose to specify the COMPILED HTML FILE to use, and the name of the FRAME or WINDOW in which the jumps display. Click NEXT.

You can change the size of the button by opening the HTML source for the file and changing the WIDTH and HEIGHT values for the <OBJECT>.

**If you are creating Related Topics,** you will see a dialog for specifying the topic files for this group. Click the ADD button and type in the TITLE that will display in the TOPICS FOUND dialog or pop-up menu, the FILE/URL that will display when the title is selected, and, if desired, an ALTERNATE URL to display if the first choice is unavailable. Click OK. You can then use the ADD, EDIT, and REMOVE buttons to add more topic files, change existing items, or remove an item. You may optionally choose to specify the name of the FRAME or WINDOW in which the jumps display. Click NEXT.

- Click FINISH to close the Wizard dialogs and return to the Workshop.

- To save the file and your changes to it, close the file by clicking the X in the *file's* top right corner and answering YES if you are asked whether you want to save your changes.

4. Compile the project and test the files to make sure all cross-references work as desired.

# Full-text search

Full-text search (FTS) is perhaps the simplest yet most powerful of HTML Help's navigation capabilities.   By simply typing in a word or part of a word, the user can immediately see a list of all topics containing that word. More sophisticated users can even use Boolean terms, wildcards, and nested expressions to specify their search terms.  And yet, the implementation of full-text search takes only a few moments.

## How it works

In a compiled HTML Help file, the user accesses full-text search from the Navigation  pane's SEARCH tab.  The user types the desired search term in the text box labeled TYPE IN THE WORD(S) TO SEARCH FOR,  then clicks the LIST TOPICS button.  After a moment's search, the window displays a list of topics and their location. To open one of the listed topics, the user can double-click the title or click the title once and then click the DISPLAY button.

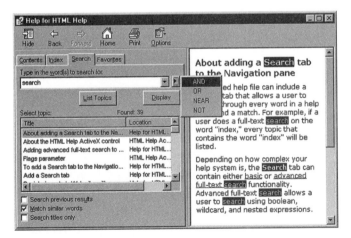

*Figure 9.3  Advanced full-text search*.  *Advanced full-text search  facilities include highlighted search terms in the topic, a full results list, and advanced options such as Boolean terms (AND, OR, NEAR, NOT) and searching within titles or previous results.*

When the selected topic opens, all occurrences of the search term(s) are highlighted (as shown in figure 9.3). The user can turn the highlighting feature on and off by selecting the OPTIONS button and toggling between SEARCH HIGHLIGHT ON and SEARCH HIGHLIGHT OFF. In a very long topic, or with a very common word (and no stop list), only the first 500 instances of the search word will be highlighted.

Figure 9.3 shows a compiled HTML Help file with advanced search features enabled by the author (from the WINDOW TYPES dialog's NAVIGATION PANE tab). Advanced search adds the ability to use Boolean operators, wildcards, and nested expressions for search terms, as well as the three search options shown at the bottom of the window: SEARCH PREVIOUS RESULTS, MATCH SIMILAR WORDS, and SEARCH TITLES ONLY.

- **Search previous results** lets the user narrow the search by adding new criteria and searching only the results of the previous search. Once chosen, this selection is retained as a user preference when the HTML Help file is next opened.

- **Match similar word**s tells the search engine to include in its search common grammatical variations of the search term, such as its plural or the addition of endings such as *-ing* or *-ed* (e.g., *add* would also find *adds, added,* and *adding*).

- **Search titles only** provides a quicker but less complete search, based only on the words in the topic titles, not on the full text of the topics. Note that this option searches all HTML topics in the project, even those without an entry in the table of contents.

If you select SEARCH PREVIOUS RESULTS during testing, be sure to deselect the option before shipping the file to customers, or they will start out with this option selected—which poses a problem when they haven't yet performed a search.

Advanced search also allows the user to create more complex searches using Boolean operators, wildcards, and nested expressions.

- **Boolean operators** can be typed directly into the text box or accessed by clicking the arrow to the right of the text box. These terms include AND, OR, NOT, and NEAR. If the user types in these terms, they must be specified in word form (AND, OR, NOT), not by their mathematical operators (&, |, !). All capitals are preferred, for clarity if nothing else.

- **AND** is the default used when no operators are specified; that is, if the user types "print pages," the search engine assumes "print AND pages," and looks only for topics containing both terms.

- **OR** finds topics with any one of the listed terms. For example, if the user types "print OR pages," the search engine displays all topics containing either the word *print* or the word *pages* or any of their grammatical variations (*prints, printing, printed, page, paging,* etc.).

- **NOT** finds all topics that contain the first term of the expression but not the second term. For example, if the user searches for "print NOT pages," the search engine displays all topics that do contain the word *print* but do not contain the word *pages*.

- **NEAR** finds all topics where the specified words exist within eight words of one another. This is different from searching for a specific phrase, which is accomplished by typing the phrase within quotation marks. For example, "print NEAR pages" finds all topics where the words *print* and *pages* appear within eight words of one another, but "print pages" (in quotes) finds only those topics in which the word *print* (or its grammatical variations) came immediately before the word *pages* (or its grammatical variations).

- **Wildcards** let the user substitute ? (question mark) and * (asterisk) for unknown characters. The question mark signifies a single unknown character (so that "wom?n" finds both *women* and *woman*), while the asterisk signifies one or more unknown characters (so that "w*n" would find *woman* and *women* as well as *widen, within,* and *wooden*).

- **Nested expressions** allow the user to control the order of the expression by using parentheses in pairs nested as many as five levels deep. Nesting changes the search order and the way the search engine combines terms. The entire realm of possibilities for nesting expressions occupies significant time in a mathematics or logic course; briefly, nesting causes the search engine to read the search terms from the innermost parentheses on out, as opposed to the American/European standard left-to-right-reading order.

# Search vs. index

HTML Help's SEARCH tab differs from the INDEX tab in that SEARCH looks for the specified terms throughout the full text of all the topics in the project, while the index displays terms explicitly specified by the HTML Help author, whether or not those terms appear in the actual topic text. Both approaches present advantages as well as challenges.

SEARCH lets the user find any word that actually appears in the help topic text, including some common variations of the search terms (such as *create, creating, creates*). If the author implements advanced search capabilities, the user can group multiple terms to create complex search parameters. In any case, SEARCH accesses *every* word in the HTML Help project *but only* those words in the project; it does not allow for synonyms.

HTML Help's INDEX, on the other hand, does allow the Help author to include a variety of synonyms (e.g., *changing* and *editing* can point to topics that actually use the word *modifying*). But the INDEX does not allow the user to combine multiple search terms. Also, because the index terms must be explicitly specified by the HTML Help author, it is more time-consuming to build an index than to implement the search features.

In merged modular projects, both the index and the full-text search from all modules are combined at run time (when the user opens the file).

# Setting up full-text search

In order to create a compiled HTML Help file with advanced full-text search capabilities, you must set the HTML Help compiler to compile the FTS information, have a window type with a navigation pane and a SEARCH tab, and enable the enable advanced search capabilities (if desired).

CHANGE PROJECT OPTIONS button

## To enable full-text search

ADD/MODIFY WINDOW DEFINITIONS button

1. Open the project file (*.hhp) in the HTML Help Workshop.

2. On the PROJECT tab, click the CHANGE PROJECT OPTIONS button (the top button) and then select its COMPILER tab. Select the COMPILE FULL-TEXT SEARCH INFORMATION check box. Do not set the COMPATIBILITY option to 1.0 if you want to merge FTS from multiple modular files. Click OK.

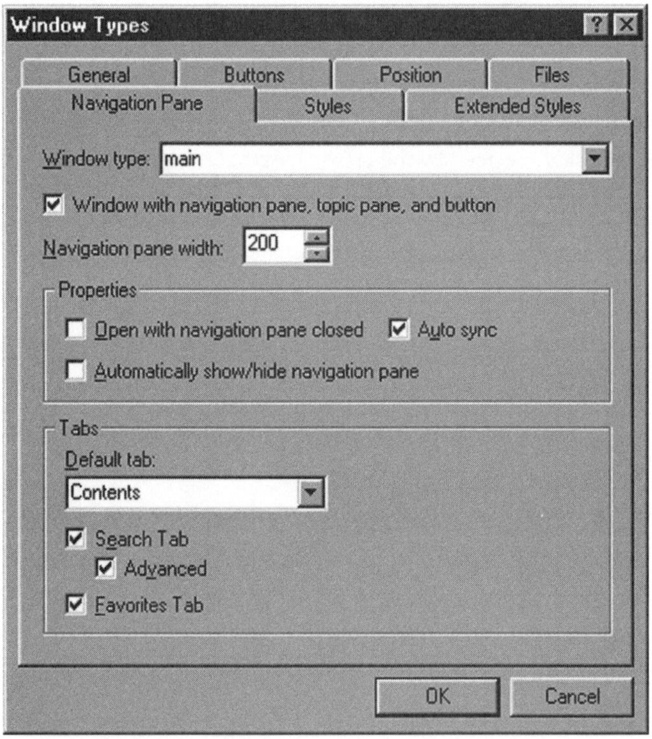

*Figure 9.4 Enabling the search tab. You must set up at least one Window Types with a SEARCH tab if you want to use full-text search.*

3. Back on the PROJECT tab, click the ADD/MODIFY WINDOW DEFINITIONS button (third from the top), and then select its NAVIGATION PANE tab. Make sure the correct WINDOW TYPE is displayed (figure 9.4).

- Click to select WINDOW WITH NAVIGATION PANE, TOPIC PANE, AND BUTTON. Also check the setting for the NAVIGATION PANE WIDTH. If this is set below 200, the SEARCH tab may not be readily visible to users (figure 9.5).

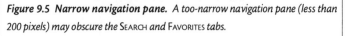

**Figure 9.5 Narrow navigation pane.** *A too-narrow navigation pane (less than 200 pixels) may obscure the* SEARCH *and* FAVORITES *tabs.*

- In the TABS section, select the SEARCH TAB box. For advanced search options, select the ADVANCED check box as well. You may also choose to make the SEARCH tab the DEFAULT TAB, if desired.

- Click OK to return to the main Workshop.

4. Finish your project, then save all files and compile the project. You must recompile the project before you will see your changes.

## To create a stop list

HTML Help also includes the ability to set "stop words," that is, words that the search engine is "stopped" from considering. A stop list tells the HTML Help compiler to leave certain words (such as *the* or *and*) out of the FTS index, thus omitting these from the user's searchers. This makes compiled HTML Help file smaller and its searches faster.

As of version 1.3x of the HTML Help Workshop, stop lists may be no larger than 512 bytes.

1. Open a plain text editor (such as Windows Notepad) and type the words for the stop list. Type each word on a new line without any punctuation. The HTML Help Workshop includes a sample stop list in its own HTML Help system. You can locate it by using the SEARCH facility to find "sample stop list," and then copy the desired stop words to your own list.

2. Save the file in the same directory as the project (`*.hhp`) file. If you are using a text editor that allows you to specify the file's extension, use `.stp` for the extension. If you are using Notepad, you will be forced to save the file with a `.txt` extension. You must then go to the file in the Windows Explorer and rename it with an `.stp` extension. Make sure that the file is *not* saved as a read-only file, or it will not be accessible from HTML Help.

3. Open the project file (`*.hhp`) in the HTML Help Workshop.

CHANGE PROJECT OPTIONS
button

4. On the PROJECT tab, click the CHANGE PROJECT OPTIONS button (the top button) and then select its FILES tab. In the text box labeled FULL TEXT SEARCH STOP LIST FILE, type the name of the file you just created, or use the BROWSE button to enter the file. Click **OK** to return to the main part of the Workshop.

5. Finish any other changes to your project, then save all files and compile the project. You must recompile the project before you will see your changes.

# Shortcuts

Shortcuts, which come under the "gee whiz" category of "amaze your friends and users," allow you to put a button in your compiled HTML Help file that automatically opens up another program in a predefined way. Shortcuts are particularly useful in walking users through a procedure, or helping them change settings in a program or a Windows Control Panel. For an example of a shortcut, look at a Windows troubleshooting topic (one is shown in figure 9.6).

Shortcuts require the compiled HTML Help format.

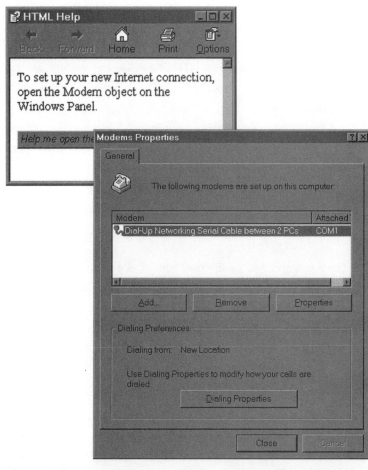

*Figure 9.6 Shortcuts. A shortcut can open a Windows Control Panel automatically.*

# To create a shortcut in a topic file

1. Open the project in the Workshop, and then open the desired topic. If the file is not yet in the project, click the PROJECT tab's ADD/REMOVE TOPIC FILES button (second from the top) and use the ADD and BROWSE buttons to locate the file and add it to the project. Once the topic file is in the project, double-click the topic file in the PROJECT tab list of included [FILES].

2. When the HTML file appears in the Workshop's right pane for editing, position the cursor within the topic at the location where you want the shortcut icon to appear.

3. From the TAGS menu, choose HTML HELP CONTROL. In the dialog that appears, use the drop-down list labeled SPECIFY THE COMMAND to choose SHORTCUT. If you are going to have other instances of the control in this file (such as a KEYWORD SEARCH or RELATED TOPICS button), or if you will use the shortcut for scripting, enter an ID name in the bottom text box. Click NEXT.

4. In the HHCTRL: DISPLAY TYPE dialog, you will normally choose to display the shortcut AS A BUTTON and then click NEXT.

5. Once you chose to display the shortcut as a button, you'll see the HHCTRL: BUTTON OPTIONS dialog. Select whether to display text, a bitmap, or an icon on the button, with the text box at the bottom changing to accommodate your selection. Make a choice and then specify the text, bitmap, or icon. When you finish, click NEXT to move to the next dialog

SHORTCUT button

- If you want to use the standard shortcut button, choose DISPLAY A BITMAP ON THE BUTTON then type shortcut in the text box labeled BITMAP (this standard button image does not require a path).

6. In the **HHCTRL: SHORTCUT** dialog, specify the main information needed to open the desired program or dialog.

- The PROGRAM is the name of the executable file for the program you wish to run. For example, if you want to open the Windows Notepad, you would type `Notepad.exe`. If the program you are opening is not in the same directory as your compiled HTML Help file, you should also enter the path to the executable.

  To open an item on the Windows Control Panel, type in its name followed by `.cpl`. For example, you can open the MODEM control panel by entering `Modem.cpl`. Not all control panels are this obviously named; to discover the name of the desired CONTROL PANEL, you can use the Windows START menu's FIND > FILES OR FOLDERS option and search for files named `*.cpl` (figure 9.7). Double-click the listed files until you find the correct CONTROL PANEL item.

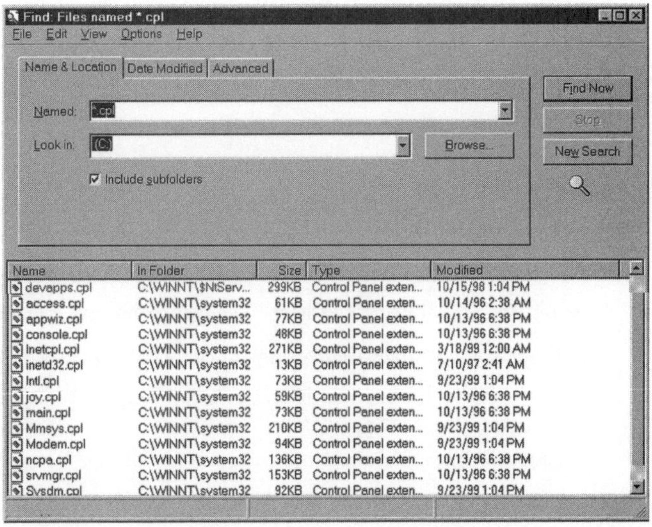

**Figure 9.7 Control Panels.** *Not all Windows control panels have obvious connections to their filenames. For example, in the graphic above,* `main.cpl` *opens the* MOUSE *control panel,* `ncpa.cpl` *opens the* NETWORK *control panel, and* `Inet.cpl` *opens the* INTERNET OPTIONS *control panel.*

- The PARAMETERS vary with the particular program. Often, you may want to open the program with a particular file loaded, so you would enter the filename here. For example, an HTML Help troubleshooting topic that you wanted to open the compiler's log file in Notepad might use the parameter `log1.log`.

- The WINDOW CLASS is the window class of the program you are calling, specified so that you will not open a new instance of the program if it is already running. If you are documenting a software application, your developers can give you this name. If you do not have a window class name, leave this field blank.

Click NEXT to move to the next dialog.

7. In the second **HHCTRL: SHORTCUT** dialog, you can specify additional parameters to open the desired program or dialog. These parameters are generally optional but may be needed when documenting a software application; ask the developers for the appropriate information. Type it in these fields, if desired, and click NEXT.

8. Click FINISH to close the Wizard and add your shortcut to the topic file.

9. If you chose to activate the shortcut with a text button, the SHORTCUT command supports a FONT parameter that is not accessible through the Wizard. To change the font on your text button, position your cursor in the HTML topic file after the closing chevron for one of the parameters, and add the following line:

```
<PARAM name="Font"
value="Face,Size,Charset,Color,Style">
```

where

    Face is the name of the desired font face

    Size is the font size in points

    Charset is the desired character set

Color is the hue of the font

Style is plain, bold, italic or underline

Do note that Size and Style work reliably; the others are less certain.

10. Save the file and your changes to it. To be sure that it is saved, close the file by clicking the X in the *file's* top right corner and answering YES if you are asked whether you want to save your changes.

11. When you next recompile the project, test that your shortcut appears in the file and works correctly.

# 10

# Making It Happen:
## Distribution & Installation

The topic pages, style sheets, and script files are written; the contents files have been created; the projects are compiled, indexed, and merged. At last, the entire compiled HTML Help system is completed, ready to teach, enlighten, and delight your users.

Well, almost.

Even after the Help author has completely finished the HTML Help system itself, there are a few elements that must be in place on the *users'* systems. While Microsoft Windows automatically includes the components required to display Windows Help, Windows versions prior to 2000 require a few additional components before they can display HTML Help.

First, users must have Internet Explorer 3.02 or higher installed on their system. IE 3.x and above supplies `shdocvw.dll,` which works with HTML Help components to display the topics in their windows. If the HTML Help system uses DHTML, users need IE 4.x or higher to access the dynamic content. Internet Explorer need not be the default browser on their system; in fact, they need never use IE itself as a Web browser but only have its components available for the HTML Help Viewer.

Second, in addition to Internet Explorer, these users must have four core HTML Help-specific files installed and registered (plus files for language support, if necessary). The HTML Help-specific files include an executable program as well as the ActiveX control that the executable calls to open the .chm and provide navigational facilities. Two additional dynamic link libraries (DLLs) provide the functionality required for the compiled HTML Help format and for search capabilities.

These issues do not arise on Windows 2000 systems, where the operating system installation includes the core IE components and the required HTML Help elements in support of their own internal help systems. (Windows 2000's method of automatically installing Internet Explorer and HTML Help 1.3x brings up a new set of challenges, as described in the section *Looking ahead: Windows 2000.*)

The minimum HTML Help installation on systems other than Windows 2000 requires installing four additional files (plus files for language support, if needed) and registering the ActiveX control, which, in its turn, registers the other files. Although the file copy and registration procedures can be done manually, the current standard approach is to run hhupd.exe as part of the installation process. HHUPD (the HTML Help Installation and Update package) is supplied with the HTML Help Workshop or can be downloaded from the Microsoft site.

# What it is & what it does

As part of its standard installation process, the HTML Help Workshop creates a `redist` subdirectory beneath its primary installation directory. The `redist` directory contains only a single file, `hhupd.exe`, a self-extracting executable known as the HTML Help Installation and Update package. This package is also available as a separate download from the Microsoft Web site.

When `hhupd.exe` is run, either by simply double-clicking the file in the Windows Explorer or as part of an application installation process, it installs the following five files, which are required to run compiled HTML Help systems:

- **HH.EXE,** the HTML Help Viewer, is the primary executable file for viewing HTML Help files. It calls `HHctrl.ocx`, the ActiveX control, and the two work together to provide most of the functionality for HTML Help systems.

  Starting with version 1.3, `hh.exe` is installed in the `Application Data\Microsoft\HTML Help` subdirectory of your Windows directory (which is usually named `Windows` or `Winnnt`). If your system is set up for multiple profiles, the HTML Help directory will be down two more levels, beneath `Windows` or `Winnnt\Profiles\YourUserID`. HTML Help versions prior to 1.3 store `hh.exe` directly in the Windows directory. (If you have a previous version of `hh.exe` installed or are running Windows NT, version 1.3x may continue to use this older location.)

- **HHCTRL.OCX,** an ActiveX control, works with the Help Viewer to provide navigational components for the compiled HTML Help file. Together with Internet Explorer (specifically, with its `Shdocvw.dll` library), they supply HTML Help's expanding and contracting table of contents, full-text searching, shortcuts, and other functionality.

The `hhupd.exe` download is available at `http://msdn.microsoft.com/library/tools/htmlhelp/wkshp/download.htm`.

The hhctrl.ocx file is installed in the system subdirectory of your Windows directory (that is, the usual installation directory is Windows\system or Winnt\system32). As part of the installation process, hhctrl.ocx must be registered with the Windows Registry, under HKEY_CLASSES_ROOT/ CLSID. Its CLSID value is ADB880A6-D8FF-11CF-9377-00AA003B7A11. If the registry item is not present, the installation process should register the OCX. If installation is performed via hhupd.exe, this registration is performed automatically. If the installation is performed via manual files copies, it is also necessary to manually register hhctrl.ocx by typing the following line at a command prompt:

```
regsvr32 hhctrl.ocx
```

- **ITIRCL.DLL** is a dynamic link library that provides functionality for HTML Help's compiled format. It is installed into the system subdirectory of your Windows directory (that is, the usual installation directory is Windows\system or Winnt\system32).

- **ITSS.DLL** is another dynamic link library; its purpose is to support the full-text search feature of HTML Help. ITSS.DLL is also installed into the system subdirectory of your Windows directory (usually, Windows\system or Winnt\system32).

- **HHCTRLUI.DLL** provides Unicode support with 28 separate satellite .dll files for each of the 28 standard Windows languages. This allows the HTML Help system's menus, commands, and other user interface (UI) elements to match the language of the operating system. It also sets up appropriate alphabetization parameters that match the conventions and character set of the operating system language. Note that these dlls do *not* automatically translate your HTML Help system content; they simply supply the necessary components for display.

The installation process creates an mui subdirectory under the Windows directory (usually, Windows\System\ or

Winnt\system32) with 28 subfolders named by their hexadecimal locale ID (for example, 0401 for Saudi Arabian Arabic or 0403 for French). Each subdirectory contains a copy of hhctrlui.dll for that language. (To check the individual languages, right-click the particular hhctrlui.dll and choose Properties from the shortcut menu. On the Version tab of the Properties dialog, click Language to see the specific language.)

**TABLE 10.1 FILES DISTRIBUTED & INSTALLED WITH HTML HELP**

| FILENAME | DESCRIPTION | INSTALLATION DIRECTORY* | PURPOSE & USE |
|----------|-------------|--------------------------|----------------|
| hhupd.exe | HTML Help Installation and Update Package | with HTML Help Workshop, in the Workshop's `redist` subdirectory | a single, freely downloadable, freely distributable file that updates the user's system to run HTML Help systems |
| hh.exe | HTML Help Viewer | `%WinDir%\ Application Data\Microsoft \HTML Help` or `%WinDir%\ Application Data\Microsoft \HTML Help\ Profiles\UserID` or `%WinDir%` | primary executable that supplies basic functionality and the HTML Help tripane window |

| FILENAME | DESCRIPTION | INSTALLATION DIRECTORY* | PURPOSE & USE |
|---|---|---|---|
| hhctrl.ocx | ActiveX control | %Windir%\ system or %WinDir%\ system32 | ActiveX module that provides help navigation and secondary window capabilities. This is the only component that must be explicitly registered (manually or via hhupd.exe) |
| itircl.dll | Dynamic link library | %WinDir%\ system or %WinDir%\ system32 | allows you to run HTML Help systems in their compiled format |
| itss.dll | Dynamic link library | %WinDir%\ system or %WinDir%\ system32 | provides FTS (full-text search) features for HTML Help |
| hhtrlui.dll | Unicode language support | %WinDir%\mui \hexadecimal locale ID | 28 versions of this file provide Unicode support in the 28 standard Windows languages; displaying GUI elements (menus, commands, etc.) in the correct language |

\*   %WinDir% stands for the Windows system directory. Typically, this is Windows under Windows 95/98 and Winnt under Windows NT and Windows 2000.

# HHUPD.EXE: The standard approach

The HTML Help Installation and Update package `hhupd.exe` provides the simplest and most common way to meet HTML Help's special system requirements. While it does not install Internet Explorer or `shdocvw.dll`, it does install and register the other necessary components. In addition, it includes a "quiet" mode that allows it to update the necessary components without user intervention.

## Getting the version right

Be sure to download the most recent version of the `hhupd.exe` file from the Microsoft Web site at `http://msdn.microsoft.com/library/ tools/htmlhelp/wkshp /download.htm`. As this book went to press, the most recent `hhupd` version was 1.31, a very minor bug fix for version 1.3, which was released in January, 2000.

Do not rely on the version of `hhupd.exe` that comes with the HTML Help Workshop, particularly with version 1.3x of the Workshop. In addition to wanting the latest, most bug-free version available, you may discover that updating the Workshop from earlier versions does not always install the 1.3x version of `hhupd`. Because of a bug in the Workshop installation program, version 1.3x does not replace the contents of the `redist` folder and some of the support dlls, especially if you have installed the new Workshop into the same folder as a previous version of the Workshop. If you have installed the Workshop, you can verify that the latest files have been installed by using the HELP menu's VERSION command. The ABOUT dialog box should show the following build numbers for versions 1.3 and 1.31 of the Workshop:

- HCTRL 4.74.8702.0 (for version 1.3) or 4.74.8793 (for version 1.31)
- ITSS 4.72.8085.0 (for version 1.3) or 4.74.8793 (for version 1.31)
- ITCC 4.72.7277.0 (for version 1.3 or 1.31)
- ITIRCL 4.72.7277.0 (for version 1.3 or 1.31)

In addition, check the version and build for hh.exe by locating it in the Windows Explorer, right-clicking on the file, and selected PROPERTIES from the shortcut menu. On the VERSION tab, it should show 4.74.8702 (for version 1.3) or 4.74.8793 (for version 1.31).

## Running HHUPD.EXE

HHUPD.EXE can be run as a one-step installation for standalone HTML Help systems or as a step within a more complex installation process for an HTML Help system that ships with a software application and its help. In either mode, HHUPD should be run from the directory in which the executable is stored. The command takes the following switches:

- **/Q** runs the installation in quiet mode; that is, it runs without any user actions. If you do not use this switch, the installation process begins with an alert asking "Do you wish to install HTML Help 1.3 Update now?" and the user must select Yes or No to proceed or to abort the process.

- **/T:<path>** defines the temporary working folder; be sure to supply the full path from the root folder.

- **/C** extracts the constituent files but does not move them to the correct system folder or install the OCX. This switch should be used together with the /T:<path> to specify the folder where the extracted files will be stored.

- **/C:<command>** allows the installation author to define an override install command.

Installing the HTML Help-specific components requires approximately 8 MB of free space on the user's drive. On a Windows NT system, installation via hhupd.exe requires an account with administrator privileges.

The installation does *not* require a system reboot. If the files are successfully copied and registered (without access denied or other error messages), the installation is complete and ready to use.

# Internet Explorer 5: an alternate approach

Internet Explorer 5.x also installs the core components required for HTML Help, so requiring users to have IE 5 installed on their systems may do away with the necessity for running hhupd, depending on the version of HTML Help you are using.

One element of the IE5 installation package is hhupd.cab, which contains the HTML-specific files (hh.exe, hhctrl.ocx, itircl, and itss.dll). If your users installed IE 5 early on, they will have version 1.1 of the HTML Help components; later releases of IE 5 may have later HTML Help versions. The 5.5 version of Internet Explorer will install version 1.3x of the HTML Help components, so that users with IE 5.5 and those with Windows 2000 should be more or less in sync.

If you want to control the HTML Help versioning issues, and if your users will allow it, you can install Internet Explorer as part of your overall installation process (at which point you need not run hhupd). You can list IE as one of the available elements of your application's installation process, or you can use a "silent install" to loads IE 5 on users' machines without user intervention. Of course, ethical practice dictates that your installation should notify the user of this step, since you will be loading new software on their system—and taking up significant space on their hard drives.

In order to install Internet Explorer as part of your own installation process, you should use the Internet Explorer Administration Kit (IEAK), which provides for customized installation of IE across a network or via the Web. IEAK used to come with complex and onerous reporting requirements, but the licensing and reporting issues have been loosened up considerably in the past year. You can find both the English version of the IEAK download and the legal requirements on Microsoft's Web site at: http://www.microsoft.com/windows/ieak/en/default.asp.

Assuming you have notified your users that you are installing Internet Explorer, you may still want to opt to install in "quiet mode" to minimize user interaction. This may be done either through a command-line executable (`ie5setup.exe`) or the Internet Explorer Customization Wizard (`ietwzd.exe`). Both support a number of command line switches, which are described in the IEAK documentation. In particular, be sure to check the following switches:

- **Quiet mode:** `/Q` for minimal user prompts; `/Q:A` for no user prompts.

- **Installation mode:** `/M:0` for minimal installation (all that is necessary to support HTML Help). You may also use **1** for a typical install, or **2** for a full install.

- **Restart mode:** `/R:N` to suppress a computer restart at the end of the installation. Use this switch only if you want to continue with the installation of other elements, and will restart at the end of all installation. IE will not be correctly set up until you do restart the computer.

- **Extra settings:** `/X` to keep IE from installing its shell, icons, or links on the Windows desktop; `/X:1` to allow IE to install its shell, icons, and links, but to keep it from setting itself as the default browser.

Be sure to check the IEAK documentation on your specific download, since these settings may be changed at any time.

# Looking ahead: Windows 2000

Microsoft has repeatedly stated that HTML Help will become the standard for online assistance. This commitment is being fulfilled in the delivery of Internet Explorer 5 and Windows 2000. In addition, the next major release of HTML Help (version 2.0) will be renamed Microsoft Help.

## Windows 2000

Microsoft Windows 2000 includes HTML Help 1.3x; so, as W2K becomes standard, HTML Help will be built in and will require no additional components. Today, the situation is available only to authors documenting Windows 2000-specific applications.

Unfortunately, "built-in" also means it is not possible to run hhupd.exe on these systems or to otherwise install new versions of HTML Help. Windows 2000 does not allow updates of elements Microsoft deems part of the core operating system. These elements—including HTML Help—are protected by the Windows File Protection (WFP). You cannot even install new versions of these files through a manual file copy; as soon as WFP determines a protected system file has been updated by an outside source, it "repairs" the problem by restoring its version of the file. So these files (such as HTML Help) can only be updated via Microsoft Service Packs.

Today, if you run hhupd.exe under Windows 2000, you will see a message saying "HTML Help 1.3 cannot be installed on Windows 2000" (under the earliest hhupd.exe release, 4.74.8702) or "HTML Help is a Windows system component and can only be updated via a service pack on this version of Windows" (under more recent versions, starting with 4.74.8703). At the moment, this situation dictates the use of version 1.3x for HTML Help systems designed for Windows 2000. In the future, as new HTML Help releases come out, authors working under Windows 2000 will have to specify service packs as part of their system requirements, or else forego the use of any features added in HTML Help versions past 1.3x.

# Index